外语教学理论选读

Selected Readings of Foreign Language Teaching Theory

卢秋萍　编著

西安交通大學出版社
XI'AN JIAOTONG UNIVERSITY PRESS

图书在版编目(CIP)数据

外语教学理论选读 / 卢秋萍编著. --西安：西安交通大学出版社，2024.11(2025.7重印). -- ISBN 978-7-5605-8031-9

Ⅰ. H09

中国国家版本馆 CIP 数据核字第 2024AH7810 号

书　　名　外语教学理论选读
　　　　　WAIYU JIAOXUE LILUN XUANDU
编　　著　卢秋萍
责任编辑　李　蕊
责任校对　庞钧颖
封面设计　任加盟

出版发行　西安交通大学出版社
　　　　　(西安市兴庆南路1号　邮政编码710048)
网　　址　http://www.xjtupress.com
电　　话　(029)82668357　82667874(市场营销中心)
　　　　　(029)82668315(总编办)
传　　真　(029)82668280
印　　刷　西安五星印刷有限公司

开　　本　880 mm×1230 mm　1/16　印张 16　字数 517千字
版次印次　2024年11月第1版　2025年7月第2次印刷
书　　号　ISBN 978-7-5605-8031-9
定　　价　55.00元

如发现印装质量问题，请与本社市场营销中心联系。
订购热线：(029)82665248　(029)82667874

前　言
Forewords

本教材具有教学理论与教学研究相结合的特点，注重培养师范类专业学生的学生观、语境观、认知观、语用观与反思观，适合英语类专业师范方向本科生或者研究生使用，能够适应基础英语教育课程改革的要求，理解英语学科核心素养的内涵，树立基于理论、创新教学的意识，不断提升科学严谨的教研精神和研究能力，培养终身学习的意识和能力。

本教材选材内容来自当前语言研究领域的顶尖学者，以及一些知名的语言学家和外语教育家。本教材的编写旨在实现三个目标：通过外语教学法的发展史、语言教学与学习的发展趋势可以了解历史、洞悉规律；通过对二语习得与授得、动态系统理论与个体差异、学习策略的学习可以学会如何研究学生、探索学习策略，使未来的教学策略有的放矢；通过语境理论、图式理论、语用失误与教学、反思性英语可以提高对教学的理性认知，在反思中获得职业发展。

本教材共分为9章，章节设置遵循从探索历史、研究学生到专业发展的教育价值体系。每章都附有练习、问题与任务，供学生与教师思考与运用。

本教材的出版得到了陕西理工大学“教材编写出版项目”的资助，以及西安交通大学出版社的大力支持，在此一并表示衷心的感谢。

由于作者水平所限，加之时间仓促，书中错误在所难免，恭请广大读者不吝赐教。

编　者

2024年8月

导 读

Introduction

第一章 外语教学方法发展史

第一章回顾了过去百余年外语教学方法的历史变迁，共介绍了 12 种教学法，包括语法翻译法、直接法、阅读法、情景法、听说法、认知法、全身反应法、沉默法、社团语言学习法、暗示法、交际法、任务型教学法。总体上，方法的变迁呈循环式，大致每 25 年出现一种新方法，每种新方法一方面对前一种方法提出了挑战，另一方面又和早期的方法有着很多的相似之处。

本章介绍部分包括三个方面：一是基于经验主义与理性主义对外语教学法发展历史的循环、演变特征等的不同解读；二是每一种教学方法中涵盖的各种问题，如每一种教学法中蕴含的“大观念”等；三是语言教学“理论”与“方法”的区别。

本章内容主要选自教育专家理查兹与罗杰斯的《语言教学的流派》、布朗的《根据原理教学：交互式语言教学》、赫德利的《在语境中教语言》、约翰逊的《外语学习与教学导论》、赛尔斯-穆尔西亚的《在语境中教语言》等。

语法翻译法

从 16 世纪起，法语、意大利语、英语开始受到重视，逐渐成为口笔译交际的主要媒体，但拉丁语仍然处于重要地位。学习拉丁语一为学习古典名著，二为分析语法，于是“拉丁语”成为学校一门主课，用于训练学生的心智、提高人文素养。“拉丁语”课程的教学过程主要是先分析语法再进行翻译，因此被称为“语法翻译法”。因其缺乏理论依据，也被称为缺乏理论的教学法。作为历史上第一个外语教学法，语法翻译法经久不衰，但该教学法易给学生带来枯燥无聊的学习情绪。

直接法

1886 年，国际语音学会的成立和国际音标的制定对推动直接法的形成和发展起到巨大的作用。1899 年，斯威特在《语言研究的实践》一书中对直接法做了系统的论述。20 世纪初直接法开始在欧洲大规模流行。第一次世界大战后，直接法的局限性暴露出来，外语教学改革创新又进入了下一个阶段。

直接法可以说是第一个引起教师和语言教学专家关注的语言教学方法，它所提供的方法似乎将语言教学带入了一个新时代，它标志着“方法时代”的开始。

阅读法

到了20世纪20年代，人们对直接法产生异议，认为只培养口语能力是不现实的，而且有限的课时难以保证熟练掌握口语，教师的口语能力和学生对口语技能的需求都与直接法的目标有距离。美国的一份研究报告(Coleman，1929)认为，外语学习更合理的路径是阅读，可以通过阅读逐步认识单词和了解语法结构。这份研究报告的结果，导致阅读成为美国大多数外语课程的授课模式，对阅读的强调成为美国外语教学的特点。自此，“阅读法”盛行近二十年之久，直到第二次世界大战。

口语法与情景法

在20世纪二三十年代，英国有一些应用语言学家研究语言教学的方法，其中的两位领军人物是英国著名外语教育家哈罗德·帕尔默和霍恩比。丹麦语言学家叶斯柏森和英国著名语言学家丹尼尔·琼斯等试图将英语教学中的口语方法发展成为一个比直接法更科学的方法，他们基于对选择和组织语言课程内容的原则和程序进行了系统研究，由此产生了情景语言教学法。该方法在前期被称为“口语法”，20世纪50年代以后改称为“情景法”。

情景法的基本特征体现在“P-P-P”模式，即一节课有三个阶段：演示(在语境中介绍一个新的语言点)、练习(控制性练习)、产出(更自由的练习阶段)。

听说法

20世纪40年代，在第二次世界大战爆发后，美国人认为有必要掌握其盟友和敌人的语言。于是，由军方资助的特殊且密集的语言课程很快得到推广，因此该课程所采用的方法也被称为“陆军法”：将直接法注入其中，聚焦听力及口语技能，几乎没有传统课程中的语法和翻译。在20世纪50年代，它被称为“听说法”，主张“听说领先”。

乔姆斯基对听说法的语言理论和学习理论进行了全面的批判。他认为，语言不是一个习惯结构，而是一个生成转换结构；人脑中有一种先天的语言习得机制，学习者通过内化规则可以创造出许多新言语，语言能力决定语言行为。由此，“听说法”跌落神坛。这是外语教学法历史上的又一次从经验论到唯理论的转换。

认知法

当20世纪60年代，“听说法”被应用于美国的外语教学和作为第二语言或外语的英语教学之中时，随即出现了两方面的批评。一方面，这种教学法因语言理论与学习理论不健全而受到抨击；另一方面，该方法的实际效果没有达到预期，学生们无法将通过听说获得的技能迁移到课堂外的真实交流中。在20世纪70年代初的一段时间里，人们对认知代码理论对语言教学的影响产生了极大的兴趣。“认知”一词被用来指代各种有意识的尝试，人们围绕语法教学大纲组织教学，同时允许有意义的语言实践。

全身反应法

全身反应法的倡导者是美国心理学家所罗门·阿希。他认为学外语应该像幼儿学母语那样轻松愉快。在课堂上，教师先发口令，并用动作把口令的意思表现出来，学生理解后，也跟着做动作，再学着把口令说出来。然后，再由学生发口令，教师做动作；学生发口令，学生做动作……直到学生全部听懂了，初步学会了，才过渡到文字，进行书面练习。

沉默法

“沉默法”也是情感人文法成员之一，是由20世纪60年代初美国数学家兼心理学家凯莱布·加特尼奥设计的一种外语教学法，其特点是教师在课堂上应尽可能保持沉默，应鼓励学习者尽可能多地创造语言。这种教学法的要素，特别是彩色图表和彩色卡牌的使用，源自加特尼奥以前作为阅读和数学项目教育设计师的经验。

社团语言学习法

“社团语言学习法”被认为是情感人文法的代表。在这种教学法的课堂里，学生坐成一圈，教师游走于圈外，学生要学的内容由老师译成目的语，学生就通过各种方式掌握运用这些译成目的语的句子。学生没有教材，教师也只有一个隐形的计划，因为该方法认为教材是学生学习的障碍。这种教学法追求的是学习内容与学生生活密切结合，学生主动大胆，有良好的心理状态，课堂气氛轻松和谐。

暗示法

20世纪60年代，保加利亚的罗扎诺夫首创“暗示法”，随后该方法形成了一股热潮。

“暗示法”认为，首先，教学要有宽松的学习环境：学生坐舒适的靠椅，墙上挂有风景画，灯光柔和等。其次，教师要使学生尽量放松：教师朗诵要伴以音乐，抑扬顿挫，学生闭眼静听。最后，信奉教师的权威和能力：教学活动要游戏化以稚化学生，使之自信。

暗示教学法对教师提出了不小的挑战。正如罗扎诺夫所说，教师必须展示对该种教学方法的绝对信任，如教师对此有怀疑，“暗示”无法发挥作用，其效果可想而知。

交际法

交际教学法起源于20世纪60年代末，当时英国的应用语言学家开始质疑情境教学法的理论假设。他们认为在语言教学中需要把重点放在交际能力上，而不是单纯地掌握语言结构。另一个推动力来自欧洲不断变化的教育现实。当时的欧洲委员会将研究开发语言教学方法视为重中之重。自20世纪70年代中期以来，交际法的范围不断扩大。美国和英国的支持者现在都把它看作是一种理论(而不仅仅是一种方法)。

所有版本的语言教学理论都是从语言和语言使用的交际模式出发，并试图将其转化为教学系统、教材、教师和学习者角色和行为以及课堂活动和技巧的设计。“交际法”成为一个多元理论的联合体，至今也没有一种定义能对其内涵做出界定。

任务型教学法

任务型教学法属于“交际法”家族。早期运用任务型教学法的两个项目，寿命都很短，但到20世纪80年代中期，有些二语习得研究者开始以任务型教学为研究对象，这些研究有力推动了任务型教学法的发展。

不过，任务型教学法的许多主张还没有得到充分证明，例如任务类型、任务顺序、对完成任务表现的评价，特别是任务型教学法的基本假设(即比其他教学方法更有效)，目前看来只是一种理想，还不是事实。

第二章　第二语言教学与学习从传统走向当代

本章综述了二语教学的发展特点。二语教学产生发展变化的主要动因是传统教学的效果不佳，以及语言学习与普通教育的缺乏关联性等。二语教学的发展变化体现在课程设计、教法、学习者的作用、语言处理、语言文本的使用、学习设备、学习方法、课堂组织、评定，以及课外活动等方面。

本章内容主要选自知名语言学家和外语教育家纽南的《第二语言教与学》第 3 章及第 4 章；部分选自语言教育者吉姆·斯克里温纳《学会教学：英语教师必备指南》第 14 章，以及二语习得国际专家李少峰教授等人的《二语习得中的个体差异：理论、研究与实践》。

课程设计

传统的教法把语言看成目的，把方法看成手段。“交际法”提高了方法的地位，认为目的和过程同样重要，因为课上的演练就是培养目标能力的方法或路径。在确定教学内容时，教师首先要了解学生需要的知识和技能，其次才能安排和设计语言项目从而实现技能的培养。

教　法

在传统教学中，教师的作用是传授知识，学生则是被动地接受知识，课堂教学由教师控制。在当代教学中，教师的主要职责是提供教学需要的条件。以交际为理念的课堂需要从高结构转向低结构，从教师控制课堂转向由教师给学生提供选择，提升了学生的自主性，学生可以结合自己的理解和认知对语言知识进行建构和重构，最终达到学习者能够在教室之外的世界中与他人交流的目标。

学习者的作用

传统教学侧重于知识的灌输和语言的练习，而现代教学则更注重功能的掌握和技能的培养。学生从被动接受者转变为积极参与者，他们不仅要进行反复的语言练习，还要学会创造性地运用语言。教室应成为语言交流的场所，而非隔绝的空间。

语言处理

传统教学法倾向于将语言学习视为线性过程，主张一次学习一个语言点。然而，学习者在实际学习中往往会同时接触多个语言点，并逐步从生疏过渡到熟练。语法教学应当使学生理解形式与功能之间的联系，并能够运用语法在真实语境中表达各种交际意图。教学中，教师应向学生传授真实的语言材料，避免使用那些专为配合语法点而人为编造的课文。

语言文本的使用

在传统课堂环境中，学习者主要通过阅读和听授课教师讲解教材文本来完成学习的过程。这些教材或文本材料通常由教科书作者(通常也是教师)创作，旨在展示特定的语法结构或教授某些特定的关键词汇。然而，学习者若禁锢于学习某本教材，则可能难以掌握在真实世界中使用语言的能力。当前教材的编写越来越注重反映生活的真实性，年长的学习者将个人的真实经历和数据带入课堂，这不仅增强了他们对学习过程的掌控性，也提高了学习者对学习内容的控制力。

学习设备

传统的语言课堂中学生仅仅依赖课本，形式、内容比较单一。在当代语言教学中，实物和真实数据的融入使教学变得更加生动。除了课本，如今的教材通常还包括自学手册、音视频素材等，这些都能够将现实世界带入课堂。

同时，信息技术和互联网的发展也为学习带来更多乐趣。学生们可以访问甚至下载各种各样的信息，通过即时聊天工具或论坛与世界各地的英语使用者建立联系，这为二语学习者提供了很多在课堂之外进行真正交流的机会。

学习方法

传统课堂的练习语境是不自然的(contrived)，而且课堂任务背后的基本策略也很少显性化。学生们如何有组织、有创意地利用已经习得的知识，更好、更有效地学习语言，这并不在教学议程上。因此，对于个体学生来说，课堂练习往往没有重点，无法针对他们需要提高的技能而展开训练。

现在教师能够将研究学习风格和策略的大量成果利用在课堂教学上，培养学生掌握有效的语言学习策略，并向学生展示如何将这些元认知策略应用于他们在课堂外的学习。通过这种方式，学生可以了解如何在正式的语言学习环境之外成为更好的语言学习者。

课堂学习更注重形式，输入材料和输出练习的数量较少，真实性较低。在数字化学习中，学习者有更多的自主权，因此学习者的自主性、积极性和乐趣也会更高。

课堂组织

传统课堂以教师为中心，学生大部分时间都在重复和操练教师提供的模型、课本和音频材料等，学生获得的是朗读和复述技能。体验式学习是基于建构主义的教育方法，其理念是通过学习者之间在课堂上的合作，以及基于任务的学习来实现的，学习者在小组中学习，以激发更丰富的语言，产生更有意义的协商。这样的模式能为学生在未来工作领域的交际打下基础。

评　定

在传统的学习环境中，评估是由外部权威机构设计、管理和评分的标准化测试。学习者在这样的体系中无法得知自己已经学到了多少，还需要学习哪些。在当代语言教学中，学习者经过系统的训练，能够具备评估自己学习进度的能力。这正是以学习者为导向的教学体系中的重要组成部分。

课外活动

在传统的教室环境中，学习者鲜有机会将所学语言技能应用于现实世界。他们唯一的实践场所通常是课堂。相比之下，在现代语言教学方法中，学习者通过参与角色扮演、模拟练习等互动课题，培养自己在课堂之外创造性地和富有想象力地运用语言的能力。

第三章　二语习得与二语授得

近年来，二语习得的研究逐渐转向二语课堂，催生了授课型二语习得，简称“二语授得”。本章主要介绍了二语习得与二语习得的研究框架、二语习得与二语授得的关系、克拉申的五个假说，以及二语授得的主要研究领域，如输入加工与加工教学法、互动假说、中介语理论与输出假说等。克拉申的五个假说是二语习得研究史上重要的里程碑。它将二语习得相关研究融入二语课堂，衍生了输入、互动、输出等一系列二语授得的研究。

本章内容主要来自克拉申、比尔·范·帕滕、苏珊·盖斯、埃利斯、肖恩·洛文、拉森-弗力曼、朗、萨维尔-特罗伊克、施罗伍、格利森、斯韦恩等人相关的研究。

二语习得的框架

研究二语习得的方法主要基于语言学、心理学和社会学的框架，侧重于语言输入和互动的作用。20 世纪 50 年代，结构主义成为主流，它强调描述语音的不同产出水平。当时最有影响力的认知学习模型来自行为主义，强调语言学习环境的刺激(如语言输入)，以及对刺激的反应、强化。结构主义与行为主义模式的交叉结合为听说法的诞生创造了条件。20 世纪中期，尽管维果茨基的社会文化理论没有被直接应用于二语习得研究，但因其强调互动在学习过程中的重要性，对二语习得方法的研究也带来了较大影响。

二语授得

洛文将 ISLA 定义为一个基于理论与实证研究的学术领域，通过对学习机制和/或学习机制的发生条件进行系统操控，促进学习者发展及习得第二语言。他的定义构成了二语授得研究的框架，包括学术领域、系统操纵、教学语境、管理对象、教学目标、教学形式等六个方面。

克拉申的监控理论

克拉申的监控理论是 20 世纪 70 年代至 80 年代初最具影响力的二语习得理论之一。他认为，二语能力有两个独立的知识系统：第一个是习得知识系统，是第一语言习得产物，是潜意识知识；第二个是学习系统，不太重要，是正式教学(通常是课堂语言教学)的产物，由“简单”有意识的知识组成。克拉申的自然顺序假说是对“语素研究”结果的综合，第二语言是以可预测的顺序习得的，并不完全由其语言的复杂性决定。

监控是克拉申监控模型的一个核心结构。他认为监控的使用必须满足三个条件：时间、关注形式、知道规则。监控在语言使用的情况下将习得和学得系统联系起来，由所学知识组成。由此可见，监控只能在产出时使用。

基于此而产生的“输入假说”回答了学习如何发生的基本问题。可理解的输入是指听到或读到的、略微高于学习者当前语法知识水平的语言表达。学习者接触到的输入必须稍微高于自身已有的水平，以便在习得方面有作用。

克拉申认为情感包括动机、态度、自信和焦虑等因素。他提出了“情感过滤器假说”：如果过滤器太高，输入就会被阻挡，习得就无法产生；如果过滤器低，输入是可以被理解的，就会到达语言习得机制，习得就会产生。

二语习得、二语授得与英语教学

二语习得理论对英语语言教学的影响可以追溯到20世纪五六十年代，当时以行为主义为支撑的听力教学法，强调操练和习惯养成。在20世纪80年代，克拉申的监控理论则提出教师应在课堂上为学生提供丰富的输入环境的建议。

虽然二语习得研究成果颇丰，但对教师来说大多数研究成果与实际课堂实践关系并不密切。基于此，学者们试图通过实证调查来影响和改进语言课堂实践。二语授得的目标是通过对课堂教学的理论主张进行实证评估，在理论、研究和教学法之间建立明确的联系。其理论和研究，尤其是从认知互动论的角度来看，可以为课堂教学提供帮助，同时教学现实对理论和研究也产生了一定的影响。

输入加工与加工教学法

范·帕滕的输入过程理论更关注初学者对语言输入的理解和加工过程，而非学生对语法规则的练习输出。他认为，语言输入应遵循五项原则：每次演示只突出一个语言点；将重点放在对意义的理解上；从单句过渡到连贯的语篇；使用口头和笔头两种形式；让学生利用输入的语言“做事”，并时刻关注学生对语言输入的加工策略。

互动与二语授得

国际二语习得研究领域著名专家迈克尔·朗的互动假设理论，指出可理解性输入应通过三种方法来实现：简化输入语言、使用语言或非语言的特征、调整会话中的交互性结构。

二语授得研究试图平衡显性知识和隐性知识的习得，其中一种方法是提倡在教学中将这两类知识纳入互动过程中。在互动过程中，学习者在语言意义和形式之间转换，这种转换有助于提升二语习得效果。

认知互动理论

认知互动理论的出现最早可追溯到迈克尔·朗提出的“互动假说”，它对ISLA的发展作出了显著的贡献。认知互动理论考察学习者接受的输入、参与的互动和产生的输出，以及互动过程所涉及的注意、语言形式与纠错性反馈、知识类型。因此，基于该理论的任务设计需要鼓励学习者在有意义的语境中使用语言，接触目标语言，并促进互动。

中介语理论

美国语言学家塞林格于1974年提出中介语理论。中介语是指学习者在学习外语过程中的一种介于母语和目的语之间的语言系统。它通常表现出五个特征：母语的干扰、教师授课与课堂活动的影响、过度使用目的语的规则、外语学习的常用策略（如背记规则和猜测等）、外语交际的常用策略（如使用手势和向他人求助等）。

斯韦恩的输出假说

美国学者斯韦恩于1985年在进行沉浸式语言教学的研究中提出了输出假说，指出准确而得体的输出对促进语言习得有三大功能：让学生发现他们想说的和能说的之间还存在差距；让学生有机会尝试使用所学的语言并在交际中进行调整；帮助学生反思自己对目的语系统的认识和所取得的进步。其后，范・帕滕区分了练习输出与交际产出。

第四章　复杂动态系统理论与个体差异

复杂动态系统理论(Complex Dynamic Systems Theory，CDST)强调系统具有动态性、复杂性、非线性、开放性等特点。个体差异研究更能体现系统性、复杂性与动态性，它涉及外在因素与内在要素，其变量通常被分为四大类：社会人口变量包括年龄；认知变量包括智力、语言能力、认知风格和学习风格；意向变量包括态度和动机；情感变量包括个性和学习者信念。

本章内容主要选自拉森-弗力曼《第二语言习得研究概况》、德尔涅伊的《语言学习动机》与《语言学习中的动机与动力》、布朗的《语言学习与语言教学的原则》、库克的《第二语言学习与教学》、洛文的《课堂二语习得》、苏珊的《第二语言习得》、埃利斯的《第二语言习得》，以及理查兹与洛克哈特的《第二语言课堂的反思性教学》等。

年　龄

关键期假说指出人类只有在两岁到十几岁之间是学习他们的第一门语言的最佳时期。这段时期与大脑的"侧化期"(lateralization)基本吻合。大脑的侧化期是大脑的语言功能在大脑左侧建立起来的时期，在此期间，大脑处于发展阶段，具有可塑性。因此，这将涉及"语言教师应该如何考虑到学生的年龄""二语教学应该何时开始""学习者要学习多长时间"等问题。

智　力

美国心理学家加德纳提出多元智能理论，包括语言智能、逻辑智能、空间智能、身体运动智能、音乐智能、人际智能、自我认知智能、自然认知智能。这八种智能既互相独立，又相互联系。

克里斯蒂森将多元智能教学分为四个阶段：通过多种感官唤醒智能；通过学生自主选取的物体、生活经验等拓展智能；通过精心设计的活动运用或发展智能；通过对前述阶段活动的反思，与现实生活中的议题或挑战建立联系，实现智能迁移。

动机

加德纳与兰伯特区分了两种不同类型的动机："融入型动机"(integrative motivation)与"工具性动机"(instrumental motivation)。2005 年，德尔涅伊提出了"二语动机自我系统"，该系统由理想自我、应该自我和二语学习经历组成。

复杂动态系统理论综合考虑了课堂上可能出现的各种动机与变量。德尔涅伊等人(2015)指出，课堂上的二语动机"如果不是复杂的和动态的，那就什么也不是。"瓦宁尔(2015)的研究指出，与课堂经验有关的主要特征要素有四个：兴趣、无聊、中度注意力和焦虑。

态　度

兰伯特依据学习态度将学习者分为增添型和消减型。增添型学习者认为学习另一种语言会给他带来好处，消减型学习者则担心学习另一种语言会让他失去已有的东西。成功的二语学习者一般是增添型的。语言教学的目标包括改变人们对其他文化的态度和有效使用第二语言。教材应该给学习者呈现成功的第二语言使用者的行为，以供学习者效仿。

天赋/学能

卡罗尔认为语言学习能力由以下四种具体能力构成：音位编码能力，学生是否能使用音标来区分语言中的音素；语法敏感性，学生是否能从句子中辨认出语法功能；语言归纳能力，学生是否能从一个个句子中归纳出其语言模式；记忆能力，学生是否能记住与翻译配对的外语词汇表。

教学中要在特定的语境中看待学生。在一个班级中表现糟糕的学生，在另一个班级中可能是有天赋的。任何班级教学都是一种折中，教学方法应适应班级中大部分学生的需求。

个　性

目前在心理学中占主导地位的个性理论是"Big Five"模型。该模型区分了个性的五个维度：开放性、严谨性、外向性、宜人性、神经质。本节在此维度分类的基础上展开叙述，内容涵盖有关个性的七个方面：自尊心、外向性与内向性、焦虑、冒险、移情、抑制、歧义容忍度。

学习者信念

学习者的信念系统受社会环境及跨文化差异的影响，受影响的层面包含学习动机、对语言学习的理解、对所学语言难易程度的期待，以及所偏好的学习策略。

学习者对语言学习本质的认识常带有相当固定的模式。他们会从不同角度来看待第二语言学习，不同的信念会带来不同的学习态度。学习者对学习和学习目标的认识会直接影响他们的课堂学习表现。在第二语言学习中，或许学习者认为有用的一些学习策略，并不是教师所鼓励的。

认知风格

对认知方式的研究主要集中在"场独立"和"场依存"的认知方式与语言学习的关系上。这组变量体现了学习者的感知方式和思维方式的差异。"场独立"的学习者具有"离群"倾向，较擅长理论性强和抽象的学习任务；"场依存"的学习者则比较"合群"，善于融入周围的环境，更依赖感性的思维方式。

学习风格

学习者有四种基本的学习感知模式：视觉学习(visual learning)，听觉学习(auditory learning)，体验学习(kin-esthetic learning)和动手操作学习(tactile learning)。有的研究者把体验学习模式和动手操作学习模式合并称为"触觉学习模式"(haptic learning)。文化和社会因素对学习者的学习风格往往会带来多方面的影响，学习者的学习风格也与动态变化的课堂有关。

第五章　学习策略

本章追溯了"策略"一词的渊源，阐释了学习策略，随后，我们将学习策略与语言学习联系起来，通过两种不同的视角，奥马利和查莫特的三要素模型与奥克斯福德的六要素模型，讲述了语言学习策略的分类。同时，本本章还介绍了科恩的四种语言使用策略、对善学者学习策略的研究、布朗的策略能力培养的10个建议、查莫特等人的策略培训的框架、如何通过任务培养学生的学习策略，以及科恩的基于策略的语言教学。

本章内容主要选自布朗、奥马利、查莫特、奥克斯福德、科恩、库克、纽南、约翰逊、施罗伍、格利森、埃利斯等的研究。

策　略

策略一词来自古希腊语的*strategia*，意思是“领兵打仗”或“战争的艺术”。更具体地说，策略涉及在一场有计划的战役中对部队、船只或飞机的最佳管理，引申到非军事环境中，策略意味着实现目标的计划、步骤或有意识的行动。

学习策略

奥克斯福德认为学习策略是学习者在语言学习中运用的某些特殊的方法或手段，是学习者获取、储存、提取和处理信息的方法和步骤。

语言学习策略

奥马利和查莫特(1990)将语言学习策略分为元认知策略、认知策略和社会/情感策略。元认知策略是高层次的行为，指学习者对语言学习进行规划、监控或评估等，对语言习得产生间接的影响。认知策略指的是对学习材料进行分析、归纳或转换时所运用的策略，指推理、演绎、组织、总结、预练等，对语言学习产生直接影响。社会/情感策略主要指合作性策略，用于人际交往或对情感的控制，具体指合作、提问、自言自语等。成功的学习者往往能较好地运用元认知策略，有意识地改进和调整自己的学习方式，并有针对性地、灵活地、恰当地运用认知学习策略。

语言使用策略

语言使用策略包括以下几个方面：

1. 检索策略：为大脑提取语言形式而采取的策略
2. 排练策略：为反复练习语言形式而采取的措施
3. 应对策略：为弥补自己语言知识不足所采取的掩盖策略
4. 交际策略：为顺利进行交际活动而采取的策略

善学者策略

学习外语，有人学得好，有人学得差。他们或者采用不同的策略，或者采用相同的策略，但是学习效率有高低。采用什么策略更好，学生自己最清楚，每个人情况不一，学习策略也不能千篇一律。教师应该鼓励学生独立思考，找到适合自己的最优学习策略。

学习者策略培训

布朗认为，在课堂上进行学习者策略训练的一个更微妙但同样有效的方法是，确保技巧尽可能地指向良好的语言学习行为。他提出了10个构建策略的方法。

另外，查莫特等人也提出了策略培训框架，该框架共包括六个步骤：准备、呈现、练习、评价、扩展。该框架能够将课堂中以教师为中心的模式逐渐转移成为以学生个体为中心的模式，从而实现培养学习策略的目的。

学习策略与任务

根据学习策略与学习任务的关系，学习策略可分成五类：认知的、人际关系的、语言的、情感的、创造的。这些不同类别的使用频率因不同学生的年龄、水平、需要培养的技能和个人需要等而各有不同。

基于策略的外语教学

将策略训练融入外语教学体现了以学习者为中心的理念。教师可以从既定的课程材料开始，然后确定嵌入哪些策略，在哪里嵌入；或是从他们关注的一种学习策略开始，围绕该策略设计活动，并在合适的时候在课程中嵌入策略。此外，教师也可以让学生选择适合自己的学习策略，并在没有教师提示的情况下自发地学习。

策略指导的目的是帮助学习者在学习和使用目标语言的过程中变得更加自如，帮助学习者提高学习效率，使其拥有个性化的第二语言学习体验。

第六章　语境理论

本章介绍了语境的规约性、语境的不同定义、语境的关联与顺应理论视角、语境的跨学科性与动态性、五个语境维度(语言、情境、互动、文化与互文)、霍尔的高低语境论、语言教学语境的各要素、语境构建的个体性与社会性。

本章内容主要选自克拉姆契的《语言教学的环境与文化》、约翰逊的《外语学习与教学导论》、梅伊的《语用学引论》、斯珀波与威尔逊的《关联：交际与认知》，以及俞理明与奥德林的《二语学习中的迁移新视角》等。

语境的规约性

语境的重要性不言而喻，每当我们用语言表达想法时，都必须考虑到语境。语言是一成不变的，但是，相同的语言可以获得完全不同，甚至截然相反的效果，这取决于规约和语境。

语境的定义

韩礼德将语境定义为“文本展开的全部环境”。这个定义是作为社会符号学的语言观点的一部分，在这个观点中，语境与文本是一种辩证关系。正如韩礼德所言，“语言是现实的一部分，是现实的塑造者，也是现实的隐喻”。语境是参考，也是行动。语境能够帮助我们理解，语境能够赋予话语真正的语用意义，并使语言具备真正的语用作用。

语境的理论视角

本节探讨了语境理论的两个关键视角：

一是关联理论。人类在接收到新信息时，对其的处理并非仅停留在表面，而是试图通过最少的认知投入，来获取最大的效益。评估新信息的相关性实际上是一种认知手段，能够使信息处理的过程更加快捷高效。

二是顺应理论。语言具有变异性、协商性和顺应性，而交际过程中的任何元素都可能成为潜在的语境关联因素。这些因素可以在心理、社会(或文化)，以及现实世界中找到，它们还涵盖了所使用的语言渠道的特性以及语言事件发生的环境。

语境的特征

语境的跨学科性。语境的概念不局限于其作为产生语词的物理环境，还包括语言、社会和认识等因素。对于语境中的不同因素是如何与语言相互关联，从而产生意义，不同学科都有各自的研究。

语境的动态性。语境以语言使用者为导向，因使用的人或群体的不同，或者使用的语言的不同，而产生差异。因此，语境是动态的：它能使参与交流的双方实现互动，并且使互动语言变得可被理解。

语境的五个维度

语境的五个维度包括语言语境、情境语境、交互语境、文化语境与互文语境。这五个维度构成了语境的相关性概念，表明语境是由不同角色与地位的人在对话中形成的。由于语言处于个人与社会、文本与话语的交汇处，因此它既反映又解释了被称为“语境”的社会现实。

高低语境

霍尔提出了低语境和高语境的概念。在一个连续体中，一端是低语境信息，语境在交流中起着最小的作用，低语境中的信息是明确的、直接的，主要通过口头语言来传达；另一端是高语境信息，语境在交流中的作用重大，高语境中的信息是隐含的、间接的，主要通过背景或社会环境来传达。

教学语境

语境是复杂的，从个体内部叙事和人际互动的微观层面语境，到教学语境特征(如教师、学习任务、教学方法等)所处的物理和社会语境，再到社会文化或区域国别等宏观层面语境，范围越来越广。外语教学者需要了解很多关于教学语境的信息，因为它非常重要。应用语言学家列出的与语言教学有关的各种因素中，总是包括一组被称为“语境”的因素。

斯特恩提出了整合教学语境因素的框架，即社会文化、历史/政治、教育、经济/技术、语言和地理。

语境与学习者复杂子系统

学习者的生态语境系统，一方面来自内部，包括认知的、情感的和语言特征，如动机、自信、焦虑、需求、意向性、语言能力与能动性等；另一方面来自外部，包括社会与环境等外在要素，如社会环境、交际话题、任务难度、会话者之间的关系等。

语境的构建

海姆斯认为言语情境包括以下八个方面：参与者的言语体裁；需要的互动和解释的规范；得体的准则和语域；对特定言语事件的一致评价；应该注意的行为序列的类型和水平；交流的

目的；参与者应该扮演的角色；整个环境或场景被赋予的意义。

教师可通过以上方式来构建学习的情境，使一堂课既有个体的活动又有社会的交往，这样学生才可以探索、发现和进行有意义的交流。学生发现的潜在意义越多，学习的效果就越好。

第七章　图式理论

这一章主要介绍了图式的定义、篇章理解所需的知识类型、图式的实例化与结构化特点、图式的内容与形式分类、图式理论在教学中语篇处理的预测、提供方向与进行推断的功能作用、图式在语篇理解中由下至上或由上至下结合的互动模型、语篇理解的两个层次(系统与图式层次)、借助先导教学手段进行基于图式的阅读和听力教学。

本章内容主要选自赫德利的《在语境中教语言》、纽南的《第二语言教与学》、卡雷尔等人的《第二语言阅读研究的交互模式》。

定　义

“图式”是由巴特利特在他的《记忆：实验和社会心理学研究》一书提出的。在书中，他证明了一个人以前的经验和知识对感知和记忆的作用。在理解过程中，以前获得的知识结构被称为图式。鲁梅尔哈特将其定义为“一个物体、事件或情景的通用概念的抽象表征”。

篇章理解所需的知识类型

我们要想理解一篇文章，至少需要具备六种知识：句法知识、词汇形态知识、一般世界知识、社会文化知识、主题知识、体裁知识。

在第二语言的理解过程中，至少有三种类型的背景知识有可能被激活：

- 语言信息知识，或一个人对目标语言代码的知识；
- 一般世界知识，包括一个人的概念储存和基于先前经验的期望。
- 语篇结构知识，或对各种类型的语篇(如对话、广播、文学作品、政治演讲、报纸和杂志故事等)一般是如何理解其组织架构的。

图式的特征

图式具备以下两种特征。

一是实例化。哈德森将图式形式的选择称为实例化。在该理论特征下，理解的过程被视为将信息的含义与心中的图式相匹配的过程。个体对信息的理解会受到经历、兴趣、先入为主的观念和文化背景的严重影响。

二是结构化。图式是抽象的知识结构，它将知识以结构化的形式展示出来，表达了知识与各个组成部分之间的关系。

图式类型

卡雷尔和埃斯特霍尔德认为，理解信息有两种基本的模式：一是内容模式，它与个体的背景知识和对物体、事件和情况的期望有关；二是形式模式，与个体对不同类型文本的修辞或话语结构的理解有关。

图式理论在教学中的功能作用

图式理论在教学中的作用体现在以下三个方面：一是有助于进行预测；二是提供理解的方向；三是有助于进行推理。

理解的互动模型

鲁梅尔哈特认为图式存在两种独立但相互关联的信息处理模式：自下而上的加工和自上而下的加工。前者指听者或读者通过解码单词去关注细节，并且试图将传入的数据实例化，寻求最适合的低层次的图式，因而是数据驱动的、从部分到整体的；后者指听者或读者从一个更高阶图式开始，根据背景知识作出预判，然后在输入中寻找适合“槽”的信息，是概念驱动的、从整体到部分的。两种处理模式同时作用于语篇的理解，构成了互动模型。

语篇理解

威多森从话语理解的角度对图式理论进行了重新阐释。他认为，任何给定的话语都有两个层面或层次：一个是系统层次，一个是图式层次。前者包括读者或听众的语言知识，后者则与背景知识有关。

基于图式理论的外语教学

基于图式理论的外语教学模式可以解决外语教学中的一些问题：

一是构建有意义的学习理论。从20世纪60年代开始，认知心理学家特别强调背景知识的意义和组织性的作用。奥苏贝尔认为，学习必须是有意义的，才是有效的和永久的。要使学习的材料有意义，它必须与学习者头脑中已有的知识构建明确的联系。

二是通过先导提升学习效果。奥苏贝尔强调，教师需要提供“先导”来促进学生对新材料的理解、学习和记忆。近年来“先导”一词被用来指一系列的教学辅助工具，包括图片、标题、主题摘要、预先提出的问题等。研究表明，图片先导对低水平的学生特别有帮助。

第八章　语用失误与外语教学

这一章介绍了语用学与外语教学的联系与应用，具体内容包括：说话者意义、语用学的不同视角、语用失误及语言语用失误与社会语用失误的根本性区别，以及语用教学等。

本章内容主要选自托马斯的《跨文化语用失误》及《语用学引论》。

说话者意义

托马斯在多个层面考察了说话者意义：抽象意义(abstract meaning)，指词、短语和语句等可能具有的意义，如词典意义；语境意义(contextual meaning)，也称话语意义(utterance meaning)，即“语句—语境”的结合体，它是说话人意义的第一个层面；用意(force)，即说话人的交际意图，它是说话人意义的第二个层面。

话语意义和说话人的交际意图是密切联系的，在理解话语意义和推导说话人的交际意图时，会出现以下情况：(1)听话人既理解了话语意义，又理解了说话人的交际用意；(2)听话人获知了话语意义，却没能理解说话人的交际用意。

语用学的不同视角

从意义互动、人际修辞、问题解决、授课型二语习得四个视角阐释了语用学概念。

托马斯认为语用学研究的是言谈互动中的意义(meaning in interaction)，意义生成是一个动态的过程，涉及说者和听者之间的意义协商、说话的语境(物理的、社会的和语言的)和说话的意义潜力。

卡斯珀与罗斯将语用学称为一种人际修辞学，关注说话者或作者如何实现交际目标，他们不仅需要把事情做成，同时还需要维护好与其他参与者的关系。利奇与托马斯将语用学分为语用语言学和社会语用学。利奇认为语用学是关于解决问题的。说话人解决的问题是：当我想向听话人传达某种信息，什么是好的传达方法？听话人解决的问题是：既然说话人说了这样那样的话，他要表达的意思是什么？听话人需要重构说话人所要表达的意义。

授课型二语习得语用学是对教学变量和学习者变量的研究，用于解决如何在第二语言或外语课堂促进学习者学习在何时、对谁、说什么及如何说的问题。

语用失误

术语“语用失误”指的是听者无法理解说者“说的话是什么意思”。其中，语言语用失误是比较容易克服的，可以作为“语法的一部分”直接讲授。社会语用失误因涉及更多知识，故必须从语用学视角，培养、提高和完善学生的元语用意识，使他们能够按照自己的选择来表达思想。

出现语法错误表示说话人是一个不太熟练的语言使用者，而产生语用失误则反映了他在行为上的失当。教师的任务是使学生能够准确地以他选择的方式来表达自己的交际意图。

语言语用失误

当一个语言符号或结构的语用意图与本族语者通常所确定的意图不一致时，就会出现语言语用错误。这些错误可能源自两个明确的源头：教学引导的偏差和语言语用的迁移。

社交语用失误

虽然根据社会价值尺度作出判断是说话者“社交能力”的一部分，但将这些判断应用于语言话语的能力——知道如何、何时和为何说话——则属于语用学的范畴。正是在评估社交距离，什么是强加于人、什么时候应该放弃“威胁面子的行为”，以及评价相对权力、权利和义务等方面的跨文化错配，导致了社会语用失误。

语用教学

在教学中，我们可以采用多种方式来提升学生的语用能力，如使用技术中介任务、提供真实的语用输入、进行语用得体性教学、提高学生元语用意识、帮助学生学会区分语言语用失误与社会语用失误等。

第九章　反思性英语教学

本章主要介绍了开展反思性教学的目的、教师反思的三种关键态度(开放的心态、责任感和全心全意)、反思的五个维度、反思性教学探讨的问题，以及在反思性教学中获取有关信息和数据的方法。本章的主要内容还包括教师在反思性教学中应关注的六个方面、反思性教学要面对的两个基本挑战(寻求多视角和学习者参与的问题),以及一些供读者参考的活动建议。

本章内容主要选自约翰·墨菲的《英语教学中的反思教学》,法雷尔的《反思性实践:重燃你的教学热情》,贝利、柯蒂斯与纽南的《追求专业化发展:以自己为资源》,以及理查兹与洛克哈特的《第二语言课堂的反思性教学》等。

相关术语的定义

理查兹与洛克哈特将反思性教学定义为第二语言课堂教学的一种方法。教师"收集有关教学的数据,检查他们的态度、信念、假设和教学实践,并将获得的信息作为批判性反思的基础",反思他们在语言课程中所付出的精力和得到的结果。

职业发展,即教师在知识、经验和态度上不断成长的过程。

弗力曼描述了以意识、态度、技能、知识为教学要素而构成的模型,他指出:"意识"引发了我们对态度、技能和知识的关注;"态度"为"对自我、活动和他人的立场";"技能"构成"如何教学",即教学的方法;"知识"体现了教学的内容。

反思教学的目的

反思性教学旨在实现三个主要目标:加深对教学和学习过程的理解;拓宽作为语言教师可采用的教学策略范围;提高在语言课堂上为学生创造更多学习机会的能力。

批判性反思

将批判性反思用于教学,即教学反思,是指教师和学生收集有关教学的数据,审视自己的态度、信念、假设和教学实践,以获得的信息为基础,对教学进行批判性反思,并促使反思进一步指导教学实践的一种方法。

教师反思的关键态度

杜威认为,教师要想成为反思型教师,必须具备三种关键的态度:开放的心态、责任感和全心全意的态度。泽切纳和利斯顿指出,"开放的心态和责任感必须是反思型教师职业生活的核心组成部分"。全心全意的教师会"定期检查他们自己的假设和信念,以及他们行动的结果,并一直秉持'可以学到新东西的态度'"。

反思的五个维度

反思分为五个层面:迅速反思(当场自觉的反思);整理(认真思考即时反思);反观(事件过去后的某个时间非正式的思考);研究(持续一段时间的更为系统化的思考);重构(根据某一的理论在较长一段时间对某一现象的思考)。经常反思可以使我们养成对自己的观念和自己的教学习惯持批判性态度。

反思型教师探索的主题

教师在反思教学时,会关注六个关键方面:课堂交际模式、教师的决策过程、学习者运用知识的方式、课堂的情感氛围、教学环境,以及教师对个人发展和成长的自我评价。

教学反思/收集信息的方法

教师使用不同工具来获取不同种类的信息。这些工具包括：来自学生或其他老师的形成性反馈、来自自身的相关信息、课程描述、学生结课时的终结性反馈、行动研究、五分钟纸条、形成性的教师评估调查、学生中心组、回顾性的现场笔记，以及来自同行的形成性反馈等。

这些可以为教师开展反思性教学提供具体的方法，帮助培养英语教师对教学过程进行分析与思考的能力。

两个要点

进行反思性教学时，教师需要面对两个基本挑战：寻求多视角和学习者参与。

一是寻求多视角。在进行反思性教学时，教师不仅要通过自己的感知和理解，还要通过参与课程的学习者及其他同行的感知，收集教与学过程的有关信息。弗力曼认为“外在”视角为我们提供了“外人所见”的信息，而“内在”视角则提供了“内人所知”的信息。

二是学习者参与。在进行反思性教学时，教师要问的第二个问题是：我是否想让学习者参与到我作为反思型教师的努力中来，如果是的话，学习者的参与程度是怎样的？

活动建议

建议一：安排两位或更多具备实践经验的语言教师进行咨询。询问他们是否听说过反思性教学或探索性教学，了解他们是否曾经参与类似教学实践。如果他们具备相关经验，则尽可能多地收集与该教学实践相关的信息；如果他们没有相关经验，就试着找出他们作为教师为其个人成长和专业发展所做的其他实践。

建议二：把自己放在一个语言学习者的位置上。如果你作为学习者，而你的语言教师采用了反思性教学的方式，你希望如何参与其中？把你愿意做的各种事情列出来。另外，你还可以想一想，在某一门具体的语言课程中，你认为有哪些话题值得老师去探讨？作为课堂上的学习者，你愿意作出哪些贡献？

目 录
Contents

CHAPTER 1

A "Methodical" History of Language Teaching

Focusing Question

- Why have language teaching methods waxed and waned in popularity?
- Why has Grammar-Translation Method been stalwart?
- What are the characteristics of the developments of language teaching?

Introduction

A glance through past century or so of language teaching gives us an interesting picture of how varied the interpretations have been of the best way to teach a foreign language. As schools of thought have come and gone, so have language teaching methods waxed and waned in popularity. Teaching methods are the application of theoretical findings and positions. They may be thought of as "theories in practice." In second language teaching some applications are in total philosophical opposition to others.

Albert Marckwardt(1972) saw these "changing winds and shifting sands" as a cyclical pattern in which a new paradigm of teaching methodology emerged about every quarter of a century, with each new method breaking from the old but at the same time taking with it some of the positive aspects of the previous paradigm.

It becomes evident that the goals and therefore the procedures of language teaching closely reflect the social, political, and intellectual climate of the times (Pennycook, 2017).

Methods, Approaches, Design and Procedures

As the study of teaching methods and procedures in language teaching assumed a more central role within applied linguistics from the 1940s on, various attempts have been made to conceptualize the nature of methods and to explore more systematically the relationship between theory and practice within a method.

Method

A method is theoretically related to an approach, is organizationally determined by a design, and is practically realized in procedure. Any language teaching method can be described in terms of the issues at the levels of approach, design, and procedure. Very few methods are explicit with respect to all of these dimensions.

Approach

Approach refers to theories about the nature of language and language learning that serve as the source of practices and principles in language teaching.

Design

In order for an approach to lead to a method, it is necessary to develop a design for an instructional system. Design is the level of method analysis in which we consider: what the objectives of a method are; how language content is selected and organized within the method, that is, the syllabus model the method incorporates; the types of learning tasks and teaching activities the method advocates; the roles of learners; the roles of teachers; the role of instructional materials.

Procedure

This encompasses the actual moment-to-moment techniques, practices, and behaviors that operate in teaching a language according to a particular method. There are three dimensions to a method at the level of procedure:

1. the use of teaching activities (drills, dialogues, information-gap activities, etc.) to present new language and to clarify and demonstrate formal, communicative, or other aspects of the target language;
2. the ways in which teaching activities are used for practicing language;
3. the procedures and techniques used in giving feedback to learners concerning the form or content of their utterances or sentences.

Essentially, procedure focuses on the way a method handles the presentation, practice, and feedback phases of teaching.

Empiricist & Rationalist

Traditionally, language practitioners in search of the "one true way" have grouped themselves along the same empiricist/rationalist continuum, aligning themselves more or less with their counterparts in theoretical linguistics. For methodologists, the basic distinction between the two ends of the continuum has been one of philosophy. Empiricists believed that language was an oral phenomenon consisting of concrete "signs" that could be described (Diller, 1978). Empiricist methodologies treated language learning as habit formation through mimicry, memorization, and drilling. Rationalists saw language not as structure, but as rule-governed creativity (Chomsky, 1965). Rationalist methodologies emphasize meaningfulness and understanding of psychologically real rules of grammar. Swaffar, Arens, and Morgan (1982), following Diller, characterize the Rationalist/ Process Approach as one in which high priority is placed on identifying form as meaningful, using problem-solving strategies. The Empiricist/Skill Approach, by contrast, places highest priority on reproduction of correct forms.

Changes in language teaching methods throughout history have reflected recognition of changes in the kind of proficiency learners need, such as a move toward oral proficiency rather than reading comprehension as the goal of language study; they have also reflected changes in theories of the nature of language and of language learning. Kelly (1976) has described a gradual evolution of language teaching over 25 centuries that is characterized by frequent shifts in focus, purpose, and practice. For the frequent swings of the pendulum that have been taking place until fairly recently is the fact that very few language teachers have a sense of history about their profession and are thus unaware of the historical bases of the many methodological options they have at their disposal.

A brief survey will encourage many language teachers to learn more about the origins of their profession. Such knowledge will ensure some perspective when teachers evaluate any so-called innovations or new approaches to methodology, which will surely continue to emerge from time to time.

Seven questions to ask about a method

It will be useful to try and identify some ways in which methods are different from each other. Here are "seven questions to ask" about any method you come across. Answers to them will help to view methods in relation to each other:

1. What are the method's "Big Ideas"?

Many are based on a small number of central insights, which act as guiding inspiration. If you can identify these "Big Ideas", you are well on the way to "understanding" the method.

2. What are the theoretical underpinnings behind the method?

In an ideal world, it would be supported by a view both of language and of language learning. This rarely happens. Sometimes just one of these—a view either of language or of language learning will be behind the method. Sometimes, shamefully, neither is there. Try to relate various methods to the theories of language and language learning.

3. How much "engagement of the mind" does the method expect?

Different learning theories have very different views about the role of the mind in learning. At one extreme is behaviorism, where the mind plays no part at all, and learning is viewed as habit formation. In mentalist views this is not true at all. A useful way of characterizing language-teaching methods is to identify how they stand in relation to this factor.

4. Is the method deductive or inductive in approach?

Deductive learning is where the learner is first given a rule. These rules are then demonstrated working in practice. The sequence is from "rule" to "example." In the contrasting sequence, examples are first given, and the learner works out the rules for herself. Often the rules are given at a last stage, and indeed are sometimes never explicitly stated at all.

5. Does the method allow use of the L1 in the classroom?

Some methods shun this at all costs; "the L1 must never be used, however desperate the struggle to communicate becomes" is a common dogma. In some others, you may find a major part of each lesson is given in the learners' L1, with the target language only making an occasional guest appearance. Sometimes the deductive versus inductive question may determine this issue. A deductive method involves giving rules, and in practice this will often have to be done in the learners' L1. It is often not practicable to explain grammatical rules to a learner (particularly at the early learning stages) in the target language.

6. Which of the four skills are given emphasis in the method?

The four skills are listening and speaking (the "spoken" skills), reading and writing (the "written" skills). Methods can differ dramatically as to where they place the emphasis. In some, learners do nothing but read and write; in others they do little other than listen and speak.

7. How much importance does the method give to "authenticity of language"?

There are methods which take great pains to make the language the learner is exposed to as "realistic" as possible. In other methods, no effort at all is made in this direction.

The Grammar-Translation Method

Background

As the status of Latin diminished from that of a living language to that of an "occasional" subject in the school curriculum, the study of Latin took on a different function. The study of classical Latin (the Latin in which the classical works of Virgil, Ovid, and Cicero were written) and an analysis of its grammar and rhetoric became the model for foreign language study from the seventeenth to the nineteenth centuries. Children entering "grammar school" in the sixteenth, seventeenth, and eighteenth centuries in England were initially given a rigorous introduction to Latin grammar, which was taught through rote learning of grammar rules, the study of declensions and conjugations, translation, and practice in writing sample sentences, sometimes with the use of parallel bilingual texts and dialogue. Once basic proficiency was established, students were introduced to the advanced study of grammar and rhetoric. School learning must have been a deadening experience for children, for lapses in knowledge were often met with brutal punishment.

The decline of Latin also brought with it a new justification for teaching Latin. Latin was said to develop intellectual abilities, and the study of Latin grammar became an end in itself.

By the nineteenth century, this approach based on the study of Latin had become the standard way of studying foreign languages in schools. A typical textbook in the mid-nineteenth century consisted of chapters or lessons organized around grammar points. Each grammar point was listed, rules on its use were explained, and it was illustrated by sample sentences. This approach to foreign language teaching became known as the Grammar-Translation Method.

Characteristics

Grammar-Translation was in fact first known in the United States as the Prussian Method. The principal characteristics were these:

1. The goal of foreign language study is to learn a language in order to read its literature or in order to benefit from the mental discipline and intellectual development that result from foreign language study. Grammar Translation is a way of studying a language that approaches the language first through detailed analysis of its grammar rules, followed by application of this knowledge to the task of translating sentences and texts into and out of the target language. It hence views language learning as consisting of little more than memorizing rules and facts in order to understand and manipulate the morphology and syntax of the foreign language. "The first language is maintained as the reference system in the acquisition of the second language." (Stern, 1983)
2. Reading and writing are the major focus; little or no systematic attention is paid to speaking or listening.
3. Vocabulary selection is based solely on the reading texts used, and words are taught through bilingual word lists, dictionary study, and memorization. In a typical Grammar-Translation text, the grammar rules are presented and illustrated, a list of vocabulary items is presented with their translation equivalents, and translation exercises are prescribed.
4. The sentence is the basic unit of teaching and language practice. Much of the lesson is devoted to translating sentences into and out of the target language, and it is this focus on the sentence that is a distinctive feature of the method. Earlier approaches to foreign language study used grammar as an aid to the study of texts in a foreign language. But this was thought to be too difficult for students in secondary schools, and the focus on the sentence was an attempt to make language learning easier.
5. Accuracy is emphasized. Students are expected to attain high standards in translation, because of the high priority attached to meticulous standards of accuracy which, as well as having an intrinsic moral value, was a prerequisite for passing the increasing number of formal written examinations that grew up during the century (Howatt, 1984).
6. Grammar is taught deductively—that is, by presentation and study of grammar rules, which are then practiced through translation exercises. In most Grammar-

Translation texts, a syllabus was followed for the sequencing of grammar points throughout a text, and there was an attempt to teach grammar in an organized and systematic way.

7. The student's native language is the medium of instruction. It is used to explain new items and to enable comparisons to be made between the foreign language and the student's native language.

Potential Drawbacks

Grammar-Translation dominated European and foreign language teaching from the 1840s to the 1940s, and in modified form it continues to be widely used in some parts of the world today.

It is remarkable, in one sense, that this method has been so stalwart among many competing models. It does virtually nothing to enhance a student's communicative ability in the language and often creates frustration for students. It is "remembered with distaste by thousands of school learners, for when foreign language learning meant a tedious experience of memorizing endless lists of unusable grammar rules and vocabulary and attempting to produce perfect translations of stilted or literary prose."

However, in another sense, one can understand why Grammar-Translation is so popular. It requires few specialized skills on the part of teachers. Tests of grammar rules and of translations are easy to construct and can be objectively scored. Many standardized tests of foreign languages still do not attempt to tap into communicative abilities, so students have little motivation to go beyond grammar analogies, translations, and rote exercises. And it is sometimes successful in leading a student toward a reading knowledge of a second language. There is no literature that offers a rationale or justification for it or that attempts to relate it to issues in linguistics, psychology, or educational theory. As we continue to examine theoretical principles, we will understand more fully the "theory lessness" of the Grammar-Translation Method.

The Direct Method

Background

Toward the mid-nineteenth century several factors contributed to a questioning and rejection of the Grammar-Translation Method. Educators recognized the need for speaking proficiency rather than reading comprehension, grammar, or literary appreciation as the goal for foreign language programs; there was an interest in how children learn languages, which prompted attempts to develop teaching principles from observation of (or, more typically, reflections about) child language learning. Toward the end of the nineteenth century, a more concerted effort arose in which the interests of reform-minded language teachers and linguists coincided. This effort became known as the Reform Movement in language teaching.

Viëtor, Sweet, and other reformers in the late nineteenth century shared many beliefs about the principles on which a new approach to teaching foreign languages should be based, although they often differed considerably in the specific procedures they advocated for teaching a language. These principles provided the theoretical foundations for a principled approach to language teaching, one based on a scientific approach to the study of language and of language learning. They reflect the beginnings of the discipline of applied linguistics—that branch of language study concerned with the scientific study of second and foreign language teaching and learning. But parallel to the ideas put forward by members of the Reform Movement was an interest in developing principles for language teaching out of naturalistic principles of language learning, such as are seen in first language acquisition. This led to what have been termed natural methods and ultimately led to the development of what came to be known as the Direct Method.

Gouin had been one of the first of the nineteenth-century reformers to attempt to build a methodology around observation of child language learning. Other reformers toward the end of the century likewise turned their attention to naturalistic principles of language learning, and for this reason they are sometimes referred to as advocates of a "natural" method. Sauveur and other believers in the Natural Method argued that a foreign language could be taught without translation or the use of the learner's native language if meaning was conveyed directly through demonstration and action.

Principles and Procedures

Enthusiastic supporters of the Direct Method introduced it in France and Germany (it was officially approved in both countries at the turn of the century), and it became widely known in the United States through its use by Sauveur and Maximilian Berlitz in successful commercial language schools. In practice it stood for the following principles and procedures:

1. Classroom instruction was conducted exclusively in the target language;
2. Only everyday vocabulary and sentences were taught;
3. Oral communication skills were built up in a carefully graded progression organized around question-and-answer exchanges between teachers and students in small, intensive classes;
4. Grammar was taught inductively;
5. New teaching points were introduced orally;
6. Concrete vocabulary was taught through demonstration, objects, and pictures; abstract vocabulary was taught by association of ideas;
7. Both speech and listening comprehension were taught;
8. Correct pronunciation and grammar were emphasized.

By the 1920s, the use of the Direct Method in noncommercial schools in Europe had consequently declined. In France and Germany, it was gradually modified into versions that combined some Direct Method techniques with more controlled grammar-based activities. In the 1920s and 1930s, applied linguists systematized the principles proposed earlier by the Reform Movement and so laid the foundations for what developed into the British approach to teaching English as a foreign language. Subsequent developments led to Audiolingualism in the United States and the Oral Approach or Situational Language Teaching in Britain.

Drawbacks

The Direct Method represented the product of enlightened amateurism. It was perceived to have several drawbacks. It required teachers who were native speakers or who had nativelike fluency in the foreign language. It was largely dependent on the teacher's skill, rather than on a textbook, and not all teachers were proficient enough in the foreign language to adhere to the principles of the method. Critics pointed out that strict adherence to Direct Method principles was often counterproductive, since teachers were required to go to great lengths to avoid using the native language, when sometimes a simple, brief explanation in the student's native language would have been a more efficient route to comprehension.

The significance

The Direct Method can be regarded as the first language teaching method to have caught the attention of teachers and language teaching specialists, and it offered a methodology that appeared to move language teaching into a new era. It marked the beginning of the "methods era."

Reading Approach

Background

The European popularity of the Direct Method in the early part of the twentieth century caused foreign language specialists in the United States to attempt to have it implemented in American schools and colleges, although they decided to move with caution.

A study begun in 1923 on the state of foreign language teaching concluded that no single method could guarantee successful results. The goal of trying to teach conversation skills was considered impractical in view of the restricted time available for foreign language teaching in schools, the limited skills of teachers, and the perceived irrelevance of conversation skills in a foreign language for the average American college student.

The study (Coleman, 1929) —published as Coleman Report—argued that a more reasonable goal for a foreign language course would be a reading knowledge of a foreign language, achieved through the gradual introduction of words and grammatical structures in simple reading texts. The main result of this recommendation was that reading became the goal of most foreign language programs in the United States. The emphasis on reading continued to characterize foreign language teaching in the United States until World War II.

Characteristics

As a reaction to the problems experienced in implementing the Direct Approach, reading was viewed as the most usable skill to have in a foreign language since not many people traveled abroad at that time; also, few teachers could use their foreign language well enough to use a direct approach effectively in class.

1. Only the grammar useful for reading comprehension is taught.
2. Vocabulary is controlled at first (based on frequency and usefulness) and then expanded.
3. Translation is once more a respectable classroom procedure.
4. Reading comprehension is the only language skill emphasized.
5. The teacher does not need to have good oral proficiency in the target language.

The Oral Approach and Situational Language Teaching

Background

The origins of this approach began with the work of British applied linguists in the 1920s and 1930s. A number of outstanding applied linguists developed the basis for a principled approach to methodology in language teaching. Two of the leaders in this movement were Harold Palmer and A. S. Hornby, two of the most prominent figures in British twentieth-century language teaching. Both were familiar with the work of such linguists as Otto Jespersen and Daniel Jones, as well as with the Direct Method. They attempted to develop a more scientific foundation for an oral approach to teaching English than was evidenced in the Direct Method. The result was a systematic study of the principles and procedures that could be applied to the selection and organization of the content of a language course (Palmer, 1917 & 1921).

Approach

Theory of language

The theory of language underlying Situational Language Teaching can be characterized as a type of British "structuralism." Speech was regarded as the basis of language, and structure was viewed as being at the heart of speaking ability.

Theory of learning

The theory is a type of behaviorist habit-learning theory. It addresses primarily the processes rather than the conditions of learning. It adopts an inductive approach to the teaching of grammar. The meaning of words or structures is not to be given through explanation in either the native language or the target language but is to be induced from the way the form is used in a situation.

Design

Objectives

The objectives are to teach a practical command of the four basic skills of language goals it shares with most methods of language teaching. But the skills are approached through structure. Accuracy in both pronunciation and grammar is regarded as crucial, and errors are to be avoided at all costs. Automatic control of basic structures and sentence patterns is fundamental to reading and writing skills, and this is achieved through speech work. Before our pupils read new structures and new vocabulary, we shall teach orally both the new structures and the new vocabulary (Pittman, 1963). Writing likewise derives from speech.

The syllabus

Basic to the teaching of English in Situational Language Teaching is a structural syllabus and a word list. A structural syllabus is a list of the basic structures and sentence patterns of English, arranged according to their order of presentation. In Situational Language Teaching, structures are taught within sentences, and vocabulary is chosen according to how well it enables sentence patterns to be taught.

Types of learning and teaching activities

Situational Language Teaching employs a situational approach to presenting new sentence patterns and a drill-based manner of practicing them.

The practice techniques employed generally consist of guided repetition and substitution activities, including chorus repetition, dictation, drills, and controlled oral-based reading and writing tasks. Other oral-practice techniques are sometimes used, including pair practice and group work.

Learner roles

In the initial stages of learning, the learner is required simply to listen and repeat what the teacher says and to respond to questions and commands. The learner has no control over the content of learning and is often regarded as likely to succumb to undesirable behaviors unless skillfully manipulated by the teacher. For example, the learner might lapse into faulty grammar or pronunciation, forget what has been taught, or fail to respond quickly enough; incorrect habits are to be avoided at all costs. Later, more active participation is encouraged. This includes learners initiating responses and asking each other questions, although teacher-controlled introduction and practice of new language is stressed throughout.

Teacher roles

The teacher's function is threefold. In the presentation stage of the lesson, the teacher serves as a model, setting up situations in which the need for the target structure is created and then modeling the new structure for students to repeat. Then the teacher "becomes more like the skillful conductor of an orchestra, drawing the music out of the performers" (Byrne, 1976)[2]. The teacher is required to be a skillful manipulator, using questions, commands, and other cues to elicit correct sentences from the learners. Lessons are hence teacher-directed, and the teacher sets the pace.

The role of instructional materials

Situational Language Teaching is dependent on both a textbook and visual aids. The textbook contains tightly organized lessons planned around different grammatical structures. Visual aids may be produced by the teacher or may be commercially produced; they consist of wall charts, flashcards, pictures, stick figures, and so on. The visual element together with a carefully graded grammatical syllabus is a crucial aspect, hence the importance of the textbook. In principle, however, the textbook should be used "only as a guide to the learning process. The teacher is expected to be the master of his textbook" (Pittman, 1963)[176].

Procedure

Classroom procedures vary according to the level of the class, but procedures at any level aim to move from controlled to freer practice of structures and from oral use of sentence patterns to their automatic use in speech, reading, and writing.

Pittman(1963)[173] gives an example of a typical lesson plan. The first part of the lesson will be stress and intonation practice. The main body of the lesson should then follow. This might consist of the teaching of a structure. If so, the lesson would then consist of five parts:

1. pronunciation
2. revision (to prepare for new work if necessary)
3. presentation of new structure or vocabulary
4. oral practice (drilling)
5. reading of material on the new structure, or written exercises

Pittman illustrates oral drilling on a pattern, using a box full of objects to create the situation. The pattern being practiced is "There's a NOUN + of + (noun) in the box." The teacher takes objects out of the box and the class repeats.

Procedures associated with Situational Language Teaching in the 1950s and 1960s were an extension and further development of well-established techniques advocated by proponents of the earlier Oral Approach in the British school of language teaching. The essential features of SLT are seen in the "P-P-P" with a lesson having three phases: Presentation (introduction of a new teaching item in context), Practice (controlled practice of the item), and Production (a freer practice phase).

The Audiolingual Method

Background

World War II broke out and suddenly the United States was thrust into a worldwide conflict, heightening the need for Americans to become orally proficient in the languages of both their allies and their enemies. The time was ripe for a language teaching revolution. The U. S. military provided the impetus with funding for special, intensive language courses that focused on the aural/oral skills; these courses came to be known as the Army Specialized Training Program (ASTP) or, more colloquially, the "Army Method." Characteristic of these courses was a great deal of oral activity—pronunciation and pattern drills and conversation practice —with virtually none of the grammar and translation found in traditional classes.

Ironically, numerous foundation stones of the discarded Direct Method were borrowed and injected into this new approach. Soon, the success of the Army Method and the revived national interest in foreign languages spurred educational institutions to adopt the new methodology. In all its variations and adaptations, the Army Method came to be known in the 1950s as the Audiolingual Method.

Approach

Theory of language

The Audiolingual Method (ALM) was firmly grounded in linguistic and psychological theory. Language was viewed as a system of structurally related elements for the encoding of meaning, the elements being phonemes, morphemes, words, structures, and sentence types. An important tenet of structural linguistics was that the primary medium of language is oral: Speech is language.

Theory of learning

Behavioristic psychologists advocated conditioning and habit-formation models of learning that were perfectly married with the mimicry drills and pattern practices of audiolingual methodology.

To the behaviorist, the human being is an organism capable of a wide repertoire of behaviors. The occurrence of these behaviors is dependent on three crucial elements in learning: a *stimulus*, which serves to elicit behavior; a *response* triggered by a stimulus; and *reinforcement*, which serves to mark the response as being appropriate (or inappropriate) and encourages the repetition (or suppression) of the response in the future (see Skinner, 1957; Brown, 1980). A representation of this can be seen in Figure 1. 1.

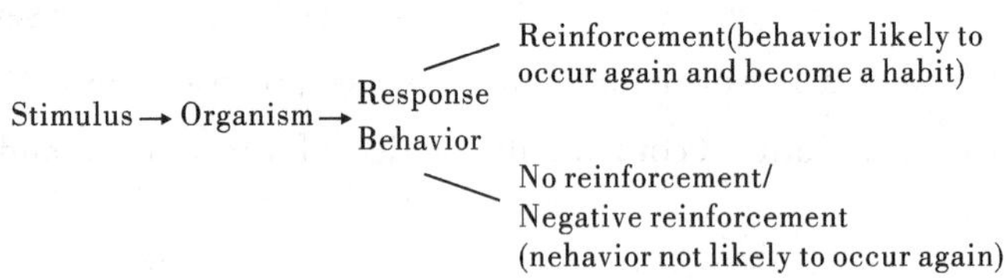

Figure 1. 1 A representation of stimulus, response and reinforcement

Design

Like the nineteenth-century reformers, audiolingualists advocated a return to speech-based instruction with the primary objective of oral proficiency, and dismissed the study of grammar or literature as the goal of foreign language teaching.

Objectives

Brooks(1964) distinguishes between short-range and long-range objectives of an audiolingual program. Short-range objectives include training in listening comprehension, accurate pronunciation, recognition of speech symbols as graphic signs on the printed page, and ability to reproduce these symbols in writing. Long-range objectives "must be language as the native speaker uses it... There must be some knowledge of a second language as it is possessed by a true bilingualist."

The syllabus

Audiolingualism is a linguistic, or structure-based, approach to language teaching. The starting point is a linguistic syllabus, which contains the key items of phonology, morphology, and syntax of the language arranged according to their order of presentation. In addition, a lexical syllabus of basic vocabulary items is usually specified in advance. The language skills are taught in the order of listening, speaking, reading, and writing. Listening is viewed largely as training in aural discrimination of basic sound patterns. The language may be presented entirely orally at first; written representations are usually withheld from learners in early stages.

When reading and writing are introduced, students are taught to read and write what they have already learned to say orally. An attempt is made to minimize the possibilities for making mistakes in both speaking and writing by using a tightly structured approach to the presentation of new language items. At more advanced levels, more complex reading and writing tasks may be introduced.

Types of learning and teaching activities

Dialogues and drills form the basis of audiolingual classroom practices. Dialogues provide the means of contextualizing key structures and illustrate situations in which structures might be used as well as some cultural aspects of the target language. Dialogues are used for repetition and memorization. Correct pronunciation, stress, rhythm, and intonation are emphasized. After a dialogue has been presented and memorized, specific grammatical patterns in the dialogue are selected and become the focus of various kinds of drill and pattern-practice exercises.

Learner roles

Learners are viewed as organisms that can be directed by skilled training techniques to produce correct responses. In accordance with behaviorist learning theory, teaching focuses on the external manifestations of learning rather than on the internal processes. Learners play a reactive role by responding to stimuli, and thus have little control over the content, pace, or style of learning. They are not encouraged to initiate interaction, because this may lead to mistakes.

Teacher roles

The teacher's role is central and active. The teacher models the target language, controls the direction and pace of learning, and monitors and corrects the learners' performance. The teacher must keep the learners attentive by varying drills and tasks and choosing relevant situations to practice structures.

The role of instructional materials

Instructional materials are primarily teacher-oriented. A student textbook is often not used in the elementary phases of a course where students are primarily listening, repeating, and responding.

Tape recorders and audiovisual equipment often have central roles in an audiolingual course. A language laboratory may also be considered essential. It provides the opportunity for further drill work and to receive controlled error-free practice of basic structures. It also adds variety by providing an alternative to classroom practice. A taped lesson may first present a dialogue for listening practice, allow for the student to repeat the sentences in the dialogue line by line, and provide follow-up fluency drills on grammar or pronunciation.

Procedure

In a typical audiolingual lesson, the following procedures would be observed:

1. Students first hear a model dialogue (either read by the teacher or on tape) containing the key structures that are the focus of the lesson. They repeat each line of the dialogue, individually and in chorus. The teacher pays attention to pronunciation, intonation, and fluency. Correction of mistakes of pronunciation or grammar is direct and immediate. The dialogue is memorized gradually, line by line. A line may be broken down into several phrases if necessary. The dialogue is read aloud in chorus, one half saying one speaker's part and the other half responding. The students do not consult their book throughout this phase.
2. The dialogue is adapted to the students' interest or situation, through changing certain key words or phrases. This is acted out by the students.
3. Certain key structures from the dialogue are selected and used as the basis for pattern drills of different kinds. These are first practiced in chorus and then individually. Some grammatical explanation may be offered at this point, but this is kept to an absolute minimum.
4. The students may refer to their textbook, and follow-up reading, writing, or vocabulary activities based on the dialogue may be introduced.
5. Follow-up activities may take place in the language laboratory, where further dialogue and drill work is carried out.

Conclusion

Audiolingualism stresses the mechanistic aspects of language learning and language use. There are many similarities between Situational Language Teaching and Audiolingualism. The order in which the language skills are introduced, and the focus on accuracy through drill and practice in the basic structures and sentence patterns of the target language, might suggest that these methods drew from each other. In fact, however, Situational Language Teaching was a development of the earlier Direct Method and does not have the strong ties to linguistics and behavioral psychology that characterize Audiolingualism. The concern for grammatical accuracy that was a focus of Audiolingualism has not disappeared, however, and continues to provide a challenge for contemporary applied linguistics.

Cognitive Approach

Background

Audiolingualism reached its period of most widespread use in the 1960s and was applied both to the teaching of foreign languages in the United States and to the teaching of English as a second or foreign language. But then came criticism on two fronts. On the one hand, the theoretical foundations were attacked as being unsound in terms of both language theory and learning theory. On the other hand, practitioners found that the practical results fell short of expectations. Students were often found to be unable to transfer skills acquired through Audiolingualism to real communication outside the classroom, and many found the experience of studying through audiolingual procedures to be boring and unsatisfying.

The theoretical attack on audiolingual beliefs resulted from changes in American linguistic theory in the 1960s. The MIT linguist Noam Chomsky (1966)[153] rejected the structuralist approach to language description as well as the behaviorist theory of language learning. "Language is not a habit structure. Ordinary linguistic behavior characteristically involves innovation, formation of new sentences and patterns in accordance with rules of great abstractness and intricacy." Chomsky's theory of transformational grammar proposed that the fundamental properties of language derive from innate aspects of the mind and from how humans process experience through language. His theories were to revolutionize American linguistics and focus the attention of linguists and psychologists on the mental properties people bring to bear on language use and language learning.

Suddenly the whole audiolingual paradigm was called into question: pattern practice, drilling, memorization. These might lead to language-like behaviors, but they were not resulting in competence. This created a crisis in American language teaching circles from which a full recovery has not yet been made. Temporary relief was offered in the form of a theory derived in part from Chomsky — cognitive code learning. In 1966, John B. Carroll, a psychologist who had taken a close interest in foreign language teaching, wrote:

> The audiolingual habit theory which is so prevalent in American foreign language teaching was, perhaps fifteen years ago, in step with the state of psychological thinking of that time, but it is no longer abreast of recent developments. It is ripe for major revision, particularly in the direction of joining it with some of the better elements of the cognitive- code learning theory (Carroll, 1966a)[105].

This referred to a view of learning that allowed for a conscious focus on grammar and that acknowledged the role of abstract mental processes in learning rather than defining learning simply in terms of habit formation. Practice activities should involve meaningful learning and language use. Learners should be encouraged to use their innate and creative abilities to derive and make explicit the underlying grammatical rules of the language. For a time in the early 1970s there was a considerable interest in the implication of the cognitive-code theory for language teaching. The term cognitive code is invoked to refer to any conscious attempt to organize materials around a grammatical syllabus while allowing for meaningful practice and use of language.

Characteristics

1. Language learning is viewed as rule acquisition, not habit formation.
2. Instruction is often individualized; learners are responsible for their own learning.
3. Grammar must be taught but it can be taught deductively (rules first, practice later) and/or inductively (rules can either be stated after practice or left as implicit information for the learners to process on their own).
4. Pronunciation is de-emphasized; perfection is viewed as unrealistic and unattainable.
5. Reading and writing are once again as important as listening and speaking.
6. Vocabulary instruction is once again important, especially at intermediate and advanced levels.
7. Errors are viewed as inevitable, to be used constructively in the learning process.
8. The teacher is expected to have good general proficiency in the target language as well as an ability to analyze the target language.

The lack of an alternative to Audiolingualism led in the 1970s and 1980s to a period of adaptation, innovation, experimentation, and some confusion. Several alternative method proposals appeared that made no claims to any links with mainstream language teaching and second language acquisition research.

Total Physical Response

Background

Total Physical Response (TPR) is a language teaching method built around the coordination of speech and action; it attempts to teach language through physical (motor) activity. Developed by James Asher, a professor of psychology at San Jose State University, California, it draws on several traditions, including developmental psychology, learning theory, and humanistic pedagogy, as well as on language teaching procedures proposed by Harold and Dorothy Palmer in 1925.

In a developmental sense, Asher(1977) sees successful adult second language learning as a parallel process to child first language acquisition. He claims that speech directed to young children consists primarily of commands, which children respond to physically before they begin to produce verbal responses. Asher shares with the school of humanistic psychology a concern for the role of affective (emotional) factors in language learning.

Approach: Theory of language and learning

TPR reflects a grammar-based view of language. Asher sees a stimulus-response view as providing the learning theory underlying language teaching pedagogy. Asher (1977) has elaborated an account of what he feels facilitates or inhibits foreign language learning. He draws on three rather influential learning hypotheses:

1. There exists a specific innate bio-program for language learning, which defines an optimal path for first and second language development.
2. Brain lateralization defines different learning functions in the left- and right-brain hemispheres.
3. Stress (an affective filter) intervenes between the act of learning and what is to be learned; the lower the stress, the greater the learning.

Design: Objectives, syllabus, learning activities, roles of learners, teachers, and materials

A TPR course aims to produce learners who are capable of an uninhibited communication that is intelligible to a native speaker.

The type of syllabus Asher uses can be inferred from an analysis of the exercise types employed in TPR classes. This analysis reveals the use of a sentence-based syllabus, with grammatical and lexical criteria being primary in selecting teaching items. Total Physical Response requires initial attention to meaning rather than to the form of items. Grammar is thus taught inductively.

Imperative drills are the major classroom activity. They are typically used to elicit physical actions and activity on the part of the learners. Conversational dialogues are delayed until after about 120 hours of instruction. Other class activities include role plays and slide presentations. Role plays center on everyday situations, such as at the restaurant, supermarket, or gas station.

Learners have the primary roles of listener and performer. They listen attentively and respond physically to commands given by the teacher. They are expected to recognize and respond to novel combinations of previously taught items, and required to produce novel combinations of their own. Learners monitor and evaluate their own progress. They are encouraged to speak when they feel ready to speak— that is, when a sufficient basis in the language has been internalized.

The teacher controls the language input the learners receive, providing the raw material for the "cognitive map" that the learners will construct in their own minds. The teacher should also allow speaking abilities to develop in learners at the learners' own natural pace. In giving feedback to learners, the teacher should follow the example of parents giving feedback to their children. Teachers should refrain from too much correction in the early stages and should not interrupt to correct errors, since this will inhibit learners. As time goes on, however, more teacher intervention is expected, as the learners' speech becomes "fine-tuned."

There is generally no basic text in a TPR course. Materials and realia play an increasing role, however, in later learning stages. For absolute beginners, lessons may not require the use of materials, since the teacher's voice, actions, and gestures may be a sufficient basis for classroom activities. Later, the teacher may use common classroom objects, such as books, pens, cups, furniture. As the course develops, the teacher will need to make or collect supporting materials to support teaching points. These may include pictures, realia, slides, and word charts.

Procedure

The activities are presented in Asher, Kusudo, and de la Torre (1974).

Listening Training. Students sit in a semicircle around the instructor. The instructor asks them to be silent, listen to commands in Spanish, and then do exactly what she does. The students are encouraged "to respond rapidly without hesitation and to make a distinct, robust response with their bodies." For example, when the teacher commands students to run by saying: Corran!, students are to run with gusto. The instructor simultaneously executes the commands as they are given, accompanied by the two students seated beside her. This routine is repeated several times until individual students indicate that they are willing to try it alone without the instructor acting as a model. Each variation of the routine is different to avoid the memorization of a fixed sequence of behaviors.

Next, commands are expanded to full sentences, such as "Walk to the door! Walk to the window! Walk to the table! Touch the table!" As students learn more vocabulary in this way, "surprises and novelty" are introduced, and the instructor begins to use playful, bizarre, and "zany" directives to keep students' interest high.

Production. Asher et al. state that after about ten hours of training in listening, students are "invited but not pressured" to reverse roles with the instructor and give their own commands in Spanish. The instructor then performs in response to the students' commands. Later, skits are prepared and performed by students, and still later, problem-solving situations are used. In this latter activity, students are presented with an unexpected difficulty in a typical survival situation or other setting in a Latin country and are expected to talk their way through the situation to a solution.

Reading and writing. The instructor wrote on the chalkboard each new vocabulary item and a sentence to illustrate the item. Then she spoke each item and acted out the sentence. The students listened as she read the material. Some copied the information in their notebooks.

Conclusion

TPR enjoyed some popularity in the 1970s and 1980s because of its support by those who emphasize the role of comprehension in second language acquisition. Krashen (1981), for example, regards provision of comprehensible input and reduction of stress as keys to successful language acquisition, and he sees performing physical actions in the target language as a means of making input comprehensible and minimizing stress. Asher stressed that TPR should be used in association with other methods and techniques. Indeed, practitioners of TPR typically follow this recommendation, suggesting that for many teachers TPR represents a useful set of techniques and is compatible with other approaches to teaching.

The Silent Way

Background

The Silent Way is devised by Caleb Gattegno (1972). It is based on the premise that the teacher should be silent as much as possible in the classroom but the learner should be encouraged to produce as much language as possible. Elements of the Silent Way, particularly the use of color charts and the colored Cuisenaire rods, grew out of Gattegno's previous experience as an educational designer of reading and mathematics programs.

Approach: Theory of language and learning

The Silent Way takes a structural approach to the organization of language to be taught. The sentence is the basic unit of teaching, and the teacher focuses on propositional meaning, rather than communicative value. Students are presented with the structural patterns of the target language and learn the grammar rules of the language through largely inductive processes.

Gattegno sees vocabulary as a central dimension of language learning and the choice of vocabulary as crucial. The most important vocabulary for the learner deals with the most functional and versatile words of the language, many of which may not have direct equivalents in the learner's native language. This "functional vocabulary" provides a key to comprehending the "spirit" of the language.

In elaborating a learning theory to support the principles of Silent Way, Gattegno makes extensive use of his understanding of first language learning. He recommends, for example, that the learner needs to "return to the state of mind that characterizes a baby's learning-surrender" (Scott et al., 1982).

Silent Way learners acquire "inner criteria, which play a central role in one's education throughout all of one's life" (Gattegno, 1976). These inner criteria allow learners to monitor and self-correct their own production. It is in the activity of self-correction through self-awareness that the Silent claims to differ most notably from other ways of language learning. It is this capacity for self-awareness that the Silent Way calls upon, a capacity said to be little appreciated or exercised by first language learners.

Design: Objectives, syllabus, learning activities, roles of learners, teachers, and materials

The general objective is to give beginning-level students oral and aural facility in basic elements of the target language. The general goal set for language learning is near-native fluency, and correct pronunciation and mastery of the prosodic elements of the target language are emphasized. An immediate objective is to provide the learner with a basic practical knowledge of the grammar.

The Silent Way adopts a basically structural syllabus, with lessons planned around grammatical items and related vocabulary. Language items are introduced according to their grammatical complexity, their relationship to what has been taught previously, and the ease with which items can be presented visually.

Learning tasks and activities in the Silent Way have the function of encouraging and shaping student oral response without direct oral instruction from or unnecessary modeling by the teacher. Basic to the method are simple linguistic tasks in which the teacher models a word, phrase, or sentence and then elicits learner responses. Learners then go on to create their own utterances by putting together old and new information. Charts, rods, and other aids may be used to elicit learner responses. Teacher modeling is minimal. Responses to commands, questions, and visual cues thus constitute the basis for classroom activities.

Learners are expected to develop independence, autonomy, and responsibility. They have only themselves as individuals and the group to rely on, and so must learn to work cooperatively rather than competitively. They need to feel comfortable both correcting one another and being corrected by one another.

Stevick defines the Silent Way teacher's tasks as to teach, to test, and to get out of the way (Stevick, 1980). By "teaching" is meant the presentation of an item once, typically using nonverbal clues to get across meanings. Testing follows immediately and might better be termed elicitation and shaping of student production, which, again, is done in as silent a way as possible. Finally, the teacher silently monitors learners' interactions with each other and may even leave the room while learners struggle with their new linguistic tools.

Silent Way materials consist mainly of a set of colored rods, color-coded pronunciation and vocabulary wall charts, a pointer, and reading/writing exercises, all of which are used to illustrate the relationships between sound and meaning in the target language. The materials are designed for manipulation by the students as well as by the teacher, independently and cooperatively, in promoting language learning by direct association.

Procedure

A Silent Way lesson typically follows a standard format. The first part of the lesson focuses on pronunciation. Depending on student level, the class might work on sounds, phrases, even sentences designated on the Fidel chart. At the beginning stage, the teacher will model the appropriate sound after pointing to a symbol on the chart. Later, the teacher will silently point to individual symbols and combinations of utterances, and monitor student utterances. The teacher may say a word and have students guess what sequence of symbols compromised the word.

The pointer is used to indicate stress, phrasing, and intonation. Stress can be shown by touching certain symbols more forcibly than others when pointing out a word. Intonation and phrasing can be demonstrated by tapping on the chart to the rhythm of the utterance.

After practice with the sounds of the language, sentence patterns, structure, and vocabulary are practiced. The teacher models an utterance while creating a visual realization of it with the colored rods. After modeling the utterance, the teacher will have a student attempt to produce the utterance and will indicate its acceptability. If a response is incorrect, the teacher will attempt to reshape the utterance or have another student present the correct model. After a structure is introduced and understood, the teacher will create a situation in which the students can practice the structure through the manipulation of the rods. Variations on the structural theme will be elicited from the class using the rods and charts.

Conclusion

Despite the philosophical and sometimes almost metaphysical quality of much of Gattegno's writings, the actual practices of the Silent Way are much less revolutionary than might be expected.

Working from what is a rather traditional structuraland lexical syllabus, the method exemplifies many of the features that characterize more traditional methods, such as Situational Language Teaching and Audiolingualism, with a strong focus on accurate repetition of sentences modeled initially by the teacher and a movement through guided elicitation exercises to freer communication.

Community Language Learning

Background

Community Language Learning (CLL) is the name of a method developed by Charles A, Curran and his associates. Curran was a specialist in counseling and a professor of psychology at Loyola University, Chicago. His application of psychological counseling techniques to learning is known as Counseling-Learning (Curran, 1972 & 1976). Community Language Learning draws on the counseling metaphor to redefine the roles of the teacher (the counselor) and learners (the clients) in the language classroom. The basic procedures of CLL can thus be seen as derived from the counselor-client relationship.

CLL techniques also belong to a larger set of foreign language teaching practices sometimes described as humanistic techniques (Moskowitz, 1978). Humanistic techniques engage the whole person, including the emotions and feelings (the affective realm) as well as linguistic knowledge and behavioral skills.

Approach: Theory of language and learning

Curran's student La Forge (1983) elaborates on the interactional view of language underlying Community Language Learning.

CLL interactions are of two distinct and fundamental kinds: interactions between learners and interactions between learners and knowers. Interactions between learners are unpredictable in content but typically are said to involve exchanges of affect. Interaction between learners and knowers is initially dependent. The learner tells the knower what he or she wishes to say in the target language, and the knower tells the learner how to say it.

The CLL view of learning is a holistic one, since "true" human learning is both cognitive and affective. This is termed whole-person learning. Learning takes place in a communicative situation where teachers and learners are involved in "an interaction... in which both experience a sense of their own wholeness" (Curran, 1972)[90].

Curran discusses what he calls"consensual validation," or "convalidation," in which mutual warmth, understanding, and a positive evaluation of the other person's worth develop between the teacher and the learner. A relationship characterized by convalidation is considered essential to the learning process and is a key element of CLL classroom procedures.

Design: Objectives, syllabus, learning activities, roles of learners, teachers, and materials

A CLL syllabus emerges from the interaction between the learner's expressed communicative intentions and the teacher's reformulations of these into suitable target-language utterances. Specific grammatical points, lexical patterns, and generalizations will sometimes be isolated by the teacher for more detailed study and analysis, and subsequent specification of these as a retrospective account of what the course covered could be a way of deriving a CLL language syllabus.

CLL combines innovative learning tasks and activities with conventional ones, including translation, group work, recording, transcription, analysis, reflection and observation, listening and free conversation.

Learners become members of a community—their fellow learners and the teacher—and learn through interacting with the community. Learners are expected to listen attentively to the knower, to freely provide meanings they wish to express, to repeat target utterances without hesitation, to support fellow members of the community, to report deep inner feelings and frustrations as well as joy and pleasure, and to become counselors of other learners.

The teacher serves as the "knower/counselor" whose role is essentially passive. He or she is there to provide the language necessary for students to express themselves freely and to say whatever it is they want to say.

Materials may be developed by the teacher as the course develops, although these generally consist of little more than summaries on the blackboard or overhead projector of some of the linguistic features of conversations generated by students.

Procedure

Based on Stevick, Curran(1976)[87-100] describes five learning stages:

Stage 1. Students make statements aloud in their native language, based on whatever they desire to communicate to the others in the group. The teacher, placing his or her hands on the student's shoulders, translates the utterance softly into the student's ear. The student then repeats the utterance after the teacher's model, recording it on tape. Another student, desiring to make a response, will signal this desire to the teacher, who then comes around the circle and provides a target-language equivalent for this student in the same way. Again, the response is recorded on tape, so that at the end of the conversation the whole dialogue is recorded. This tape-recorded script is used later in the class session as a source of input for the analysis and practice of the language.

Stage 2. In this "self-assertive stage," the students try to say what they want to without constant intervention and help from the teacher.

Stage 3. In this "birth stage," students increase their independence from the teacher and speak in the new language without translation, unless another student requests it.

Stage 4. The "adolescent" or "reversal" stage is one in which the learner has become secure enough to welcome corrective feedback from the teacher or other group members.

Stage 5. This "independent" stage is marked by free interaction between students and teacher(s): Everyone offers corrections and stylistic improvements in a community spirit. By this time, the trust level is high, and no individual is threatened by this type of feedback from others in the group. At all times, the atmosphere is one of warmth, acceptance, and understanding.

Conclusion

CLL places unusual demands on language teachers. They must be highly proficient and sensitive to nuance in both LI and L2. They must be familiar with and sympathetic to the role of counselors in psychological counseling. The teacher must also be relatively nondirective and must be prepared to accept and even encourage the "adolescent" aggression of the learner as he or she strives for independence. The teacher must operate without conventional materials, depending on student topics to shape and motivate the class.

Critics of CLL question the appropriateness of the counseling metaphor on which it is predicated. Questions also arise about whether teachers should attempt counseling without special training. Other concerns have been expressed regarding the lack of a syllabus, which makes objectives unclear and evaluation difficult to accomplish, and the focus on fluency rather than accuracy, which may lead to inadequate control of the grammatical system of the target language. Supporters of CLL, on the other hand, emphasize the positive benefits of a method that centers on the learner and stresses the humanistic side of language learning, and not merely its linguistic dimensions.

Suggestopedia

Background

Suggestopedia, also known as Desuggestopedia, is a method developed by the Bulgarian psychiatrist-educator Georgi Lozanov. It is a specific set of learning recommendations derived from Suggestology, which Lozanov describes as a "science ... concerned with the systematic study of the nonrational and/or nonconscious influences" that human beings are constantly responding to. Suggestopedia tries to harness these influences and redirect them so as to optimize learning.

Lozanov acknowledges ties in tradition to yoga and Soviet psychology. From raja-yoga Lozanov has borrowed and modified techniques for altering states of consciousness and concentration, and the use of rhythmic breathing. From Soviet psychology Lozanov has taken the notion that all students can be taught a given subject matter at the same level of skill. He claims that his method works equally well whether or not students spend time on outside study. He promises success through Suggestopedia to the academically gifted and the ungifted alike.

A most conspicuous feature of Suggestopedia is the centrality of music and musical rhythm to learning. It thus has a kinship with other functional uses of music, particularly therapy.

Approach: Theory of language and learning

Suggestion is at the heart of the theory of learning underlying Suggestopedia.

Authority

Lozanov appears to believe that scientific-sounding language, highly positive experimental data, and true-believer teachers constitute a ritual placebo system that is authoritatively appealing to most learners. Well-publicized accounts of learning success lend the method and the institution authority, and commitment to the method, self-confidence, personal distance, acting ability, and a highly positive attitude give an authoritative air to the teacher.

Infantilization

Authority is also used to suggest a teacher-student relation like that of parent to child. In the child's role the learner takes part in role playing, games, songs, and gymnastic exercises that help "the older student regain the self-confidence, spontaneity and receptivity of the child" (Bancroft, 1972).

Double-planedness

The learner learns not only from the effect of direct instruction but from the environment in which the instruction takes place. The bright decor of the classroom, the musical background, the shape of the chairs, and the teacher personality are considered as important in instruction as the form of the instructional material itself.

Intonation, rhythm, and concert pseudo-passiveness

Both intonation and rhythm are coordinated with a musical background. This helps to induce a relaxed attitude, which Lozanov refers to as concert pseudo-passiveness. This state is felt to be optimal for learning, in that anxieties and tension are relieved and power of concentration for new material is raised.

Design: Objectives, syllabus, learning activities, roles of learners, teachers, and materials

The objectives are to deliver advanced conversational proficiency quickly. It bases its learning claims on student mastery of prodigious lists of vocabulary pairs and, indeed, suggests to the students that it is appropriate that they set such goals for themselves. Lozanov emphasizes, however, that increased memory power is not an isolated skill but is a result of "positive, comprehensive stimulation of personality."

A Suggestopedia course lasts 30 days and consists of ten units of study. Classes are held 4 hours a day, 6 days a week. The central focus of each unit is a dialogue consisting of 1,200 words or so, with an accompanying Suggestopedia vocabulary list and grammatical commentary. The dialogues are graded by lexis and grammar.

Learning activities used in the method include imitation, question and answer, and role play. The type of activities that are more original to Suggestopedia are the listening activities, which concern the text and text vocabulary of each unit. These activities are typically part of the "presession phase," which takes place on the first day of a new unit. The students first look at and discuss a new text with the teacher. In the second reading, students relax comfortably in reclining chairs and listen to the teacher read the text in a certain way.

Learners' roles are carefully prescribed. Learners must maintain a pseudo-passive state, in which the material rolls over and through them. Students are expected to tolerate and in fact encourage their own "infantilization."

Groups of learners are ideally socially homogeneous, twelve in number, and divided equally between men and women. Learners sit in a circle, which encourages face-to-face exchange and activity participation.

The primary role of the teacher is to create situations in which the learner is most suggestible and then to present linguistic material in a way most likely to encourage positive reception and retention by the learner. Lozanov lists several expected teacher behaviors that contribute to these presentations.

1. Show absolute confidence in the method.
2. Display fastidious conduct in manners and dress.
3. Organize properly and strictly observe the initial stages of the teaching process—this includes choice and play of music, as well as punctuality.
4. Maintain a solemn attitude toward the session.
5. Give tests and respond tactfully to poor papers (if any).
6. Stress global rather than analytical attitudes toward material.
7. Maintain a modest enthusiasm.

Materials consist of direct support materials, primarily text and tape, and indirect support materials, including classroom fixtures and music.

The text is organized around the ten units. The textbook should have emotional force, literary quality, and interesting characters. Language problems should be introduced in a way that does not worry or distract students from the content. "Traumatic themes and distasteful lexical material should be avoided". Each unit should be governed by a single idea featuring a variety of subthemes.

The environment (the indirect support materials) comprises the appearance of the classroom (bright and cheery), the furniture (reclining chairs arranged in a circle), and the music (Baroque largo).

Procedure

Bancroft (1972) notes that the 4-hour language class has three distinct parts.

The first part we might call an oral review section. Previously learned material is used as the basis for discussion by the teacher and twelve students in the class. All participants sit in a circle in their specially designed chairs, and the discussion proceeds like a seminar. This session may involve what are called micro-studies and macro-studies. In micro-studies specific attention is given to grammar, vocabulary, and precise questions and answers.

In the second part of the class new material is presented and discussed. This consists of looking over a new dialogue and its native language translation and discussing any issues of grammar, vocabulary, or content that the teacher feels important or that students are curious about. Bancroft notes that this section is typically conducted in the target language, although student questions or comments will be in whatever language the student feels he or she can handle. Students are led to view the experience of dealing with the new material as interesting and undemanding of any special effort or anxiety. The teacher's attitude and authority are considered critical to preparing students for success in the learning to come. The pattern of learning and use is noted (i. e. , fixation, reproduction, and new creative production), so that students will know what is expected.

The third part the seance or concert session—is the one by which Suggestopedia is best known. we quote Lozanov(1978) as to how this session proceeds.

> At the beginning of the session, all conversation stops for a minute or two, and the teacher listens to the music coming from a tape-recorder. He waits and listens to several passages in order to enter into the mood of the music and then begins to read or recite the new text, his voice modulated in harmony with the musical phrases. The students follow the text in their textbooks where each lesson is translated into the mother tongue. Between the first and second part of the concert, there are several minutes of solemn silence. In some cases, even longer pauses can be given to permit the students to stir a little. Before the beginning of the second part of the concert, there are again several minutes of silence and some phrases of the music are heard again before the teacher begins to read the text. Now the students close their textbooks and listen to the teacher's reading. At the end, the students silently leave the room. They are not told to

do any homework on the lesson they have just had except for reading it cursorily once before going to bed and again before getting up in the morning.

Conclusion

Lozanov maintains that placebos do both cure and teach when the patient or pupil credits them with the power to do so. Perhaps, then, it is not productive to further belabor the science/nonscience, data/double-talk issues and instead, as Bancroft and Stevick have done, try to identify and validate those techniques from Suggestopedia that appear effective and that harmonize with other successful techniques in the language teaching inventory.

Communicative Language Teaching

Background

The origins of Communicative Language Teaching (CLT) are to be found in the changes in the British language teaching tradition dating from the late 1960s. Just as the linguistic theory underlying Audiolingualism was rejected in the United States in the mid-1960s, British applied linguists began to call into question the theoretical assumptions underlying Situational Language Teaching.

Chomsky(1957) had demonstrated that the current standard structural theories of language were incapable of accounting for the fundamental characteristic of language—the creativity and uniqueness of individual sentences. British applied linguists emphasized another fundamental dimension of language that was inadequately addressed in approaches to language teaching at that time—the functional and communicative potential of language.

Another impetus for different approaches to foreign language teaching came from changing educational realities in Europe. The Council of Europe was active in promoting the formation of the International Association of Applied Linguistics. The need to develop alternative methods of language teaching was considered a high priority.

Practitioners from different educational traditions identify with Communicative Approach, and interpret it in different ways. Common to all versions is a theory of language teaching that starts from a communicative model of language and language use, and that seeks to translate this into a design for an instructional system, for materials, for teacher and learner roles and behaviors, and for classroom activities and techniques.

Approach

Theory of language

The goal of language teaching is to develop what Hymes (1972a) referred to as "communicative competence." Canale and Swain (1980) identified four dimensions of communicative competence:

Grammatical competence refers to what Chomsky calls linguistic competence and what Hymes (1972a) intends by what is "formally possible." It is the domain of grammatical and lexical capacity.

Sociolinguistic competence refers to an understanding of the social context in which communication takes place, including role relationships, the shared information of the participants, and the communicative purpose for their interaction.

Discourse competence refers to the interpretation of individual message elements in terms of their interconnectedness and of how meaning is represented in relationship to the entire discourse or text.

Strategic competence refers to the coping strategies that communicators employ to initiate, terminate, maintain, repair, and redirect communication.

Theory of learning

Elements of an underlying learning theory can be discerned in some CLT practices.

1. The communication principle:
   Activities that involve real communication promote learning.
2. The task principle:
   Activities in which language is used for carrying out meaningful tasks pro mote learning (Johnson, 1982).
3. The meaningfulness principle:
   Language that is meaningful to the learner supports the learning process.

Savignon (1983) surveys second language acquisition research as a source for learning theories and considers the role of linguistic, social, cognitive, and individual variables in language acquisition.

Krashen and other second language acquisition theorists typically stress that language learning comes about through using language communicatively, rather than through practicing language skills.

Johnson(1984) and Littlewood (1984) consider an alternative learning theory that they also see as compatible with CLT—a skill-learning model of learning. According to this theory, the acquisition of communicative competence in a language is an example of skill development.

Design

Objectives

Piepho (1981)[8] discusses the following levels of objectives:

1. an integrative and content level (language as a means of expression)
2. a linguistic and instrumental level (language as a semiotic system and an object of learning)
3. an affective level of interpersonal relationships and conduct (language as a means of expressing values and judgments about oneself and others)

4. a level of individual learning needs (remedial learning based on error analysis)
5. a general educational level of extra-linguistic goals (language learning within the school curriculum)

These are proposed as general objectives, applicable to any teaching situation.

The syllabus

Discussions of the nature of the syllabus have been central in Communicative Language Teaching. There is extensive documentation of attempts to create syllabus and proto-syllabus designs. Descriptions of interactional strategies have been given, for example, for interactions of teacher and student and doctor and patient. Although interesting, these descriptions have restricted the field of inquiry to two- person interactions in which there exist reasonably rigid and acknowledged superordinate-to-subordinate role relationships.

Some designers of communicative syllabuses have also looked to task specification and task organization as the appropriate criteria for syllabus design.

Types of learning and teaching activities

The range of exercise types and activities compatible with a communicative approach is unlimited, provided that such exercises enable learners to attain the communicative objectives of the curriculum, engage learners in communication, and require the use of such communicative processes as information sharing, negotiation of meaning, and interaction. Classroom activities are often designed to focus on completing tasks that are mediated through language or involve negotiation of information and information sharing.

Littlewood (1981) distinguishes between "functional communication activities" and "social interaction activities" as major activity types in Communicative Language Teaching. Functional communication activities include such tasks as learners comparing sets of pictures and noting similarities and differences; working out a likely sequence of events in a set of pictures; discovering missing features in a map or picture; one learner communicating behind a screen to another learner and giving instructions on how to draw a picture or shape, or how to complete a map; following directions; and solving problems from shared clues. Social interaction activities include conversation and discussion sessions, dialogues and role plays, simulations, skits, improvisations, and debates.

Learner roles

Breen and Candlin(1980)[110] describe the learner's role in the following terms:

> The role of learner as negotiator — between the self, the learning process, and the object of learning emerges from and interacts with the role of joint negotiator within the group and within the classroom procedures and activities which the group undertakes. The implication for the learner is that he should contribute as much as he gains, and thereby learn in an interdependent way.

The cooperative (rather than individualistic) approach to learning stressed in CLT may likewise be unfamiliar to learners. CLT methodologists consequently recommend that learners learn to see that failed communication is a joint responsibility and not the fault of speaker or listener. Similarly, successful communication is an accomplishment jointly achieved and acknowledged.

Teacher roles

Breen and Candlin (1980)[99] describe teacher roles in the following terms:

> The teacher has two main roles: the first role is to facilitate the communication process between all participants in the classroom, and between these participants and the various activities and texts. The second role is to act as an independent participant within the learning-teaching group. The latter role is closely related to the objectives of the first role and arises from it. These roles imply a set of secondary roles for the teacher; first, as an organizer of resources and as a resource himself, second as a guide within the classroom procedures and activities. ... A third role for the teacher is that of researcher and learner, with much to contribute in terms of appropriate knowledge and abilities, actual and observed experience of the nature of learning and organizational capacities.

Other roles assumed for teachers are as follows:

1. Needs analyst

The CLT teacher assumes a responsibility for determining and responding to learner language needs. This may be done informally and personally through one-to-one sessions with students, in which the teacher talks through such issues as the student's perception of his or her learning style, learning assets, and learning goals. It may be done formally through administering a needs assessment instrument, such as those exemplified in Savignon (1983). Typically, such formal assessments contain items that attempt to determine an individual's motivation for studying the language.

2. Counselor

The teacher-counselor is expected to exemplify an effective communicator seeking to maximize the meshing of speaker intention and hearer interpretation, through the use of paraphrase, confirmation, and feedback.

3. Group process manager

CLT procedures often require teachers to acquire less teacher-centered classroom management skills. It is the teacher's responsibility to organize the classroom as a setting for communication and communicative activities. Guidelines for classroom practice suggest that during an activity the teacher monitors, encourages, and suppresses the inclination to supply gaps in lexis, grammar, and strategy but notes such gaps for later commentary and communicative practice. At the conclusion of group activities, the teacher leads in the debriefing of the activity, pointing out alternatives and extensions and assisting groups in self-correction discussion.

The role of instructional materials

A wide variety of materials have the primary role of promoting communicative language use. We will label these text-based, task-based, and realia.

1. Text-based materials

A typical lesson consists of a theme (e. g., relaying information), a task analysis for thematic development (e. g., understanding the message, asking questions to obtain clarification, asking for more information, taking notes, ordering and presenting information), a practice situation description (e. g., "A caller asks to see your manager. He does not have an appointment. Gather the necessary information from him and relay the message to your manager."), a stimulus presentation (in the preceding case, the beginning of an office conversation scripted and on tape), comprehension questions (e. g. , "Why is the caller in the office?"), and paraphrase exercises.

2. Task-based materials

A variety of games, role plays, simulations, and task-based communication activities have been prepared to support Communicative Language Teaching classes. These typically are in the form of one-of-a-kind items: exercise handbooks, cue cards, activity cards, pair-communication practice materials, and student-interaction practice booklets. In pair communication materials, there are typically two sets of material for a pair of students, each set containing different kinds of information. Sometimes the information is complementary, and partners must fit their respective parts of the "jigsaw" into a composite whole. Others assume different role relationships for the partners (e. g. , an interviewer and an interviewee). Still others provide drills and practice material in interactional formats.

3. Realia

Many proponents have advocated the use of "authentic," "from-life" materials in the classroom. These might include language-based realia, such as signs, magazines, advertisements, and newspapers, or graphic and visual sources around which communicative activities can be built, such as maps, pictures, symbols, graphs, and charts. Different kinds of objects can be used to support communicative exercises, such as a plastic model to assemble from directions.

Procedure

Finocchiaro and Brumfit (1983)[107-108] offer a lesson outline for teaching the function "making a suggestion" for learners in the beginning level of a secondary school program that suggests CLT procedures are evolutionary rather than revolutionary:

1. Presentation of a brief dialog or several mini-dialogs, preceded by a motivation (relating the dialog situation[s] to the learners' probable community experiences) and a discussion of the function and situation-people, roles, setting, topic, and the informality or formality of the language which the function and situation demand, (At beginning levels, where all the learners understand the same native language, the motivation can well be given in their native tongue.)
2. Oral practice of each utterance of the dialog segment to be presented that day (entire class repetition, half-class, groups, individuals) generally preceded by your model. If mini-dialogs are used, engage in similar practice.
3. Questions and answers based on the dialog topic(s) and situation itself.

(Inverted *wh-* or *or-* questions.)

4. Questions and answers related to the students' personal experiences but centered around the dialog theme.
5. Study one of the basic communicative expressions in the dialog or one of the structures which exemplify the function. You will wish to give several additional examples of the communicative use of the expression or structure with familiar vocabulary in unambiguous utterances or mini-dialogs (using pictures, simple real objects, or dramatization) to clarify the meaning of the expression or structure...
6. Learner discovery of generalizations or rules underlying the functional expression or structure. This should include at least four points: its oral and written forms (the elements of which it is composed, e.g., "How about + verb + ing?"); its position in the utterance; its formality or informality in the utterance; and in the case of a structure, its grammatical function and meaning...
7. Oral recognition, interpretative activities (two to five depending on the learning level, the language knowledge of the students, and related factors).
8. Oral production activities-proceeding from guided to freer communication activities.
9. Copying of the dialogs or mini-dialogs or modules if they are not in the class text.
10. Sampling of the written homework assignment, if given.
11. Evaluation of learning (oral only), e.g., "How would you ask your friend to ________? And how would you ask me to ________?"

Such procedures clearly have much in common with those observed in classes taught according to Structural-Situational and Audiolingual principles. Traditional procedures are not rejected but are reinterpreted and extended.

Conclusion

Communicative Language Teaching is best considered an approach rather than a method. It refers to a diverse set of principles that reflect a communicative view of language and language learning and that can be used to support a wide variety of classroom procedures.

These principles include:

- Learners learn a language through using it to communicate.
- Authentic and meaningful communication should be the goal of classroom activities.
- Fluency is an important dimension of communication.
- Communication involves the integration of different language skills.
- Learning is a process of creative construction and involves trial and error.

Johnson et al. (1998) identify five core characteristics that underlie current applications of communicative methodology:

1. *Appropriateness.* Language use reflects the situations of its use and must be appropriate to that situation depending on the setting, the roles of the participants, and

the purpose of the communication, for example. Thus learners may need to be able to use formal as well as casual styles of speaking.

2. *Message focus*. Learners need to be able to create and understand messages, that is, real meanings. Hence the focus on information sharing and information transfer in CLT activities.
3. *Psycholinguistic processing*. CLT activities seek to engage learners in the use of cognitive and other processes that are important factors in second language acquisition.
4. *Risk taking*. Learners are encouraged to make guesses and learn from their errors. By going beyond what they have been taught, they are encouraged to employ a variety of communication strategies.
5. *Free practice*. CLT encourages the use of "holistic practice" involving the simultaneous use of a variety of subskills, rather than practicing individual skills one piece at a time.

These address very general aspects of language learning and teaching that are now largely accepted as self-evident and axiomatic throughout the profession. Some focus centrally on the *input* to the learning process. Some teaching proposals focus more directly on *instructional* factors. Other more recent proposals take learners and *learning factors* as the primary issues to address in teaching and learning.

Outcome is another dimension of the process of communication and is central in Competency-Based Language leaching. Outcomes are the starting point in program planning with this approach.

Today, Communicative Language leaching continues in its "classic" form, as is seen in the huge range of course books and other teaching resources based on the principles of CLT. In addition, it has influenced many other language teaching approaches and methods that subscribe to a similar philosophy of language teaching.

Task-Based Language Teaching

Background

Task-Based Language Teaching (TBLT) refers to an approach based on the use of tasks as the core unit of planning and instruction in language teaching. Some of its proponents present it as a logical development of Communicative Language Teaching since it draws on several principles that formed part of the communicative language teaching movement from the 1980s.

An interest in tasks as potential building blocks of second language instruction emerged when researchers turned to tasks as SLA research tools in the mid-1980s. SLA research has focused on the strategies and cognitive processes employed by second language learners. This research has suggested a reassessment of the role of formal grammar instruction in language teaching. There is no evidence, that the type of grammar-focused teaching activities used in many language classrooms reflects the cognitive learning processes employed in naturalistic language learning situations outside the classroom.

Engaging learners in task work provides a better context for the activation of learning processes than form-focused activities, and hence ultimately provides better opportunities for language learning to take place. Language learning is believed to depend on immersing students not merely in "comprehensible input," but in tasks that require them to negotiate meaning and engage in naturalistic and meaningful communication.

Approach

Theory of language

TBLT is motivated primarily by a theory of learning rather than a theory of language. However, several assumptions about the nature of language can be said to underlie current approaches to TBLT. These are:

Language is primarily a means of making meaning.

In common with other realizations of communicative language teaching, TBLT emphasizes the central role of meaning in language use. Skehan notes that in task-based instruction (TBI), "meaning is primary... the assessment of the task is in terms of outcome and that task-based instruction is not concerned with language display" (Skehan, 1998)[98].

Multiple models of language inform TBI.

Advocates of task-based instruction draw on structural, functional, and interactional models of language. This seems to be more a matter of convenience than of ideology. For example, *structural* criteria are employed by Skehan in discussing the criteria for determining the linguistic complexity of tasks:

> Language is simply seen as less-to-more complex in fairly traditional ways, since linguistic complexity is interpretable as constrained by structural syllabus considerations (Skehan, 1998)[99].

Other researchers have proposed *functional* classifications of task types. For example, Berwick uses "task goals" as one of two distinctions in classification of task types.

Finally, task classifications proposed by those coming from the SLA research tradition of interaction studies focus on interactional dimensions of tasks. Pica (1994) distinguishes between interactional activity and communicative goal.

TBLT is therefore not linked to a single model of language but rather draws on all three models of language theory.

Lexical units are central in language use and language learning.

In recent years, vocabulary has been considered to play a more central role in second language learning than was traditionally assumed. Vocabulary is here used to include the consideration of lexical phrases, sentence stems, prefabricated routines, and collocations, and not only words as significant units of linguistic lexical analysis and language pedagogy. Many task-based proposals incorporate this perspective, Skehan(1996b)[21-22], for example, comments:

> Although much of language teaching has operated under the assumption that language is essentially structural, with vocabulary elements slotting in to fill structural patterns, many linguists and psycholinguists have argued that native language speech processing is very frequently lexical in nature. This means that speech processing is based on the production and reception of whole phrase units larger than the word (although analyzable by linguists into words) which do not require any internal processing when they are "reeled off"... Fluency concerns the learner's capacity to produce language in real time without undue pausing for hesitation. It is likely to rely upon more lexicalized modes of communication, as the pressures of real-time speech production met only by avoiding excessive rule-based computation.

"Conversation" is the central focus of language and the keystone of language acquisition.

Speaking and trying to communicate with others through the spoken language drawing on the learner's available linguistic and communicative resources is considered the basis for second language acquisition in TBI; hence, the majority of tasks that are proposed within TBI involve conversation.

Theory of learning

TBLT shares the general assumptions about the nature of language learning underlying Communicative Language Teaching. However, some additional learning principles play a central role in TBLT theory. These are:

Tasks provide both the input and output processing necessary for language acquisition.

Krashen has long insisted that comprehensible input is the one necessary (and sufficient) criterion for successful language acquisition. Others have argued, however, that productive output and not merely input is also critical for adequate second language development. Tasks, it is said, provide full opportunities for both input and output requirements, which are believed to be key processes in language learning. Other researchers have looked at "negotiation of meaning" as the necessary element in second language acquisition. "It is meaning negotiation which focuses a learner's attention on some part of an [the learner's] utterance (pronunciation, grammar, lexicon, etc.) which requires modification. That is, negotiation can be viewed as the trigger for acquisition."

Tasks are believed to foster processes of negotiation, modification, rephrasing, and experimentation that are at the heart of second language learning. This view is part of a more general focus on the critical importance of conversation in language acquisition (e.g., Sato, 1988). Drawing on SLA research on negotiation and interaction, TBLT proposes that the task is the pivot point for stimulation of input-output practice, negotiation of meaning, and transactionally focused conversation.

Task activity and achievement are motivational.

Tasks are also said to improve learner motivation and therefore promote learning. This is because they require the learners to use authentic language, they have well-defined dimensions and closure, they are varied in format and operation, they typically include physical activity, they involve partnership and collaboration, they may call on the learner's past experience, and they tolerate and encourage a variety of communication styles.

Learning difficulty can be negotiated and finetuned for particular pedagogical purposes. Another claim for tasks is that specific tasks can be designed to facilitate the use and learning of particular aspects of language. Long and Crookes (1992)[43] claim that:

> Tasks provide a vehicle for the presentation of appropriate target language samples to learners—input which they will inevitably reshape via application of general cognitive processing capacities—and for the delivery of comprehension and production opportunities of negotiable difficulty.

Skehan suggests that in selecting or designing tasks there is a trade-off between cognitive processing and focus on form. More difficult, cognitively demanding tasks reduce the amount of attention the learner can give to the formal features of messages, something that is thought to be necessary for accuracy and grammatical development. In other words, if the task is too difficult, fluency may develop at the expense of accuracy. He suggests that tasks can be designed along a cline of difficulty so that learners can work on tasks that enable them to develop both fluency and an awareness of language form. He also proposes that tasks can be used to "channel" learners toward particular aspects of language:

> Such channeled use might be towards some aspect of the discourse, or accuracy, complexity, fluency in general, or even occasionally, the use of particular sets of structures in the language(Skehan, 1998)[97-98].

Design

Objectives

There are few published (or perhaps, fully implemented) examples of complete language programs that claim to be fully based on most recent formulations of TBLT. The literature contains mainly descriptions of examples of task-based activities. However, as with other communicative approaches, goals in TBLT are ideally to be determined by the specific needs of particular learners. Selection of tasks, according to Long and Crookes (1993), should be based on a careful analysis of the real-world needs of learners.

The syllabus

A TBLT syllabus specifies the tasks that should be carried out by learners within a program. The intrinsic difficulty of tasks has been proposed as a basis for the sequencing of tasks, but task difficulty is itself a concept that is not easy to determine. Honeyfield (1993)[129] offers the following considerations:

1. Procedures, or what the learners have to do to derive output from input
2. Input text
3. Output required
   - Language items: vocabulary, structures, discourse structures, processability, and so on
   - Skills, both macro-skills and subskills
   - World knowledge or "topic content"
   - Text handling or conversation strategies
4. Amount and type of help given
5. Role of teachers and learners
6. Time allowed
7. Motivation
8. Confidence
9. Learning styles

This list illustrates the difficulty of operationalizing the notion of task difficulty: One could add almost anything to it, such as time of day, room temperature, or the aftereffects of breakfast!

Types of learning and teaching activities

There are many different views as to what constitutes a task. Consequently, there are many competing descriptions of basic task types and of appropriate classroom activities.

For Prabhu, a task is "an activity which requires learners to arrive at an outcome from given information through some process of thought, and which allows teachers to control and regulate that process." Reading train timetables and deciding which train one should take to get to a certain destination on a given day is an appropriate classroom task according to this definition. Crookes defines a task as "a piece of work or an activity, usually with a specified objective, undertaken as part of an educational course, at work, or used to elicit data for research" (Crookes 1986)[1]. This definition would lead to a very different set of "tasks" from those identified by Prahbu, since it could include not only summaries, essays, and class notes, but presumably, in some language classrooms, drills, dialogue readings, and any of the other "tasks" that teachers use to attain their teaching objectives.

In the literature on TBLT, several attempts have been made to group tasks into categories, as a basis for task design and description. Pica, Kanagy, and Falodun (1993) classify tasks according to the type of interaction that occurs in task accomplishment and give the following classification:

1. *Jigsaw tasks.* These involve learners combining different pieces of information to form a whole (e.g., three individuals or groups may have three different parts of a story and have to piece the story together).
2. *Information-gap tasks.* One student or group of students has one set of in formation

and another student or group has a complementary set of information. They must negotiate and find out what the other party's information is in order to complete an activity.

3. *Problem-solving tasks*. Students are given a problem and a set of information. They must arrive at a solution to the problem. There is generally a single resolution of the outcome.
4. *Decision-making tasks*. Students are given a problem for which there are a number of possible outcomes and they must choose one through negotiation and discussion.
5. *Opinion exchange tasks*. Learners engage in discussion and exchange of ideas. They do not need to reach agreement.

Learner roles

Primary roles that are implied by task work are:

1. Group participant

Many tasks will be done in pairs or small groups. For students more accustomed to whole-class and/or individual work, this may require some adaptation.

2. Monitor

In TBLT, tasks are not employed for their own sake but as a means of facilitating learning. Class activities have to be designed so that students have the opportunity to notice how language is used in communication. Learners themselves need to "attend" not only to the message in task work, but also to the form in which such messages typically come packed. A number of learner-initiated techniques to support learner reflection on task characteristics, including language form, are proposed in Bell and Burnaby (1984).

3. Risk-taker and innovator

Many tasks will require learners to create and interpret messages for which they lack full linguistic resources and prior experience. In fact, this is said to be the point of such tasks. Practice in restating, paraphrasing, using paralinguistic signals (where appropriate), and so on, will often be needed. The skills of guessing from linguistic and contextual clues, asking for clarification, and consulting with other learners may also need to be developed.

Teacher roles

Additional roles are also assumed for teachers in TBI, including:

1. Selector and sequencer of tasks

A central role of the teacher is in selecting, adapting, and/or creating the tasks themselves and then forming these into an instructional sequence in keeping with learner needs, interests, and language skill level.

2. Preparing learners for tasks

Most TBLT proponents suggest that learners should not go into new tasks "cold" and that some sort of pretask preparation or cuing is important. Such activities might include topic introduction, clarifying task instructions, helping students learn or recall useful words and phrases to facilitate task accomplishment, and providing partial demonstration of task procedures. Such cuing may be inductive and implicit or deductive and explicit.

3. Consciousness-raising

If learners are to acquire language through participating in tasks they need to attend to or notice critical features of the language they use and hear. This is referred to as "Focus on Form." TBLT proponents stress that this does not mean doing a grammar lesson before students take on a task. It does mean employing a variety of form-focusing techniques, including attention-focusing pretask activities, text exploration, guided exposure to parallel tasks, and use of highlighted material.

The role of instructional materials

1. Pedagogic materials

Instructional materials play an important role in TBLT because it is dependent on a sufficient supply of appropriate classroom tasks, some of which may require considerable time, ingenuity, and resources to develop. Materials that can be exploited for instruction in TBLT are limited only by the imagination of the task designer. Many contemporary language teaching texts cite a "task focus," or "task-based activities" among their credentials, though most of the tasks are familiar classroom activities for teachers who employ collaborative learning, Communicative Language teaching, or small-group activities. Several teacher resource books are available that contain representative sets of sample task activities that can be adapted for a variety of situations. A number of task collections have also been put into textbook form for students use.

2. Realia

A wide variety of realia can also be used as a resource for TBLT. TBLT proponents favor the use of authentic tasks supported by authentic materials wherever possible. Popular media obviously provide rich resources for such materials as newspapers, television, and Internet.

Procedure

The way in which task activities are designed into an instructional bloc can be seen from the following example from Richards (1985). The example comes from a language program that contained a core component built around tasks. The program was an intensive conversation course for Japanese college students studying on a summer program in the United States. Needs analysis identified target tasks the students needed to be able to carry out in English, including:

- basic social survival transactions
- face-to-face informal conversations
- telephone conversations
- interviews on the campus
- service encounters

A set of role-play activities was then developed focusing on situations students would encounter in the community and transactions they would have to carry out in English. The following format was developed for each role-play task:

Pretask activities

1. Learners first take part in a preliminary activity that introduces the topic, the situation, and the "script" that will subsequently appear in the role-play task. Such activities are of various kinds, including brainstorming, ranking exercises, and problem-solving tasks. The focus is on thinking about a topic, generating vocabulary and related language, and developing expectations about the topic. This activity therefore prepares learners for the role-play task by establishing schemata of different kinds.
2. Learners then read a dialogue on a related topic. This serves both to model the kind of transaction the learner will have to perform in the role-play task and to provide examples of the kind of language that could be used to carry out such a transaction.

Task activity

Learners perform a role play. Students work in pairs with a task and cues needed to negotiate the task.

Posttask activities

Learners then listen to recordings of native speakers performing the same role-play task they have just practiced and compare differences between the way they expressed particular functions and meanings and the way native speakers performed.

Research on Task-based language teaching in China

The TBLT approach has both strengths and weaknesses when used in China. According to Shu Dingfang and Zhuang Zhixiang (2008), the strengths of TBLT include introducing China to new views of language learning and language teaching that place learners in the center as the primary participants taking responsibility for their own learning. Teachers are not only knowledge-providers but also helpers and facilitators, who design proper tasks and organize class activities based on students' needs. Another strength of TBLT is that it bridges the gap between classroom and real life by creating simulated real-life tasks. A further advantage of TBLT is its goal of teaching students how to learn so that they can become lifelong learners.

As for TBLT's weaknesses when used in China, Shu Dingfang and Zhuang Zhixiang (2008) believe that TBLT takes an extreme stance on the learning process, overemphasizing learners' initiative and autonomy and undervaluing the function of instruction. For Chinese learners, especially beginning learners who have limited exposure to the target language, instruction on language forms and rules are important. In addition, the selection and sequence of tasks in class is problematic as they are often done based on teachers' assumptions. Next, TBLT is more suitable for a second language context than for a foreign language one, as it requires learners to understand and induce rules in the process of living in and using the target language. In China, English exposure is rather limited; thus, the applicability of TBLT becomes a problem.

Like anywhere, the China task-based innovation experience constitutes a unique social, cultural, geographical, and educational context. Yet despite traditional classroom culture, language context, exam-oriented instruction and learning, etc., the voices of the informants reveal their wisdom in their teaching. They are willing to accept and utilize TBLT, and they overcome those challenges by designing appropriate tasks for students to create natural learning environment, adopting flexible teaching procedures, applying TBLT creatively, exploring task-based language assessment, and integrating TBLT with traditional teaching. The practitioners make changes when adopting TBLT in English classroom, and experiment with tasks in sophisticated ways, in an effort to make their language teaching more functional, more usage-based, and more powerful, aiming to cultivate students' English language abilities and core competencies. (Liu Chunyan et al., 2020).

Conclusion

Few would question the pedagogical value of employing tasks as a vehicle for promoting communication and authentic language use in second language classrooms, and depending on one's definition of a task, tasks have long been part of the mainstream repertoire of language teaching techniques for teachers of many different methodological persuasions. TBLT, however, offers a different rationale for the use of tasks as well as different criteria for the design and use of tasks. It is the dependence on tasks as the primary source of pedagogical input in teaching and the absence of a systematic grammatical or other type of syllabus that characterizes current versions of TBIT. Many aspects of TBLT have yet to be justified, such as proposed schemes for task types, task sequencing, and evaluation of task performance. And the basic assumption of Task-Based Language Teaching—that it provides for a more effective basis for teaching than other language teaching approaches—remains in the domain of ideology rather than fact.

Exercises, Questions and Tasks

1. Multiple Choices.

(1) ________ often creates frustration for students.

A. Audiolingual Method　　B. Situational Language Teaching

C. Grammar-Translation Method　　D. Community Language Learning

(2) ________ can be regarded as the first language teaching method to have caught the attention of teachers and language teaching specialists, and it offered a methodology that appeared to move language teaching into a new era.

A. Grammar-Translation Method　　B. Audiolingual Method

C. Situational Language Teaching　　D. The Direct Method

(3) The theory of language underlying Situational Language Teaching can be characterized as a type of ________.

A. structuralism　　B. behaviorism

C. cognitivism　　D. constructivism

(4) ________ stresses the mechanistic aspects of language learning.

A. Audiolingualism B. Communicative Language Teaching

C. Task-Based Language Teaching D. Community Language Learning

(5) ________ is undemanding in terms of linguistic production and involves game like movements reduces learner stress.

A. Suggestopedia B. Total Physical Response (TPR)

C. The Silent way D. Community Language Learning

(6) It is in the activity of self-correction through self-awareness that ________ claims to differ most notably from other ways of language learning.

A. Suggestopedia B. Total Physical Response (TPR)

C. The Silent Way D. Community Language Learning

(7) ________ view of learning is a holistic one, since "true" human learning is both cognitive and affective.

A. Community Language Learning B. Total Physical Response (TPR)

C. The Silent Way D. Suggestopedia

(8) A most conspicuous feature of ________ is the centrality of music and musical rhythm to learning.

A. Community Language Learning B. Total Physical Response (TPR)

C. The Silent Way D. Suggestopedia

(9) Which of the following is least likely to be a CLT principle?

A. The communication principle B. The accuracy principle

C. The task principle D. The meaningfulness principle

(10) Which of the following is not a task based on TBLT?

A. Information-gap tasks B. Problem-solving tasks

C. Opinion exchange D. substitution tasks

2. Fill in each blank with an appropriate word.

(1) Changes in language teaching methods throughout history have reflected recognition of changes in the kind of ________ learners need.

(2) TPR focuses on meaning interpreted through ________, in which the learner is said to be liberated from self-conscious and stressful situations and is able to devote full energy to learning.

(3) One conspicuous feature of Suggestopedia is students are expected to tolerate and in fact encourage their own ________.

(4) The focus on ________ and comprehensibility in Communicative Language Teaching may cause anxiety among teachers accustomed to seeing error suppression and correction as the major instructional responsibility.

(5) It is the ________ on tasks as the primary source of pedagogical input in teaching and the absence of a systematic grammatical or other type of syllabus that characterizes current versions of TBLT.

(6) Grammar Translation method is remembered with ________ by thousands of school learners in that it often creates frustration for students.

(7) The whole audiolingual paradigm might lead to language like behaviors, but they were not resulting in ________.

(8) In the Silent Way, learners are expected to develop independence, ________, and responsibility.

(9) Tasks are believed to foster processes of ________, modification, rephrasing, and experimentation that are at the heart of second language learning.

(10) The goal of Communicative Language Teaching is to develop learners' gram-matical competence, sociolinguistic competence, ________ competence and strategic competence.

3. Mark "True" or "False" for the following statements and explain why.

(1) Grammar Translation Method is so popular partly because it requires few specialized skills on the part of teachers.

(2) The Direct Method emphasized the similarities between naturalistic first language learning and classroom foreign language learning.

(3) Situational Language Teaching adopts an inductive approach to the teaching of grammar.

(4) Audiolingualists advocated a return to grammar-based instruction with the primary objective of listening proficiency.

(5) In TPR, Asher views the verb, and particularly the verb in the imperative, as the central linguistic motif around which language use and learning are organized.

(6) The Silent Way takes a structural approach to the organization of language to be taught.

(7) The CLL view of language is the interactional.

(8) Suggestopedia shows a view of language in which grammar is central and in which grammar translation rather than contextualization is stressed.

(9) Communicative Language Teaching is best considered a method rather than an approach.

(10) Tasks are believed to foster processes of negotiation, modification, rephrasing, and experimentation that are at the heart of second language learning.

4. Discuss the following questions.

(1) Why have language teaching methods waxed and waned in popularity?

(2) How can you interpret Grammar-Translation Method? Do you think it has been stalwart? Why?

(3) What aspects of the audiolingualism are still practised today (whatever they are actually called)?

(4) If communicative teaching is about transferring information, what information do you feel should be conveyed during the language lesson?

(5) Which of these methods do you have a strong feeling about? What are your impressions? What is your assessment of its effectiveness?

Suggested Readings

BROWN H D, 2001. Principles of language learning and teaching[M]. 3rd ed. Beijing: Foreign

Language Teaching and Research Press.

BROWN H D, 2002. Teaching by principles. An interactive approach to language pedagogy[M]. Beijing: Foreign Language Teaching and Research Press.

CELCE-MURCIA M, 2006. Language teaching approaches: An overview [M]// CELCE-MURCIA M. Teaching English as a second or foreign language[M]. Beijing: Foreign Language Teaching and Research Press, 3-11.

HADLEY A O, 2012. Teaching language in context[M]. Beijing: Foreign Language Teaching and Research Press.

JOHNSON K, 2011. An introduction to language learning and teaching[M]. Beijing: Foreign Language Teaching and Research Press.

LIU CHUNYAN, GUO RUI, 2020. A Study of localization of Task-Based Language Teaching in China[J]. Chinese Journal of Applied Linguistics, 43(2): 205-218.

LIU DAOYI, WU ZHAOYI, 2015, English language education in China: Past and present[M]. Beijing: People's Education Press.

NUNAN D, 2014. Task-based language teaching[M]. Beijing: Foreign Language Teaching and Research Press.

PENNYCOOK A, 2017. Critical approaches to English language teaching [M]. Shanghai: Shanghai Foreign Language Education Press.

RICHARDS J C, RODGERS T S, 2008. Approaches and methods in language teaching[M]. 2nd ed. Beijing: Foreign Language Teaching and Research Press.

CHAPTER 2

From the Traditional to the Contemporary in Second Language Teaching and Learning

Focusing Question

- Why are changes in teaching practice evolutionary rather than revolutionary?
- How do you feel about the efficiency of ELT in China?
- Why does the author list these factors for contemporary trends? Can you add some other to the list? Why?

Introduction

Insights from theory and research have led to some fundamental changes in our beliefs about the nature of language and learning, and this has led inevitably to a change in the ways in which we go about the business of language teaching. However, current trends are basically **evolutionary** rather than **revolutionary** in nature, as methodologists and curriculum developers seek to add value to tried and tested practices rather than to subvert or reject them.

This chapter shows how contemporary trends have added value to practice, or have prompted a reassessment and reevaluation of practice in the areas of syllabus design, approaches to teaching, the role of the learner, approaches to language, the role of texts, resources, and approaches to learning, classroom organization, and assessment.

Stimuli for Change

Ineffectiveness of traditional approaches

A perennial stimulus for change in language education has been a dissatisfaction with the results obtained by traditional methods, often at great cost to schools and language systems, and the expenditure of tremendous effort by students and teachers. In grammar-translation classrooms, learners typically spent years learning English and yet many of them were still unable to use the language effectively. They often knew a good deal about the language but were unable to use this knowledge to communicate appropriately. In systems where grammar- translation gave way to audiolingualism, students were able to parrot responses in predictable situations of use, but had difficulty communicating effectively in the relatively unpredictable world beyond the classroom.

Many concluded that it was a poor investment if all that work seemed to offer so little practical result. Students had a basic foundation of language knowledge but they did not know how to put that knowledge to active use. Learners needed to understand that language is not just a list of grammatical patterns and a collection of words. Language as communication involves the active use of grammar and vocabulary to listen and read effectively and to speak with and write to other people. Language needs to be learned functionally so that learners are able to see that different forms communicate different meanings.

One response to the perception that language educators are relatively ineffective was to question the value of learning another language. In a world that is increasingly intermeshed economically, environmentally, and electronically, the ability to communicate effectively is crucial.

Relevance of language teaching to general education

It is through language that we can communicate with each other, share our ideas, tell people what we have experienced, express our wishes and desires, solve complex problems by drawing on information we read or hear, and, above all, communicate in the workplace and across cultures with people from other countries. To achieve these objectives, we need to learn language as communication, not just as a list of facts to be memorized or a set of symbols to be manipulated. This has been an important force in the evolution of a new approach to language learning, one that begins from the active use of language and involves learners in cooperative learning tasks using language, helped by their teachers and specially designed learning materials. This is a central aim of contemporary approaches to language teaching.

The skills developed through the application of active, cooperative learning principles can extend to other subjects as well. Effective foreign language learning produces learners with the social and cognitive problem-solving skills that can be used in other subjects in the school curriculum. If only we could get language teachers and subject teachers communicating with each other, it might be possible to fashion a new type of school curriculum, one in which the familiar elements are not jettisoned but recombined. The relevance of the intellectual knowledge, learning skills, interpersonal development and intercultural sensitivities fostered in the language classroom might be appreciated by others with a vested interest in education.

Syllabus Design

Traditionally, the field of curriculum development has been divided into syllabus design, methodology and evaluation (Tyler, 1949). Syllabus design has to do with selecting and sequencing content, methodology with selecting and sequencing appropriate learning experiences and evaluation with appraising learners and determining the effectiveness of the curriculum as a whole.

Difficulty of separating content and process in a communicative syllabus

Stenhouse (1975) changed perspectives with a compelling rationale for the elevation of process (traditionally the domain of methodology) to the same status as content. His ideas found their way into language education through people such as Mike Breen (1984) and Leo van Lier (1988). Breen used the metaphor of the journey to describe his approach to language teaching. Traditionally, he argued, content was seen as the destination ("We want learners to know how to contrast the simple past and perfect tenses"). Methodology was the route, the means whereby we reach the destination ("We'll get learners to do a set of substitution drills involving present perfect and simple past"). However, with the emergence of a communicative, skills-based approach ("We want learners to be able to give an informal oral presentation on a subject of their choice"), a rigid separation became difficult to sustain because, if our method of achieving the target performance is to rehearse that performance in class, then the route *becomes* the destination. This reconceptualization changed the way that course designers and materials writers go about their jobs.

In traditional language teaching, syllabus design issues (what students learn) and methodology (how they learn) were decided with reference to the classroom rather than with reference to learners' real communicative needs in actual situations in the world outside. As a result, learners often had difficulty using what they learned beyond the classroom. With grammar-translation and audiolingual drills, it was often difficult for learners to make the conceptual leap from the classroom to genuine communication outside the classroom. This is not to say that drills of various kinds, and even translation tasks, have no place in the language classrooms, but that, in and of themselves, they are insufficient.

Syllabus

A syllabus consists of lists of content to be taught through a course of study. Key tasks for the syllabus designer are the selection of the items and their sequencing and integration.

In writings on second language teaching, it is possible to identify two views on the nature of syllabus design. The narrow view draws a clear distinction between the selection and sequencing of content (the domain of syllabus design) and the selection and sequencing of learning tasks and activity (the domain of methodology). With the emergence of CLT has come a group of curriculum specialists who take a broader view, and who question the sustainability of this strict separation.

Linguistic specification as a second-order activity

Syllabus designers begin by choosing language content and learning experiences that match the needs of learners as users of language beyond the classroom. In designing courses they are guided by specified communicative tasks that learners can perform at the end of their period of learning. In consequence, it is easier for learners to apply what they have learned in class to the challenge of communicating in the real world, and for employers to know what learners can do. In practical terms, syllabus designers no longer begin with a structurally graded list of linguistic items, and then cast around for ways of teaching those items. Instead, they begin with an inventory of target skills and ask what learners need to know and be able to do in order to perform those skills. Listing, sequencing, and integrating target items becomes a second-order activity rather than the first thing that they do.

Approach to Teaching

Transmission versus interpretation models of learning

In traditional language classrooms, learners are taught chiefly about language and its rules. They learn facts about language rather than how to use it communicatively to express ideas, to talk and write to other people, to read and listen to real language, and to learn how to cooperate with others. In educational systems functioning under a transmission model, the primary role of the learner is as a relatively passive recipient of knowledge. The teacher's role is to provide that knowledge by transmitting it to the learner, largely through lockstep, teacher-fronted modes of learning.

High-structure versus low-structure teaching

Generally speaking, classrooms informed by current communicative views on language pedagogy will involve a change in teaching approach away from a high- structure orientation towards a more low-structure orientation.

High-structure versus low-structure teaching

High-structure teaching situations are those in control of the instructional process. In these situations, learners have relatively little power or control over either the content or process of learning. Low-structure situations, on the other hand, provide learners with numerous options and a great deal of autonomy. According to Biggs and Telfer (1987) all instructional decision making can be located on a continuum, which has 'high-structure' decisions at one extreme and "low-structure" decisions at the other.

In contemporary classrooms, while direct instruction and high-structure tasks are not eschewed, much more time will be devoted to low-structure tasks. In addition, direct instruction when it occurs, will be integrated into instructional sequences in which learners are actively involved in using the language, guided and helped by their teachers.

The teacher's primary role is the provision of pedagogical opportunities through which learners might structure and restructure their own understanding. The ultimate goal is to enable the learner to communicate with others in the world beyond the classroom where they will not have a teacher on hand. In helping learners achieve this goal, however, teachers need to redefine their approach to teaching.

Role of Learners

Passive versus active language roles

Learners in classrooms characterized by a transmission model of learning are cast in a relative passive role. They are passengers, being carried forward in the learning experience by the teacher. They practice patterns provided by teachers, textbooks, and tapes. They are thus cast into passive, reproductive roles. Rather than learning how to use language creatively themselves, they spend most learning time copying and reproducing language written down by others. They learn how to communicate in model and predictable situations, but they don't learn how to respond appropriately in novel and authentic communicative situations. Such a drill-based pedagogical culture is most commonly associated with audioingualism, and, although audiolingualism is supposedly dead and buried, the drill-based culture is very much alive and well, as is evident in most so-called communicative curricula.

Reproductive language tasks

The following task is an example of a task that is purportedly a communicative exercise, but is, in reality a reproductive exercise practicing comparative adjectives.

Instructions: Working with a partner take turns asking and answering these questions. If you agree on the answer, circle the word. If you disagree, put your initials next to the answer that you think is correct.

Q: Which is taller, the Sears Building, or the Empire State Building?
A: The Sears Building is taller.
1. Which has more sides, a pentagon or a rectangle?
2. Which country has more cars per person, Japan or Singapore?
3. Which is closer to the equator, Singapore or Malaysia?
4. Which is bigger, the Earth or the Moon?
5. Which country has the larger population, Pakistan or the U. S. A. ?
6. Which country has more television sets per person, Australia or Singapore?
7. Which planet is closer to the Earth, Venus or Mars?
8. Which is an older capital city, Madrid or Rome?

There is nothing wrong with drills, and there is certainly nothing wrong with exercises such as the one above. They are an essential ingredient in the learning process for most learners, and provide the enabling skills for later communicative performance. However, by themselves, they do not go far enough in equipping learners to communicate. In addition to reproducing language models provided by others, even in disguised forms such as the task above, learners need opportunities for creative language use. By creativity Nunan (2001) does not mean that we should have learners writing poetry in class (although the use of imaginative literature could be used much more extensively than it is). Rather, by creativity he means the recombination of familiar elements into new, and previously unrehearsed, forms.

Encouraging creative language use

In classrooms and textbooks in which the creativity principle is activated, learners are given structured opportunities to use the language that they have been practicing in new and unexpected ways. They are provided with the language that they will need to take part in genuine communicative tasks, and they are given opportunities to respond appropriately in new situations outside the classroom.

Creative language use

Creative language use involves the recombination of familiar elements (words, structures, and prefabricated patterns) in new ways to produce utterances that have never been produced before by that particular individual (for that individual, they are therefore unique.) In role plays, simulations, and problem solving tasks, learners are given opportunities for creative language use.

Tasks allow learners to practice identifying the key grammar and vocabulary in real-world texts and to develop the skills of reading, writing, speaking, and listening in an integrated way just as in authentic communicative situations. Tasks also give learners practice in cooperating with other learners and their teachers, making creative use of the language they have learned. In this way, classrooms themselves act as a bridge to the outside world rather than as a linguistic quarantine station where learners are protected from the risks involved in having to engage in genuine communication.

Understanding learner roles is crucial to an understanding of problems and potential solutions in contemporary language classrooms (Wright, 1987).

Approach to Language

Shortcomings of grammar-translation and audiolingualism

Grammar-translation and audiolingualism adopted very different approaches to the treatment of grammar. In fact, audiolingualism developed partly in reaction to grammar-translation's excessively deductive approach to the teaching of grammar. Audiolingual methodology was based on an inductive approach in which rules were "caught" rather than "taught" (Richards et al., 1986). "Get students to learn by analogy, not analysis," "Language is a set of habits," and "Teach the language, not about the language," were pedagogical catchcries when audiolingualism was most popular as a teaching method (Moulton, 1963).

Despite their marked differences, grammar-translationand audiolingualism did share one thing in common. They both separated the teaching of grammatical form from communicative meaning. In grammar-translation classrooms, grammar was taught as a set of rules to be memorized and repeated. In audiolingual classrooms, learners were expected to come to an inductive understanding of the rule through processes of analogy. In both approaches, it was difficult for learners to make connections between different parts of the grammatical system and to see how to apply the grammar they had learned in communication. Words were usually learned as individual items in lists so that learners did not develop an understanding of how they are grouped by their meanings into semantic sets.

The other thing that they both shared was an assumption that acquiring a second language was a linear process, that learners learn one item at a time, mastering the simple items first, and then moving on, in a step-by-step fashion to more complex items. However, this is an oversimplification (and, in some ways, a misrepresentation) of the way that second language grammar is actually acquired.

An organic metaphor describes second language acquisition as more like growing a garden than building a wall. Learners do not learn one thing perfectly one item at a time, but learn numerous things simultaneously (and imperfectly). The linguistic flowers do not all appear at the same time, nor do they all grow at the same rate. Some even appear to wilt, for a time, before renewing their growth. The rate and speed are determined by a complex interplay of factors related to speech processing constraints, pedagogical interventions, acquisitional processes and the influence of the discourse environment in which the items occur.

Teaching grammar communicatively

In a teaching methodology that reflects what we currently know about second language acquisition, grammar and vocabulary are taught communicatively. Grammatical patterns are matched to particular communicative meanings so that learners can see the connection between form and function. Learners learn how to choose the right pattern to express the ideas and feelings that they want to express. They learn how to use grammar to express different communicative meanings. Words are grouped meaningfully and are taught through tasks involving semantic networking, concept mapping, and classifying. Such a methodology enables learners to recombine the familiar in unique ways and thus achieve the creativity in language use.

Using Language Texts

In traditional classrooms, learners listen to and read specially written classroom texts. These texts are usually produced by textbook writers and teachers to exemplify particular grammatical points, or to teach core vocabulary items. For example, the following text (Molinsky et al., 1989) is designed to teach prepositions of place (next to, across from, between) existential there, and core vocabulary associated with neighborhoods, and it is difficult to imagine a context other than a language teaching textbook in which the text could conceivably appear.

> Jane's apartment building is in the center of town. Jane is very happy because the building is in a very convenient place.
>
> Across from the building, there's a laundromat, a bank, and a post office. Next to the building, there's a drug store and a restaurant. Around the corner from the building, there are two gas stations.
>
> There's a lot of noise near Jane's apartment building. There are a lot of cars on the street and there are a lot of people walking on the sidewalk all day and night.
>
> Jane isn't very upset about the noise, though. Her building is in the center of town. It's a very busy place, but for Jane, it's a very convenient place to live.

There is nothing wrong in introducing texts such as this into the classroom. They demonstrate target language items within controlled contexts. However, learners who only encounter texts such as this frequently have difficulty understanding the language and the texts that are used by speakers and writers authentically in the real world.

Authenticity

Learners can study spoken and written texts brought into the classroom from authentic contexts outside the classroom. In fact, learners are strongly encouraged to bring in their own samples of authentic language data. They practice listening to and reading genuine language drawn from a wide variety of contexts, including TV and radio broadcasts, conversations, discussions and meetings of all kinds, talks, and announcements. They read magazines, stories, printed material and instructions, hotel brochures and airport notices, bank instructions, and a wide range of written messages. This practice helps them cope successfully with genuine communication outside the classroom.

Authenticity

Authentic texts are those that have been produced in the course of genuine communication, not specially written for purposes of language teaching. They provide learners with opportunities to experience language as it is used beyond the classroom. Of course, there is a great deal of language generated within the classroom itself that is authentic, and this can very often be used for pedagogical purposes.

Exercises and tasks help even the learners at the lower levels to make sense of these real texts, and to develop effective learning strategies for reading and listening, speaking and writing. Some years ago, when writing a series aimed at beginning and post-beginning learners, Nunan drew on a wide variety of authentic texts, including the materials listed in Table 2. 1.

Table 2. 1 Authentic texts

Spoken Data	Written Data
casual conversations	invitations
telephone conversations	airline tickets
answering machine messages	postcards
office conversations	enrollment forms
public announcements	business cards
stories and anecdotes	family trees
oral histories	classified advertisements
descriptions	airline boarding passes
directions	licenses
store announcements	handwritten notes
advertisements	movie reviews
interviews	maps
	business letters
	menus

Student-generated data

With appropriate guidance and support, even low level learners can benefit from opportunities to work with everyday spoken and written texts such as these. Older learners can be given a greater sense of ownership and control over their own learning by being encouraged to bring their own authentic data into the classroom. Bringing authentic data into the classroom can assist learners to see how grammatical forms operate in context and enable speakers and writers to make communicative meanings. Another advantage of using authentic data is that learners encounter target language items in the kinds of contexts that they naturally occur, rather than in contexts that have been concocted by a textbook writer. Ultimately, this assists the learner because he/she will experience the language item in inter- action with other closely related grammatical and discourse elements. By distorting the contexts of use in which grammatical items occur, nonauthentic language, in some respects, actually makes the task for the language learner more difficult.

Facilities for Learning

Many of young students have grown up with 21st-Century digital technology; it is just a part of their normal world: familiar and well understood. Mark Prensky calls them "digital natives." They have sophisticated phones, music players, game consoles, netbooks, home computers, GPS systems, digital personal video recorders and media centres (Scrivener, 2020).

In traditional classrooms, learners usually have to rely only on the textbook as an aid to language learning. Often these textbooks are not especially provided with interesting visuals and supporting material, and rapidly become boring and uninteresting to the learner.

Textbooks and support resources

In contemporary approaches to language teaching, the design of textbooks has become much more sophisticated. The incorporation of realia and authentic data brings the content to life, and helps learners make connections between the classroom world and the world beyond it. In addition to classroom texts, published textbook series these days typically contain self-study workbooks, cassette tapes, and videotaped materials that bring the real world into the classroom. For example, the highly innovative *Grammar Dimensions* (Larsen-Freeman, 1995), which introduces a new approach to the teaching of grammar, contains the following components in addition to the student text:

instructor's manual; audio tape; student workbooks; tests;

World Wide Web site for interactive grammar and writing

Information technology and the Internet

Suddenly, new technology is widely available, much cheaper, in schools, in people's homes and in their pockets. It also works and is genuinely useful. This means that teaching is just beginning to undergo a huge change. Technology is at the heart of education now (Scrivener, 2020).

Increasingly access to the Internet brings the world into the classroom. Students can access and even download a wide range of informative, educational, and entertaining information. They can also establish contact with other first and second speakers of English around the world through chat lines and pen pal links. In addition to increasing their intercultural awareness and sensitivities, this also provides them with opportunities for genuine communication beyond the classroom. Such opportunities are not always easy to find in foreign language settings, and so the explosion in Internet usage has been particularly valuable to EFL students.

Once learners discover and begin to tap the potential of the Internet and the World Wide Web, they may find it both liberating and empowering. Students also can submit their assignments and class journals to teachers on e-mail. In the case of the assignments, the teacher can embed comments on their work, and return the assignments to them, without the red ink scribbles that necessitate lengthy time-consuming, and often wasteful retyping. Having them submit their journals electronically saves class time, and increases the amount of time that they devote to working on their English out of class.

Approach to Learning

Learning styles and strategies

In traditional classrooms, learners typically did not learn how to become better language learners on their own once they left a school or college. While they learned how to memorize individual words and grammatical patterns, and to practice them in contrived contexts, the underlying strategies behind the classroom tasks were rarely made explicit. As a result, students rarely learned how to make use of this stored knowledge in an organized and creative way. Ways of learning language better and more effectively was not on the pedagogical agenda, and practice was therefore often unfocused and not directed at those skills they needed to improve.

Adding a process dimension

A substantial amount of research has now been carried out on learning styles and strategies, and, in classrooms where teachers have been able to draw on this research, their students are able to develop a range of effective language learning strategies. They learn how to read and listen effectively, how to work out what texts mean, how to gather important information, how to work well in cooperation with others, how to use what they know in new and unpredictable situations, how to speak and write appropriately and so on. They learn metacognitive strategies for monitoring and reflecting on their learning (Oxford, 1990). These strategies are explicitly taught as part of the curriculum, and learners are shown how to apply these strategies to their own learning outside the classroom. In this way, they learn how to become better language learners outside of formal language learning contexts.

Classroom learning & Digital learning

Learning in a digital setting (abbreviated as "digital learning") involves mechanisms that are different from classroom learning. Digital learning is characterized by an abundance of authentic audio and visual input materials and opportunities for real-world communication with other learners and native speakers.

Classroom learning is more form-oriented and controlled, and the amount of input materials and output practice is smaller and less authentic. In digital learning, learners are more likely involved in offline learning activities that learners complete at their own pace.

Classroom learning is more explicit and therefore it is more likely to involve cognitive factors in the explicit paradigm such as explicit aptitude, which consists of memory, phonetic coding, and analytic ability. Conversely, digital learning is more facilitative of incidental and implicit learning, and naturally implicit language aptitude—the ability to learn the probabilistic relationships between linguistic units via exposure to a large amount of input—is more important in this setting. Also, in digital learning, learners have more agency, which may increase learner autonomy, motivation, and enjoyment (Li et al., 2022).

Classroom Organization

Teacher-fronted versus small group classrooms

The traditional mode of classroom organization was a teacher-fronted one, with learners sitting in rows facing the teacher. They spent most of their time repeating and manipulating models provided by the teacher, the textbook and the tape, and developed skills in choral speaking and repeating. The physical set-up of classrooms was (and, in many schools, still is) predicated on this mode of organization, with desks set out in rows, and even, in many cases, screwed to the floor, thus making any other mode of organization almost impossible. Students in such classrooms do not learn how to express their own ideas and to share these ideas by communicating in small groups.

Experiential learning was based on a constructivist approach to education. Such a philosophy is realized at a classroom level by cooperative, task-based learning, with learners working in small groups and pairs. Students become skilled at cooperating with others, and express their own opinions, ideas, and feelings, guided by the teacher. They learn how to solve language problems in a systematic way and to decide what language to use in the different situations that their teachers present in the classroom. Role plays and simulations help to make the task-based classroom a lively and rich language environment for learners of all abilities. Tasks such as those stimulate the production of a much richer array of language functions than teacher-fronted modes of classroom organization. They also result in the negotiation of meaning, something that is largely absent in teacher-fronted tasks.

Communication in the workplace

Skills of communicating and cooperating in groups are increasingly required in the workplace. Over the last few years, the old, hierarchical models of production in which communication is a one-way, downward process from line managers to workers on the shop floor, are giving way to small, integrated production teams in which communication occurs horizontally between members of the team.

However, many educational institutions have not kept pace with changes in the workplace and in society at large. Educational institutions are inherently conservative, and it is probably fair to say that most are still predicated on a transmission mode of education, a mode that is even reflected in the physical setting of the classroom. Within such institutions there is often an ideological tussle between the dominant, transmission ideology of the institution itself, and the interpretative, constructivist approach advocated by the language teacher.

Group Work

Group work is essential to any classroom that is based on principles of experiential learning. Through group work, learners develop their ability to communicate through tasks that require them, within the classroom, to approximate the kinds of things they will need to be able to do to communicate in the world beyond the classroom.

Assessment

Shortcomings of standardized tests

In traditional learning environments, assessment practices are characterized by standardized tests designed, administered, and graded by outside authorities. Teachers have little control of what is assessed, or how it is assessed, and the examination system has a disproportionate influence over the curriculum.

In such environments, learners do not develop their own ability to assess how much they have learned and how much they need to learn. As a result, they often do not know exactly what they have learned and how much they still have to learn. The assessment is typically through quizzes and tests that do not reflect actual language use.

Assessment and evaluation

Evaluation is the collection and interpretation of information about aspects of the curriculum (including learners, teachers, materials, learning arrangements, etc.) for decision making purposes.

Assessment is a subcomponent of evaluation. It refers to the tools, techniques, and procedures for collecting and interpreting information about what learners can and cannot do. In evaluating one's teaching, it is obviously important to include assessment data. This tells us what learners can and cannot do as a result of the instructional process. However, in order to make sense of this information, and to decide what worked and what did not work, it is important to collect other information that will tell us whether it was the teaching materials, instructional procedures, or some other aspect of the instructional process that needs to be changed.

Student self-assessment

In contemporary language teaching, learners are trained systematically in ways of assessing their own learning progress. Learners can identify their own strengths better, and where they need more help from the teacher. When they leave the program we can indicate their proficiency level in the language they have been studying, and also provide a profile of their strengths and weaknesses in many other factors that influence effective communication. In this way, learners, parents, and employers can see precisely what progress has been made and what communicative tasks learners can successfully carry out. Increasingly, portfolios of work, providing concrete instances of learner achievement, are being accepted by employers and educational institutions. Student-centered records of work can be built up over time. These records have a number of purposes. In the first place, they serve to remind learners of the content covered in the unit. Secondly, over time, they provide a record of achievement, as well as reminding learners of work still to be done. Finally, and most importantly, they develop skills in self-assessment and self-evaluation, skills that are important ingredients in a learner-oriented instructional system.

Language out of Class

In traditional classrooms, learners are rarely encouraged to make use of their language skills in the real world. The only practice they have is in class. However, one of the things that characterizes good language learners is their ability to find opportunities to activate their language outside of the classroom.

Strategies for activating language out of class

In contemporary approaches to language teaching, learners are involved in role plays and practice simulations, and through these develop an ability to carry out creative and imaginative learning projects outside of the language classroom. These projects are carefully connected to the kinds of language tasks that they will have to perform when they complete their studies. In this way they develop independence, they learn how to function as communicators themselves, and they learn to use language as a working tool to achieve their objectives outside of the classroom.

In teaching, Nunan tries to structure out-of-class learning opportunities for students on a ratio of three to one. In other words, for every hour they spend with him, he tries to find ways in which they will spend three hours outside the classroom systematically working on their language. In addition to increasing the overall quantity of language use, this sends the message to the learners that they have power and control over their own learning. It also shows them that, even in foreign language situations, there are many opportunities for them to practice their language.

Out-of-class tasks include:

1. engaging in peer review sessions, in which they collaborate with a fellow student to

review projects and assignments;

2. conducting dialogue journals with me via the Internet;
3. taking part in conversation exchanges with foreigners who want to practice their Chinese (students are paired with foreigner, and arrange, at their own convenience, to spend forty minutes a week in conversation, twenty minutes in English and twenty minutes in Chinese);
4. projects and surveys, (in which they collect information in English, and bring it back to a subsequent class);
5. doing language improvement projects in the independent learning center (in these projects they identify an aspect of their English they want to improve, they formulate a learning objective, and write up a learning contract, which they carry out independently).

Conclusion

Nunan has illustrated the changes that have been brought about to pedagogical practice as a result of changing views on the nature of language and learning, and also through the incorporation into classroom teaching of insights from research. The ideology driving the view of education presented here is that learners have a right to be involved in curriculum decision making, that is, selecting content, learning activities and tasks. It is also predicated on a belief that learners learn best if the content relates to their own experience and knowledge. At the level of implementation, there is a belief that learners who have developed skills in "learning how to learn" are the most effective students, and that learners have different learning styles and strategies that need to be taken into consideration in developing learning programs.

Table 2.2 summarizes the major shifts that have taken place in language pedagogy over the last thirty years.

Table 2.2 The traditional and the contemporary in language education

Dimensions	Traditional	Contemporary
Syllabus design	Content & methodology decided with reference to the classroom rather than with reference to learners' real communicative needs.	Content & methodology match learner needs beyond the classroom. Process and content are integrated.
Approach to teaching (methodology)	Learners are taught about language and its rules, learning facts about language.	Learners are taught how to use language communicatively and they are actively involved in using language.
Role of the learners	Learners spend their time copying and reproducing language written down by others.	Learners learn how to use language creatively responding in novel and authentic communicative situations.

Continued

Dimensions	Traditional	Contemporary
Approach to language	Grammar is taught as rules to be memorized.	Grammar and vocabulary are taught communicatively so learners can use the grammar to express different communicative meanings.
Using language texts	Learners listen to and read specially written classroom texts. They have difficulty comprehending authentic language outside the classroom.	Learners study authentic texts and learn to use genuine language outside the classroom.
Resources for learning	Learners have to rely only on the textbook as an aid to language learning.	Learners use a specially written well-illustrated textbook plus self-study workbooks, cassette tapes, and video-taped materials.
Approach to learning	Learners don't learn how to become better language learners on their own.	Learners learn effective language learning strategies and are shown how to apply these strategies to their own learning outside the classroom.
Classroom organization	Learners sit in rows facing the teacher and spend most of their time repeating what the teacher says.	Learners work in small groups and pairs, learning skills of cooperating with others and how to express their own opinions, ideas, and feelings.
Assessment	Teacher alone assesses the student's progress. Learners do not develop ability to assess what they have learned.	Learners are trained to assess their own learning progress, and can identify their own strengths and weaknesses.

Exercises, Questions and Tasks

1. Multiple Choices

(1) In traditional language classrooms, learners are taught chiefly about ________.

A. language and its rules

B. how to read and listen to real language

C. how to use it communicatively to express ideas

D. how to talk and write to other people

(2) In traditional classrooms, students ________.

A. typically learned how to become better language learners on their own

B. rarely learned how to make use of stored knowledge in an organized way

C. were taught how to become better language learners on their own

D. learned how to make use of stored knowledge in a creative way

(3) In the traditional mode of classroom organization, students ________.

A. are working in small groups and pairs

B. share their own ideas by communicating in small groups

C. spend most of their time repeating and manipulating models

D. become skilled at cooperating with others, and express their own opinions

(4) In contemporary approaches to language teaching, learners ________.

A. are rarely encouraged to make use of their language skills in the real world

B. learn facts about language

C. learn to use language to express their intention only in class

D. develop an ability to carry out imaginative learning projects outside of the language classroom

(5) In traditional language classrooms, the teacher's role is to ________.

A. provide pedagogical opportunities for students to restructure their own understanding

B. teach how to use the language communicatively

C. provide knowledge by transmitting it to the learner

D. teach students how to cooperate with others

(6) The changes to theory and practice in language and learning are that ________.

A. learners practice skills they will need in class

B. learners are actively involved in learning through teacher's explaining

C. learners communicate authentically and learn to use language appropriately

D. learners can see the connection between form and function

(7) In contemporary approaches to language teaching, learners ________.

A. listen to and read authentic texts of different kinds

B. develop strategies to become better language learners

C. work together in small cooperative groups

D. develop skills in self-assessment and self-evaluation

E. learn how to take their language into the real world beyond the classroom

(8) In contemporary approaches to language teaching, teachers ________.

A. help learners to learn useful language and to become better learners

B. provide models of the language they are learning and share their knowledge about the language

C. actively cooperate in providing a varied program of instruction

D. continuously assess learners' performance and provide a detailed profile of their skills

(9) In traditional learning environments, ________.

A. assessment practices are characterized by standardized tests designed, administered, and graded by outside authorities.

B. teachers have control of what is assessed

C. teachers have little control of how it is assessed

D. the examination system has a proportionate influence over the curriculum

(10) Strategies such as ________ should be explicitly taught as part of the curriculum.

A. how to read and listen effectively

B. how to work out what texts mean

C. how to gather important information

D. how to work well in cooperation with others

E. how to use what they know in new and predictable situations

2. Fill in each blank with an appropriate word.

(1) In grammar-translation classrooms, learners often knew a good deal about the language but were unable to use this knowledge to communicate ________.

(2) The ________ of the intellectual knowledge, learning skills, interpersonal development and intercultural sensitivities fostered in the language classroom might be appreciated by others with a vested interest in education.

(3) Syllabus design has to do with selecting and sequencing content, methodology, appropriate learning experiences, and evaluation with appraising learners and determining the ________ of the curriculum as a whole.

(4) In educational systems functioning under a transmission model, the primary role of the learner is as a relatively passive ________ of knowledge.

(5) Students in classrooms characterized by a transmission model of learning learn how to communicate in model and ________ situations, but they don't learn how to respond appropriately in novel and authentic communicative situations.

3. Mark "True" or "False" for the following statements and explain why.

(1) Current trends in language teaching are basically evolutionary rather than revolutionary in nature.

(2) Students had a basic foundation of language knowledge and they knew how to put that knowledge to active use.

(3) Effective foreign language learning produces learners with the social and cognitive problem-solving skills.

(4) In traditional language teaching, what students learn and how they learn were decided with reference to learners' real communicative needs.

(5) Classrooms informed by current communicative views on language pedagogy will involve a change in teaching approach to a more high-structure orientation.

(6) One of the things that characterizes good language learners is their ability to find opportunities to activate their language outside of the classroom.

(7) Many educational institutions have kept pace with changes in the workplace and in society at large.

(8) Experiential learning was based on a behaviorist approach to education.

(9) The explosion in Internet usage has been particularly valuable to EFL students for a wide range of informative, educational, and entertaining information.

(10) The incorporation of realia helps learners make connections between the classroom world and the world beyond it.

4. Discuss the following questions.

(1) What was the major conceptual shift brought about by Stenhouse to the field of syllabus design?

(2) List three characteristics of a "high-structure" classroom and three characteristics of a "low-structure" classroom.

(3) hat is the essential difference between a "reproductive" and a "creative" learning task?

(4) Why is it desirable to introduce learners to authentic data? List ten sources or, potential sources, of authentic data in your current teaching situation.

(5) What media, in addition to commercial texts, are you using/do you have the potential to use in your current teaching situation?

(6) Identify three ways in which learning strategies could be integrated into your current teaching situation.

(7) Identify three impediments to group work in some teaching situations, and brainstorm solutions to these.

(8) List and discuss three ways in which some students can activate their language skills out of class.

Suggested Readings

LI S F, HIVER P, PAPI M, 2022. Individual differences in second language acquisition: Theory, research, and practice[J]. The Routledge Handbook of Second Language Acquisition and Individual Differences, 3 - 34.

NUNAN D, 2001. Second language teaching and learning[M]. Beijing: Foreign Language Teaching and Research Press.

SCRIVENER J. 2020. Learning teaching: The guide to English language teaching[M]. 2nd ed. Beijing: Foreign Language Teaching and Research Press.

CHAPTER 3

Theories in SLA & ISLA

Focusing Question

- What does the child do that makes L1 acquisition so quick and successful?
- How do the adults who talk to the child behave? What assistance do they give to the acquisition process?
- What are the important aspects of the acquisition environment?

Introduction

There are two immediately obvious sorts of language acquisition. The first is first language (L1) acquisition, which every normal child manages at an early age. The second is foreign language (FL) acquisition where someone, child or adult, picks up a language, for example while they are living in the target-language (TL) country (Johnson, 2002)[75].

In the case of second language acquisition (SLA), the language plays an institutional and social role in the community (i. e. it functions as a recognized means of communication among members who speak some other language as their mother tongue). In contrast, foreign language learning takes place in settings where the language plays no major role in the community and is primarily learnt only in the classroom (Ellis, 2013)[6].

Whatever psycholinguistic processing takes place in a naturalistic situation presumably takes place in a classroom situation as well. For learners in a foreign-language setting, not only is there limited input, but a large part of the input comes from classmates whose knowledge of the foreign language is restricted. Interactional opportunities are also often severely restricted.

Researchers have posed a range of questions related to classroom language/ input, the type or types of instruction that are most effective (e. g. , explicit vs. implicit), the duration and intensity of instructional effects, and whether those effects might interact with or be moderated by, other variables, such as learner proficiency or the types of L2 features being taught (Gass, 2020)[460].

Frameworks of SLA

Second Language Acquisition (SLA) refers both to the study of individuals and groups who are learning a language subsequent to learning their first one as young children, and to the process of learning that language. The additional language is called a second language (L2), even though it may actually be the third, fourth, or tenth to be acquired. It is also commonly called a target language (TL), which refers to any language that is the aim or goal of learning.

The scope of SLA includes informal L2 learning that takes place in naturalistic contexts, formal L2 learning that takes place in classrooms, and L2 learning that involves a mixture of these settings and circumstances (Savill-Troike, 2008)[2].

Interest in second language learning and use dates back many centuries (McCarthy, 2001), but it is only since the 1960s that scholars have formulated systematic theories and models to address the basic questions in the field of SLA:

1. What exactly does the L2 learner know?
2. How does the learner acquire this knowledge?
3. Why are some learners more successful than others?

Different approaches to the study of SLA can be categorized as primarily based on *linguistic*, *psychological*, and *social* frameworks. There are extensive interrelationships among them.

Prior to the 1960s, interest in L2 learning was tied almost exclusively to foreign language teaching concerns. The dominant linguistic model through the 1950s was Structuralism (Bloomfield, 1933), which emphasized the description of different levels of production in speech: phonology (sound systems), morphology (composition of words), syntax (grammatical relationships of words within sentences, such as ordering and agreement), semantics (meaning, and lexicon).

The most influential cognitive model of learning applied to language acquisition at that time was Behaviorism (Skinner, 1957), which stressed the notion of habit formation resulting from S-R-R: stimuli from the environment (such as linguistic input), responses to those stimuli, and reinforcement if the responses resulted in some desired outcome. The intersection of these two models formed the disciplinary framework for the Audiolingual Method, which emphasized repetition and habit formation that was widely practiced in much of the world at least until the 1980s.

Although it had not yet been applied to second language concerns, Vygotsky's Sociocultural Theory was also widely accepted as a learning theory by mid-century, emphasizing interaction with other people as critical to the learning process. This view is still influential in SLA approaches which are concerned with the role of input and interaction (Savill-Troike, 2008)[24-25].

Instructed Second Language Acquisition

In spite of some non-pedagogically related areas, a large component of SLA research is concerned with what happens in the classroom. In fact, there has been an increase in the use of the phrase instructed second language acquisition (ISLA) to specify a field of research that directly investigates what happens in the L2 classroom(Loewen et al., 2019)[3].

According to Long (2017)[8], ISLA includes "incidental and intentional, and/or implicit and explicit, second language (L2) or second dialect (D2) learning when the learning processes are influenced, or at least intended to be influenced, by teachers, classmates, or pedagogic materials."

Loewen (2015) defines ISLA as a theoretically and empirically based field of academic inquiry that aims to understand how the systematic manipulation of the mechanisms of learning and/or the conditions under which they occur enable or facilitate the development and acquisition of an additional language.

The two definitions converge on instruction as a common denominator in ISLA, but Long's conception of ISLA is oriented more toward instruction in the real world, while Loewen's is more confined to experiments carried out in a lab (Han, 2023).

According to Loewen et al. (2017), ISLA focuses on the following key aspects.

An academic field

ISLA is an academic endeavor, meaning that it is based on a rigorous and scientific process of accumulating knowledge about L2 learning. To that end, theories and hypotheses have been and are being proposed about general or specific aspects of the L2 learning process (see VanPatten et al, 2015); furthermore, these theories and hypotheses are investigated using data that researchers gather and interpret.

Because researchers rely on specific skills and methods to research L2 learning (e.g., Larson-Hall, 2010; Mackey et al., 2015; Paltridge et al., 2015), ISLA includes examination of research methodology, not because it necessarily has a direct impact on L2 learning (although in some cases it might, such as action research), but because research methods are lenses that provide information from specific epistemological perspectives. Consequently, methodology impacts the credibility and trustworthiness of research findings that ultimately inform pedagogical practice.

Systematic manipulation

The systematic manipulation of the learning environment and learning processes separates ISLA from what has been called, among other things, uninstructed or naturalistic L2 acquisition; in this, learners are simply surrounded by the target language but make no or little conscious effort to learn the language.

Instructional contexts

The prototypical context for ISLA is the language classroom, which may take many different shapes: from introductory lessons for children in elementary school that aim to give kids a taste of an L2, to required university foreign language courses, to private language schools whose sole purpose is to promote L2 learning.

The physical classroom is not the only context of interest for ISLA because there is considerable L2 learning that occurs outside of the four walls of a classroom (Leow, 2015). For instance, the virtual L2 classroom is an increasingly popular L2 learning context, with both hybrid and fully online options (see Benson et al., 2011). In addition, there are other circumstances, such as learner self-study, in which there is systematic manipulation of the learning conditions.

Another context that is included in ISLA is study abroad, even though the amount of manipulation may be minimal if students are placed in content classes taught in the target language and left to their own devices; however, many study abroad programs provide considerable structure for L2 learning. In such cases, learners are exposed to both intentional and incidental learning conditions (see Perez-Vidal, 2014).

Learning contexts may also affect the effectiveness of instruction because language instruction is a culturally bound endeavor. It is necessary to conduct research in different learning contexts that may challenge existing ISLA theories or provide alternative perspectives. As an example, the different perspectives between task-based language teaching with its emphasis on student-centered activities (see Shehadeh et al., 2012) and, in contrast, more teacher-centered educational cultures require ISLA researchers to consider how larger social, political, or ideological variables may affect the classroom (see Block, 2014).

Target of manipulation

The mechanisms of learning include the processing and internalization of input; the restructuring, consolidation and storage of L2 knowledge; and the production of L2 output. However, not all learning mechanisms are of equal interest to ISLA researchers because some mental processes are not open to manipulation. For example, Universal Grammar (UG) or innatist perspectives of L2 acquisition are not primarily focused on instruction because arguably there is little that can be done to alter the makeup of the cognitive system.

In general, therefore, ISLA research is concerned with L2 learning processes that are hypothesized to be or have been found to be amenable to intervention.

Goals of instruction

Overall, the goal of many in the ISLA endeavor is for learners to develop communicative competence in the L2, that is the ability to use the L2 for communicative purposes (e.g., Littlewood, 2014).

There is what has been called explicit knowledge, declarative knowledge, or knowledge about language, all of which consist of information that learners are consciously aware of (DeKeyser, 2015; Rebuschat, 2013).

However, the difficulty with explicit or declarative knowledge is that it is not readily available for use in spontaneous, real-time communication. For that, learners need to possess a type of knowledge that has been referred to variously as implicit knowledge, proceduralized knowledge, or knowledge "of" language, which is held unconsciously by the learner. In other words, learners are not aware of this knowledge, and they cannot verbalize it; however, learners are able to access it rapidly to communicate in spontaneous, real-time contexts.

In sum, implicit knowledge is the primary contributor to communicative competence; therefore, it is the type of knowledge that many L2 learners wish to obtain and the type of knowledge that ISLA is primarily concerned with.

Although ISLA has been concerned with linguistic knowledge, there has also been a concern, especially among teachers and learners, with the language skills, especially productive skills. Consequently, some ISLA researchers conceptualize the goal of instruction in skill domains such as listening, reading, writing, and speaking.

Type of instruction

Currently, much ISLA research is ultimately concerned, either directly or indirectly, with the optimal combination of attention to language forms and language meaning in the classroom.

It is important to acknowledge that there are numerous variables, both internal and external to the learner, which moderate and influence the effectiveness of instruction. Such individual differences are both interesting and challenging to ISLA researcher (as well as teachers and learners) who are trying to account for the effects of instruction. Learner-internal factors that have received considerable ISLA investigation include motivation, language aptitude, and foreign language anxiety, while learner-external factors include the micro- and macro-social contexts in which learners find themselves (see The Douglas Fir Group, 2016). Furthermore, teachers' characteristics may affect the ultimate effect of instruction.

This overview provides an overarching framework for ISLA, while introducing the rich array of concerns and interests that comprise ISLA research.

Krashen's Monitor Theory

One of the best known and most influential theories of SLA in the 1970s and early 1980s was Krashen's Monitor Theory (MT). MT began life not as a theory of SL acquisition, but as a model of SL performance (Krashen, 1976).

The acquisition-learning hypothesis

Krashen (1976) claimed that two separate knowledge systems underlay SL performance. The first and most important, the acquired system, was the product of application by learners of the same (unspecified) language-learning abilities children used for first language acquisition, and consists of subconscious knowledge of the SL grammar, like the subconscious knowledge NSs have of their first language. The second and less important knowledge system, the learned system, was the product of formal instruction (typically classroom language teaching), and comprised conscious knowledge of "easy" SL grammatical rules, such as those for subject-verb agreement or for pluralizing NPs in English.

The acquired system was typically the only knowledge source speakers could use in real-time communication, when they were attending to meaning, not form; the learned system served only as a planner and editor with which to inspect, or monitor, the output of the acquired system (Larsen-Freeman et al., 2002)[240].

For Krashen, learning is particularly marked by two characteristics. First, there is error correction. When learners make mistakes, it is normal for the classroom teacher to draw explicit attention to them, and to correct the errors. The second characteristic is what Krashen calls rule isolation. In the language-teaching classroom it is normal for a lesson to focus on one language point. It may be a grammatical item like a particular tense, or a pronunciation point, or some "rule of use." The word "isolation" indicates that in this procedure language points are dealt with one by one, in isolation(Johnson, 2002)[77].

The natural order hypothesis

This hypothesis says that SL rules are acquired in a predictable order, one apparently not determined solely by linguistic complexity, and certainly not by the order in which the items appear in teaching syllabuses. Acquisition orders, that is, do not reflect instructional sequences. Krashen's "natural order" is his synthesis of the findings of the "morpheme studies," studies which actually addressed accuracy, or difficulty, orders, not acquisition orders (Larsen-Freeman et al., 2002)[242].

The monitor hypothesis

The Monitor is a construct central to Krashen's Monitor Model. There are three conditions that must be met for Monitor usage (Krashen, 1985):

1. **Time**: Learners need time to consciously think about and use the rules available to them in their learned system.
2. **Focus on form**: Although time may be basic, one must also be focused on form. Learners must be paying attention to how they are saying something, not just to what they are saying.
3. **Know the rule**: In order to apply a rule, one has to know it. In other words, one has to have an appropriate learned system in order to apply it.

Although he claimed that, whereas these are necessary conditions, they are not necessarily sufficient, because the Monitor may not be activated, even when all three conditions have been satisfied.

The Monitor is intended to link the acquired and learned systems in a situation of language use. The Monitor consists of learned knowledge, and the only function of learned knowledge is to edit utterances. Following from this is the idea that the Monitor can only be used in production; it is useless in comprehension. How, then, do learners in a classroom setting ever comprehend the L2, as, for all intents and purposes, they have no acquired system (Gass, 2020)[147]?

Krashen claimed that ("small m") monitoring, self-correcting using conscious or subconscious general awareness of language, could be done by "feel" judgements, using the acquired system. Learners might pause to see whether a word or construction looked or sounded right, in the same way that NSs sometimes compare mental images of two possible spellings of a word they are unsure of, say, "ceiling" and "cieling," or even write out both versions to see which looks correct. (Monitoring with the learned system —"big M" Monitoring—on the other hand, would be equivalent to accessing a rule of English spelling the NS happens to know, like "i before e, except after c.") Knowledge from one system could not pass into the other, however. The two systems, like the processes which produced them, acquisition and learning, operated separately; there was no "cross-over" or "interface," e. g. through some "consciousness-raising" process (Sharwood-Smith, 1981; Rutherford, 1987; Schmidt, 1990). Finally, learners varied in their use of the Monitor, some being underusers, some optimal users (those who used the learned system to improve accuracy without too great a loss of fluency), and some over-users (Krashen, 1978; Larsen-Freeman et al., 2002).

The modification of speech patterns, particularly in situations where there is form-focus, is known as monitoring. Krashen applies the concept to FL learning. He (along with others) notices that there is much variability in FL learners' language production. Sometimes for example they will get a structure right while on another occasion they will get it wrong. He conjectures that on some occasions learners will be making a particular effort with their language (for example when they are writing something formal, talking to someone important, doing a language test). On other occasions, as when chatting informally to friends, they will be more interested in what they are saying than in how they are saying it. In these former situations, we may say that the learners are monitoring their own speech—checking it carefully before they produce it. In the latter situations there is no monitoring.

Krashen links FL monitoring to the learning/acquisition distinction. He says that in informal speech the language the FL learner produces is the result of an acquisition process—the learner uses the language she has "picked up." It is only in more formal situations that what has been learned comes into play and, even then, it is in a rather restricted role. That role is to monitor production, to inspect and sometimes to alter output generated by the acquired system.

An example of FL monitoring: there is a notoriously unfriendly rule of English grammar which says that most verbs take an -s in the third person singular of the simple present tense—so we say "She likes," in contrast to "I like," "They like." The rule is simplicity itself, and is usually taught early on in language-teaching courses. But, although the rule is simple, we describe it as "unfriendly," because learners are highly liable to forget it when communicating naturally. So they will practise sentences like "She likes" ad infinitum (and indeed ad nauseam) in the language classroom, but then—to the teacher's fury—stroll out of the class and slip "She like" into their conversation. Why? Because in class the learner is alert to things linguistic, and is attending to her own language as she produces it. Her internal monitoring device is at its highest setting. It is then that what she has learned in class comes into play. Outside class she uses the form often acquired by those living in the target-language environment: "She like" (Johnson, 2002)[91-92].

The input hypothesis

Input refers to the language (in spoken, written, or signed forms) the learner is exposed to in communicative contexts. It is language that learners hear, read, or see that carries some sort of message. Input must be communicatively embedded and it must, in some way, be comprehensible for it to be of use for language acquisition. Input as language embedded in a communicative event suggests that acquisition is a by-product of learners actively trying to comprehend language. Differing theories about what underlies language acquisition converge on what the basic data are for acquisition: communicatively embedded input (VanPatten et al., 2020).

In Krashen's view, the Input Hypothesis answers the basic question of how learning takes place. If there is a natural order, what mechanism exists to allow learners to move from one point to another? L2s are acquired "by understanding messages," or "by receiving comprehensible input" (Krashen, 1985)[2].

Krashen defined comprehensible input in a particular way. Essentially, comprehensible input is that bit of language that is heard/read and that is slightly ahead of a learner's current state of grammatical knowledge. Language containing structures a learner already knows essentially serves no purpose in acquisition. Similarly, language containing structures way ahead of a learner's current knowledge is not useful. A learner does not have the ability to "do" anything with those structures. Krashen (1985)[2] defined a learner's current state of knowledge as i and the next stage as i+1. Thus the input a learner is exposed to must be at the i+1 level in order for it to be of use in terms of acquisition. "We move from i, our current level to i+1, the next level along the natural order, by understanding input containing i+1."

Krashen assumed a Language Acquisition Device (LAD), that is, an innate mental structure capable of handling both first and second language acquisition. The input activates this innate structure, but only input of a very specific kind (i+1) will be useful in altering a learner's grammar(Gass, 2020)[148].

In Krashen's view, the Input Hypothesis is central to all of acquisition and also has implications for the classroom:

1. Speaking is a result of acquisition and not its cause. Speech cannot be taught directly, but "emerges" on its own, as a result of building competence via comprehensible input.
2. If input is understood and there is enough of it, the necessary grammar is automatically provided. The language teacher need not attempt deliberately to

> teach the next structure along the natural order—it will be provided in just the right quantities and automatically reviewed, if the student receives a sufficient amount of comprehensible input.

The teacher's main role, then, is to ensure that students receive comprehensible input. However, despite its attractiveness (and clearly no one would deny the importance and significance of input), there are numerous difficulties with the concept.

First, the hypothesis itself is not specific as to how to define levels of knowledge. Thus, if we are to validate this hypothesis we must know how to define a particular level (say level 1,340), so that we can know whether the input contains linguistic level 1,341, and, if so, whether the learner, as a result, moves to level 1,341.

Second is the issue of quantity. Krashen states that there has to be sufficient quantity of the appropriate input. But what is sufficient quantity? How do we know whether the quantity is sufficient or not? One token, two tokens, 777 tokens? And, perhaps the quantity necessary for change depends on developmental level, or how ready the learner is to acquire a new form.

Third, how does extralinguistic information aid in actual acquisition, or internalization of a linguistic rule, if by *understanding* Krashen meant understanding at the level of meaning? We may be able to understand something that is beyond our grammatical knowledge, but how does that translate into grammatical acquisition? As Gregg (1984)[88] stated: "I find it difficult to imagine extra-linguistic information that would enable one to 'acquire' the third person singular *-s*, or *yes/no* questions, or indirect object placement, or passivization" (Gass, 2020)[148-149].

The affective filter hypothesis

Affect, from Krashen's perspective, is intended to include factors such as motivation, attitude, self-confidence, and anxiety. Krashen proposed an Affective Filter. If the filter is up, input is prevented from passing through; if input is prevented from passing through, there can be no acquisition. If, on the other hand, the filter is down, or low, and if the input is comprehensible, the input will reach the acquisition device, and acquisition will take place. This is schematized in Figure 3. 1.

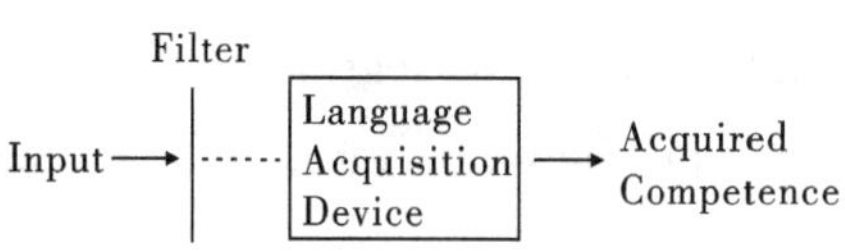

Figure 3. 1 The affective filter

According to Krashen, the Affective Filter is responsible for individual variation in SLA and differentiates child language acquisition from SLA, because the Affective Filter is not something children have/use. Two conditions are necessary for acquisition: comprehensible input and a low or weak Affective Filter.

The Affective Filter hypothesis captures the relationship between affective variables, on the one hand, and the process of SLA, on the other, by positing that learners vary with respect to the strength or level of their Affective Filters. Those whose attitudes are not optimal for SLA will not only tend to seek less input, but they will also have a high or strong Affective Filter—even if they understand the message, the input will not reach that part of the brain responsible for language acquisition, or the Language Acquisition Device. Those with attitudes more conducive to SLA will not only seek and obtain more input, they will also have a lower or weaker filter. They will be more open to the input, and it will strike "deeper" (Krashen, 1982)[31].

The Affective Filter, which shields the Language Acquisition Device from input necessary for acquisition, is what differentiates one individual from another; it is intended to explain why some learners learn and others do not. It is also intended to explain child-adult differences. The filter is not present (or, at least, not operative) in children, but is present in adults. But how does it work? Here, we are left without explanation. How is the input filtered out by an unmotivated learner? One of the functions of the filter noted by Dulay et al. (1982) is that it will determine what parts of the language will be attended to and in what order. However, a question to ask is: How can affect be selective in terms of grammatical structures?

The following diagram is adapted by Cook (2021)[54] from Gregg (1984), who combines Krashen's diagrams of production and acquisition into one.

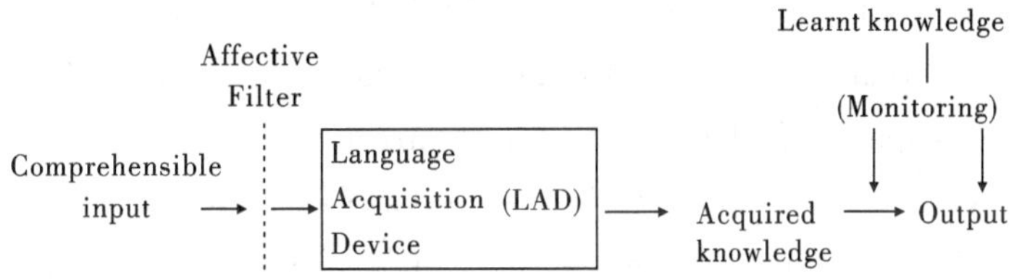

Figure 3.2 The input hypothesis model of L2 learning and production (adapted from Krashen, 1982, and Gregg, 1984)

Gregg (1984) gave the example of a Chinese NS with near-native-like knowledge of English. This speaker, however, had not acquired certain rules, such as third person singular *-s*. In Krashen's view, this incomplete knowledge of English would be due to the Affective Filter, but there is no explanation as to how the filter could let most of the input pass through and filter out third person singular.

Putting the parts of Krashen's model together, we can find difficulty in relating one part to another in a meaningful way. In general, the hypotheses are dependent on one another, and the arguments for one depend on the arguments for the others. For example, the Monitor is needed to account for discrepancies in the natural order; a learning-acquisition distinction is needed to justify the use of the Monitor. Thus, the argumentation is circular, rendering it vacuous (Gass, 2020)[149-151].

SLA, ISLA & ELT

SLA & ELT pedagogy

The influence of second language acquisition (SLA) theory on ELT pedagogy can be seen as far back as the 1950s and 1960s when behaviorism was the theoretical support for audiolingualism, with its emphasis on drills and habit formation (VanPatten et al., 2015). Later, in the 1980s, Stephen Krashen and Tracy Terrell (1983) developed the natural approach and the monitor model (Krashen, 1982; Krashen et al., 1983), which are arguably some of the first modern theories that apply specifically to SLA. The five hypotheses of the monitor model (acquisition-learning hypothesis, input hypothesis, affective filter hypothesis, natural order hypothesis, and interface hypothesis) were evident in the ELT classroom through the strong and weak versions of communicative language teaching, with a move away from rote language practice and explicit language instruction. Indeed, Krashen recommended that teachers provide an input-rich environment for their students in the classroom. More recently, the influences of focus on form (Long, 1991; 1996) and task-based language teaching (Willis, 1996) can be seen in the movement to include attention to both communication and linguistic structures in the classroom.

However, not all aspects of SLA theory relate directly to the classroom. Some areas of research, such as universal grammar (White 2015), processability theory (Pienemann, 1998; Pienemann et al., 2015), and usage-based learning approaches (Ellis et al., 2015), have somewhat limited relevance to the L2 classroom (Ortega, 2015) because these theories are concerned primarily with the relationship between the learner's cognitive system, the input that it receives, and how that input is processed and restructured in the brain. These theories typically view cognition as a ballistic system which is generally outside the control of the learner; consequently, there is little that teachers or learners can do to change how the cognitive system functions. As a result, some questions that researchers have about how individuals learn or acquire an L2 will have a limited impact on the classroom even though the answers are important for SLA in general. For example, the role of innate linguistic knowledge in the acquisition of an L2 is of great interest to some SLA researchers (e. g., White, 2015), but there is very little that teachers can do to influence any such innate knowledge (Loewen et al., 2019)[2-3].

SLA & ISLA

A frequent topic of position papers in applied linguistics is the research-pedagogy interface. Over the years, there have been multiple assessments of how far apart or close together research and language teaching are or should be with varying degrees of optimism for the future (Bardovi-Harlig et al., 2022).

Ellis (2015) and Ellis et al. (2014) claimed that the relationship between teaching and research can be examined at least in three ways:

1. applying research findings to language-teaching practice in the classroom,
2. identifying teaching problems and examining them from the perspective of SLA,
3. promoting action research.

Although SLA research has been quite prolific, most of its findings have generally been either difficult for teachers to access or of little relevance to actual classroom practice, which has resulted in limited L2 practitioners' engagement with research. In the past decades, though, scholars have grown more aware of the pedagogical implications of their studies and have therefore tried to influence and improve language classroom practices through empirical investigations. Furthermore, academics have become more aware of their responsibility to guarantee that research and its results are not only of use in the classroom but are also accessible to L2 teachers. The book—*The Routledge Handbook of Instructed Second Language Acquisition* (2017) is concrete evidence of this growing tendency, with the editors calling for a more fruitful "research - pedagogy dialogue" (Porcellato, 2020)[96].

ISLA & ELT

The relationship between instructed second language acquisition (ISLA) research, on the one hand, and English language teaching (ELT) pedagogy, on the other, is not always clear and is sometimes contentious. While ISLA researchers hope to inform English second language (L2) pedagogy, teachers may feel that theory and research are of limited use in their classrooms(Loewen et al, 2019)[1].

An underlying assumption of ISLA is that there is a relationship between the interests of ISLA researchers and ELT practitioners.

The goal of ISLA is to make explicit links among theory, research, and pedagogy by empirically evaluating theoretical claims about classroom instruction. ISLA theory and research, particularly from a cognitive-interactionist perspective, can bring to the classroom, while also considering the influence that pedagogical realities can have on theory and research.

There are many benefits to a dialog between ISLA researchers and ELT instructors. ISLA researchers obviously need L2 teachers and learners in order to conduct research. However, they should also listen to teachers' concerns and perspectives in order to better understand the classroom context. Conversely, teachers can benefit from the systematic investigation into ISLA. Obviously, they should not blindly accept all research; however, with the growing number of research syntheses and meta-analyses, teachers are in a better position to benefit from the aggregated effects of ISLA research. Having such input allows teachers to focus on their task at hand, knowing that their practices are informed by evidence about effective teaching (Loewen et al., 2019).

Input Processing & Processing Instruction

Input for acquisition is language that learners hear or see in a communicative context that they process for meaning (propositional content and intent) (VanPatten, 2017)[167]. When input is simplified and tailored to the level of the learner, learners are better able to make connections between form and meaning and thus convert input to intake (a filtered, processed version of the *input*). This intake is then incorporated by the learner in developing a linguistic system that is subsequently used to produce output in the language (Shrum, et al., 2004).

Input processing

Input processing(IP) is concerned with how learners come to make form-meaning connections or parse sentences, the reason being that acquisition is, to a certain degree, a by-product of comprehension (Truscott & Sharwood Smith, 2004). Although comprehension cannot guarantee acquisition, acquisition cannot happen if comprehension does not occur. Why? Because a good deal of acquisition is dependent upon learners making appropriate form-meaning connections during the act of comprehension. A good deal of acquisition is dependent upon learners correctly interpreting what a sentence means (Carroll, 2001; VanPatten et al., 2014; White, 1987).

IP theory claims that lexical items are privileged in input processing (i. e., the Primacy of Content Words Principle), and that learners' initial orientation toward input is to process it for meaning; that is, they do what they can to extract basic meanings from sentences.

VanPatten (2017)[169-170] has sketched out a general model of input processing that includes three basic principles of input processing (and their corollaries) to capture basic strategies that guide learners' processors:

1. The primacy of meaning principle

Learners' comprehension of input is driven by a focus on meaning and not a focus on form. That is, learners do not consciously or unconsciously approach comprehension with the intent of seeking out formal properties of language. Instead, their intent is to figure out the meaning of what they hear or see.

2. The lexical preference principle

In the case of something like the past tense, learners will first seek out and process words and phrases that are tense indicators (e. g., *right now*, *everyday*, *last week*, *next year*) to comprehend the temporal reference of an utterance or discourse. The idea underlying this principle is that most grammatical inflections are redundant in nature; that is, markers of such things as plurality, person and number, tense, and so on, are almost always recoverable in the input from lexical information (e. g., two, many = plural; John, he = third person singular, yesterday = past).

3. The first-noun principle

Learners tend to process the first noun (or pronoun) they encounter as the subject/agent of a sentence.

Processing instruction

Processing Instruction (PI) is actually a type of focus on form or better yet, a pedagogical intervention. As such it is not a method with an underlying approach but instead an intervention that can be used by any communicative approach that seeks a supplemental or periodic focus on the formal features of language (VanPatten, 2017)[166].

VanPattenet al. (1993) argued that beginning language learners need structured input activities that enable them to focus on meaning while attending to form before they are expected to use the language to produce output. In their view, instruction may be more beneficial when it focuses on how learners perceive and process input rather than when it focuses on having learners practice linguistic structures by means of output. VanPatten (1993) suggests the following guidelines in developing structured input activities:

1. present one thing at a time;
2. keep meaning in focus;
3. move from sentences to connected discourse;
4. use both oral and written input;
5. have the learner "do something" with the input;
6. keep the learner's processing strategies in mind.

One of the most well-known outcomes of the model of IP is VanPatten's processing instruction.

Interaction & ISLA

Interaction, simply put, refers to the conversations that learners participate in.

Interactions are important because it is in this context that learners receive information about the correctness and, more important, about the incorrectness of their utterances (VanPatten et al., 2020).

Long's Interaction Hypothesis

Building on Hatch's (1978) claims of the importance of carrying out conversations in language learning, the original version of Long's Interaction Hypothesis posited that conversation features increase input comprehensibility for L2 learners. This view was highly influenced by various research trends such as Krashen's Input Hypothesis (Krashen, 1980) and foreigner talk research (Ferguson, 1971). According to Long (1983), input can be made "comprehensible" in three ways:

1. by simplifying the input, i. e., using familiar structures and vocabulary;
2. by using linguistic and extralinguistic features, i. e., familiar structures, background knowledge, gestures;
3. by modifying the interactional structure of the conversation.

This third element is the basis of Long's (1981) Interaction Hypothesis, which takes into account both input and learner production in promoting acquisition. The hypothesis claims that it is in the interaction process that acquisition occurs: learners acquire through talking with others.

Long (1983) maintains that speakers make changes in their language as they interact or"negotiate meaning" with each other. Negotiation of meaning has been characterized as "exchanges between learners and their interlocuters as they attempt to resolve communication breakdown and to work toward mutual comprehension." Speakers negotiate meaning to avoid conversational trouble or to revise language when trouble occurs. Through negotiation of meaning, interactions are changed and redirected, leading to greater comprehensibility.

What exactly does it mean to negotiate meaning? In the classroom this means that both parties in a teacher-student and student-student interaction must seek clarification, check comprehension, and request confirmation that they have understood or are being understood by the other. This process is often difficult to achieve in the classroom, given the traditional roles between teachers and students. Since students are often hesitant to question or counter-question the teacher, negotiation of meaning may not occur often. Although teachers often work to provide comprehensible input through a variety of techniques (visuals, simplified input, mime, etc.), this process does not necessarily imply or lead to the negotiation of meaning. For this type of interaction to occur, both interlocutors must have equal rights in asking for clarification and adjusting what they say. Thus, Long's theory implies that learners cannot simply listen to input, but that they must be active conversational participants who interact and negotiate the type of input they receive in order to acquire language (Shrum, et al., 2004)[56].

Interaction plays a role as the cognitive processes of learners interact with the input to which they pay attention. Input can become implicit, or automatic language, when learners notice specific features of it, compare these features to those of their own output, and integrate the features into their own developing language system.

Long's (1996)[451] updated Interaction Hypothesis states: "Negotiation for meaning, and especially negotiation that triggers interactional adjustments by the native speaker or more competence interlocutor, facilitates acquisition because it connects input, internal learner capacities, particularly selective attention, and output in productive ways." Since the proposal of the updated Interaction Hypothesis, the field of SLA has witnessed an explosion of empirical studies with the overarching goal of investigating how interaction facilitates L2 learning.

Today, we have ample evidence that interaction does foster L2 development. Gasset al. (2007)[176] claimed that "it is now commonly accepted within the SLA literature that there is a robust connection between interaction and learning." Therefore, as a field, there is agreement that what was once viewed as a hypothesis (i. e., Interaction Hypothesis) can now be viewed as an approach to SLA (Mackey et al., 2013).

Interaction and instructed second language acquisition (ISLA)

One way that ISLA research has tried to balance the development of explicit and implicit knowledge is to advocate instruction that incorporates both types of knowledge during interaction (Loewen et al., 2018).

This theoretical and pedagogical framework has been most commonly referred to as *focus on form* (Long 1996) or *form-focused instruction* (Ellis, 2001; Spada, 1997). The premise of the framework is that learners' attention is shifted to specific linguistic structures while their primary focus is on meaning. For example, when conducting an information and opinion gap task in which learners have to discuss the relative merits of various scholarship candidates, and then decide which one should receive the scholarship, learners might be exposed to various grammatical structures (e. g. , conditionals) and vocabulary items that are useful for completing the task. During the interaction, learners might need to pause briefly to think about the grammatical forms or vocabulary words they need to use to express their meaning. Thus, learners are shifting between meaning and form.

Such attention shifts are beneficial for developing implicit knowledge. From the cognitive-interactionist perspective, the combination of meaning and form during communication helps develop implicit knowledge because it provides learners with the opportunity to notice linguistic items and structures at the very moment they are most needed for communication (Long, 1996).

Cognitive-Interactionist Approach

Among the various approaches to SLA, cognitive-interactionist approach has made clear suggestions for optimal features of L2 instruction and contributed most notably to the development of ISLA. Its roots can be found in Long's initial formulations of the Interaction Hypothesis (Long, 1981). It is concerned with the types of knowledge that L2 learners need to develop to communicate proficiently in the L2. This issue has most recently been framed in terms of the description and measurement of either implicit and explicit knowledge (e. g. , Ellis, 2005) or declarative and procedural knowledge (DeKeyser, 2015). The two sets of terms are not isomorphic, but there is considerable overlap (Lowen, 2021)[311].

The major constructs

The major constructs of cognitive-interactionist approaches to L2 learning cover the following key concepts:

1. Input: The language that is available to a learner through any medium (e. g. , listening, reading). It provides positive evidence.
2. Interaction: Conversation in which the learners engage. It can be carried out in person, online, or through other mobile-mediated communication settings.
3. Output: The oral or written language that is produced by learners.
4. Noticing: Paying attention to linguistic input with some level of awareness.
5. Corrective feedback: A written or oral response to learners' errors. It provides negative evidence (i. e. , information about what is not possible in a target language).
6. Focus on form: Spontaneous attention to linguistic forms during meaning-oriented activities.

7. Modified output: Learners' response to feedback that is more target-like than the original utterance.

From a theoretical perspective, an interactionist approach to SLA values the role of corrective feedback in language development because it promotes noticing of linguistic forms in unobtrusive ways. Pedagogically speaking, it addresses long-standing concerns related to a lack of accuracy development in communicative language teaching. Recent development in interaction research involves exploring intervening variables that affect the role of corrective feedback such as feedback types (e.g., recasts vs. elicitation; Nassaji, 2009), individual differences (e.g., working memory, aptitude, anxiety, proficiency; Li, 2013), and target linguistic features (e.g., questions, passives; Mackey, 2006). For instance, working memory has been increasingly examined, and research has shown that individual differences in working memory capacity is associated with the role of corrective feedback in language learning (e.g., Goo, 2012; Li, 2013; Mackey et al., 2002; Mackey et al., 2012).

In terms of learner-learner interaction, we have strong evidence that it is beneficial in classrooms. What seems to be the most important at the present stage is to train learners to become autonomous interaction participants, given that recent training studies demonstrate the benefits of training (Fujii et al., 2016; Kim, 2013; Sato et al., 2012).

Task design features can also impact the degree of interaction-driven language learning. Tasks need to be designed to encourage learners to use language in meaningful contexts, to engage with target language, and to facilitate interaction. For instance, when task complexity is increased in a way that it encourages learners to use target features, learners might pay more attention to target linguistic features while carrying out collaborative tasks (Kim, 2012). Also, the use of specific techniques as a part of guided planning seems to encourage learners to pay attention to target forms during interaction. Finally, encouraging learners to work collaboratively to identify gaps and actively work to identify solutions for their language-related episodes (LREs; instances in the interactions where learners talk about, question, and/or self-or-other correct language use: Swain & Lapkin, 1998) or form-focused episodes (FFEs) may be helpful for L2 development.

Technology-Mediated Interaction

A notable development in cognitive-interactionist research is the expansion of interactional contexts. The use of diverse instructional technology in educational contexts and the creation of online courses have contributed to the expansion of interaction research (see McDonough & Mackey, 2013).

Besides face-to-face interaction in classroom contexts, computer-mediated communication (CMC) interaction settings have received increasing attention in the interactionist research domain (Ziegler, 2016). In particular, synchronous computer-mediated communication (SCMC) has been attracting much attention in the SLA literature for its purported benefits for L2 development (Smith, 2005). SCMC refers to real-time interaction between people over a computer network (Stockwell, 2010), and it can be oral (voice chat) or written (text chat) modes.

In SCMC, unlike face-to-face interaction, learners have more time to understand and process what they see or hear. Previous studies have demonstrated that unique features of SCMC (e. g. , text-based and computer mediated interaction, slower rate of interaction, little competition over turn-taking) may allow for advantages within SCMC contexts over face-to-face interaction contexts. Because SCMC interaction allows for a self-correction before sending messages, researchers have claimed that learners might be less intimidated.

Interlanguage Theory

Interlanguage (IL) is the "language of the learner," a system in development and not yet a totally accurate approximation of native speaker language (Shrum, et al. , 2004)[6-7]. Selinker (1974) defines interlanguage as an individual linguistic system created by second language learners as a result of five cognitive processes:

1. interference from the native language;
2. effect of instruction (approach, rules provided by the teacher, classroom activities, etc.);
3. overgeneralization of target language rules (application of rules to contexts where they do not apply);
4. strategies involved in second language learning, such as rote memorization, use of formal rules, and guessing in context;
5. strategies involved in second language communication, such as circumlocution, use of gestures, appeal for assistance from a conversational partner.

This system is composed of numerous elements, not the least of which are elements from the NL and the TL. There are also elements in the IL that do not have their origin in either the NL or the TL. It is important that the learners themselves impose structure on the available linguistic data and formulate an internalized system (IL). Patterns in IL systems are both consistent and dynamic. What we eventually want to understand is: What is the nature of the IL system, how does it come to be, and why does it generally fail to be the same as a system underlying native speaker knowledge. With regard to the latter, an important question is: why are learners exposed to something (often many times) but still remain unable to reproduce it in a way that matches that of native speakers?

Central to the concept of IL is the concept of **fossilization**, which generally refers to the cessation of learning. The *Random House Dictionary of the English Language* (Flexner et al. , 1988)[755] defines fossilization of a linguistic form, feature, rule, and so forth in the following way: "to become permanently established in the interlanguage of a second language learner in a form that is deviant from the target-language norm and that continues to appear in performance regardless of further exposure to the target language"(Grass, 2020)[13].

Because of the difficulty in determining when learning has ceased, one frequently refers to **stabilization** of linguistic forms, rather than fossilization or cessation of learning. In SLA, one often notes that IL plateaus are far from the TL norms. Furthermore, it appears to be the case that fossilized or stabilized ILs exist, no matter what learners do in terms of further exposure to the TL (Gass, 2020)[13].

Current theories of L2 acquisition maintain that learners modify their own interlanguage only when they integrate into their long-term memories the input to which they attend, that is, construct new hypotheses in order to incorporate the noticed features into the interlanguage system (Ellis, 1997; Gass, 1988).

Output

Input alone is not sufficient for acquisition, because, when one hears language one can often interpret the meaning without the use of syntax.

Learners are pushed or stretched in their production as a necessary part of making themselves understood. In so doing, they might modify a previous utterance, or they might try out forms that they had not used before (Gass, 2020)[412-413].

Swain's Output Hypothesis

Swain (1985), based on her research in Canadian immersion contexts, claimed that while comprehensible input is necessary for L2 development, on its own, it is insufficient. She argued that language production is necessary because it forces learners to move beyond semantic processing of language during comprehension and focuses their attention toward syntactic use of language.

According to Swain's Output Hypothesis (Swain, 1995), producing output thus plays a critical role in L2 acquisition because it encourages learners to notice gaps in their interlanguage system (i. e. , noticing), gives learners a chance to test their linguistic hypotheses (i. e. , hypothesis testing), and fosters the co-construction of knowledge when learners use language to reflect on language use (i. e. , metalinguistic awareness).

Comprehensible output refers to the need for a learner to be "pushed toward the delivery of a message that is not only conveyed, but that is conveyed precisely, coherently, and appropriately" (Swain, 1985)[249].

Swain (1995) suggests that "pushed output" (i. e. , output that is accurate and socio-linguistically appropriate) may be necessary for learners to achieve higher levels of linguistic and sociolinguistic competence. Pushed output facilitates acquisition, as it:

1. helps learners to discover that there is a gap between what they want to say and what they are able to say,
2. provides a way for learners to try out new rules and modify them accordingly,
3. helps learners to actively reflect on what they know about the target language system.

Output as practice verses communicative output

When learners produce output, they are not engaged in comprehension as they are with input. They are doing something else (VanPatten et al., 2020)[119-120].

One kind of output is what we might call "practice," in the traditional sense of the term. Learners repeat something after the instructor (or the voice on the software program they are using). Learners translate a sentence from the L1 to the L2. Learners are asked to make a sentence in the past tense to show they can make the past tense. Learners are asked to write full sentences as answers to particular prompts (e.g., "Where do you live?" "I live in London."). What all of these output events have in common is that learners are producing language for the sake of producing language. This is output as practice.

The other major kind of output can be termed communicative output or communicatively embedded output. It refers to the kind of language learners produce in order to express meaning to someone else in a given context for a given purpose.

When a learner says to an instructor "Professor, I don't understand this word" and points to a word on a page, that learner is engaged in communicative output. When a learner witnesses an accident and the police interview that learner-witness, the learner engages in communicative output during the interchange. What all of these scenarios have in common is communicative purpose and not practice.

Learners are speaking not because they are practicing sentence structure, verb forms, or vocabulary—they are speaking because some kind of meaning-making is relevant to the task or situation at hand. Those learners need information, are seeking help, or are asked to supply some kind of information for a given task.

Exercises, Questions and Tasks

1. Multiple Choices.

(1) Which of the following is not a condition that must be met for Monitor usage in Krashen's view?

A. There was time. B. The learner was focused on form.

C. When the learner knew the rule. D. The learner was focused on meaning.

(2) The Affective Filter Hypothesis ascribes variation between learners to their ________ states.

A. psychological B. psychic

C. psychiatric D. physiological

(3) Comprehensible input relies on ________.

A. the comprehensible language forms B. the incomprehensible language forms

C. the total message D. the parts learners understand

(4) According to the Natural Order Hypothesis, we acquire the rules of language in a(n) ________ order.

A. unpredictable B. linear

C. predictable D. accessible

(5) The minimal condition for acquisition to occur is ________.

A. practice sentences B. rote memory

C. output D. participation in communication

(6) In Krashen's view of the Input Hypothesis, which of the following is not an implication for the classroom?

A. Speech cannot be taught directly.

B. The teacher's main role is to provide comprehensible input.

C. The student receives a sufficient amount of comprehensible input.

D. The teacher need to teach the text structure along the natural order.

(7) Which of the following is a guideline in developing structured input activities according to VanPatten?

A. keep form in focus

B. move from words to sentences

C. use oral input

D. keep the learner's processing strategies in mind

(8) According to Long, input can be made "comprehensible" in the following ways except ________.

A. using familiar structures and vocabulary

B. modifying the interactional structure of the conversation

C. complicating the input

D. using gestures

(9) Interlanguage is an individual linguistic system created by second language learners as a result of the following cognitive processes except ________.

A. contextualized learning

B. interference from the native language

C. effect of instruction

D. overgeneralization of target language rules

(10) Pushed output might not concern ________.

A. fluency

B. sociolinguistically appropriateness

C. accuracy

D. how to work well in cooperation with others

2. Fill in each blank with an appropriate word.

(1) For Krashen, learning is a ________ process, and it usually takes place in the language classroom.

(2) Comprehensible input and the ________ of the filter are the true causes of second language acquisition.

(3) Those with attitudes more conducive to SLA will not only seek and obtain more input, they

will also have a lower or weaker ________.

(4) There is much ________ in FL learners' language production. Sometimes they will get a structure right while on another occasion they will get it wrong.

(5) When input is simplified and tailored to the level of the learner, learners are better able to make connections between form and meaning and thus convert input to ________.

3. Mark "True" or "False" for the following statements and explain why.

(1) When learners make mistakes, it is normal for the classroom teacher to draw explicit attention to them, and to correct the errors.

(2) Those whose attitudes are not optimal for SLA will not only tend to seek less input, but they will also have a lower or weaker Affective Filter.

(3) The "natural order" was determined by a synthesis of the results of the morpheme studies and is a result of the acquired system.

(4) On occasions when chatting to friends, learners are monitoring their own speech-checking it carefully before they produce it.

(5) Monitoring uses acquired knowledge as a quality check on speech originating form learnt knowledge.

4. Discuss the following questions.

(1)Why are young learners better at L2 acquisition over the long term?

(2) Why is acquisition not equally successful for all L2 learners, even when they receive apparently identical comprehensible input?

(3) What might work out a more beneficial instruction for beginning language learners in terms of input processing theory?

(4) In what situations do learners modify their own interlanguage?

(5)Why does Swain believe that pushed output facilitates acquisition?

Suggested Readings

BARDOVI-HARLIG K, COMAJOAN-COLOMÉ L, 2022. The relation of second language acquisition, instructed second language acquisition, and language teaching from the lens of second language tense-aspect[J]. Language Teaching, 55(3): 289-345.

COOK V, 2021. Linguistics and Second Language Acquisition[M]. Beijing: Foreign Language Teaching and Research Press.

ELLIS R, 2013. The study of second language acquisition[M]. 2nd ed. Shanghai: Shanghai Foreign Language Education Press.

GASS S M, 2020. Second language acquisition: An introductory course[M]. 4th ed. Beijing: Tsinghua University Press.

HAN Z H, 2023. Issues of narrowness and staticity in ISLA[J]. Instructed Second Language Acquisition, 7(1): 3-26.

JOHNSON K, 2002. An introduction to foreign language learning and teaching[M]. Beijing:

Foreign Language Teaching and Research Press.

KIM Y J, 2017. Cognitive-interactionist approaches to L2 instruction// LOEWEN S, SATO M. The Routledge handbook of instructed second language acquisition[M]. New York: Routledge, 166-180.

LARSEN-FREEMAN D, Long M H, 2000. An introduction to second language acquisition Research[M]. Beijing: Foreign Language Teaching and Research Press.

LOEWEN S, SATO M, 2017. Instructed second language acquisition (ISLA): An overview [M]// LOEWEN S, SATO M. The Routledge handbook of instructed second language acquisition[M]. New York: Routledge, 1 - 12.

LOEWEN S, SATO M, 2018. Interaction and instructed second language acquisition[J]. Language Teaching, 51(3): 285 - 329.

LOEWEN S, SATO M, 2019. Instructed Second Language Acquisition and English Language Teaching: Theory, Research, and Pedagogy [J]. Second Handbook of English Language Teaching, 1131 - 1148.

LOEWEN S, 2021. Was Krashen right? An instructed second language acquisition perspective [J]. Foreign Language Annals, 54(2): 311 - 317.

PORCELLATO A M, 2020. Evidence-based second language pedagogy: A Collection of instructed second language acquisition studies edited by M. Sato and S. Loewen [J]. Instructed Second Language Acquisition, 4(1): 96 - 99.

SAVILLE-TROIKE M, 2008. Introducing second language acquisition[M]. Beijing: Foreign Language Teaching and Research Press.

SHRUM J L, GLISAN E W, 2004. Teacher's handbook: Contextualized language instruction [M]. Beijing: Foreign Language Teaching and Research Press.

VANPATTEN B, 2017. Processing instruction// LOEWEN S, SATO M. The Routledge handbook of instructed second language acquisition[M]. New York: Routledge, 126 - 145.

VANPATTEN B, SMITH M, BENATI A G, 2020. Key questions in second language acquisition: An introduction[M]. 2nd ed. Cambridge: Cambridge University Press.

VANPATTEN B, WILLIAMS J, 2015. Theories in second language acquisition: An introduction[M]. 2nd ed. New York: Routledge.

CHAPTER 4

Dynamic Systems Theory & Individual Differences

Focusing Question

- How can one cater for different personality types in the same classroom?
- Why do you think some people are good at learning other languages?
- Do you think the same people learn a language well in the classroom as learn it well in a natural setting, or do these demand different qualities?

Introduction

Individual difference (ID) variables are learner traits and characteristics that may have an impact on learning processes, behaviors, and outcomes.

Li et al. (2022) divide the ID factors covered into four categories: cognitive, conative, affective, and sociocultural/demographic differences. Affective has to do with feelings and emotions. Conative has to do with goal setting and the will. And cognitive refers to analysis and interpretation. It includes reasoning, remembering, and using symbols (Cronbach, 2002).

In this taxonomy, sociodemographic variables in this chapter subsume age; cognitive variables include intelligence, language aptitude, cognitive styles, learning styles; conative variables comprise attitude and motivation; affective variables encompass personality and learner beliefs. There may be an overlap between certain categories, especially between conative and affective variables (Li et al., 2022).

These variables, both internal and external to the learner, moderate and influence the effectiveness of instruction. Such individual differences are both interesting and challenging to ISLA researcher (as well as teachers and learners) who are trying to account for the effects of instruction (Loewen et al., 2017)[6]. Learner-internal factors that have received considerable ISLA investigation include motivation, language aptitude, and foreign language anxiety (see Dörnyei et al., 2015), while learner-external factors include the micro- and macro-social contexts in which learners find themselves (see The Douglas Fir Group, 2016).

CDST & Individual Differences

Complexity Theory is a transdisciplinary ecological metatheory, which is centrally concerned with the study of nonlinear change in open systems. As applied to second language development (SLD), it has been called the Complex Dynamic Systems Theory (CDST). CDST researchers seek to trace the patterns in a learner's developing language resources as they continuously emerge over time and are constructed in interactions with others (Li et al., 2022)[12].

While the main trajectory of SLA is determined by language acquisitional processes, relatively stable and monolithic learner attributes—called individual differences cause systematic deviations from the overall trend. However, when we look at them more closely, individual learner characteristics appear to be rather different from the meaning we tend to assign to them in everyday parlance or in traditional professional discourse: they are not at all stable but show salient temporal and situational variation, and they are not monolithic either but constitute complex constellations that are made up of different parts that interact with each other and the environment synchronically and diachronically. As a result, simple cause-effect relationships are unable to do justice to these multi-level interactions and temporal changes. Individual learner variation can be better accounted for in terms of the operation of a complex dynamic system in the sense that high-level mental attributes and functions are determined by an intricate set of interconnected components that continuously evolve over time and which also interact with the environment in an ongoing manner. The value of each constituent keeps changing depending on the overall state of the system and in response to external influences, making ID factors dynamic system variables (Dörnyei, 2012)[276].

Age Differences

The critical period hypothesis

Undoubtedly, children are popularly believed to be better at learning second languages than adults. This belief in the superiority of young learners was enshrined in the critical period hypothesis (CPH): the claim that human beings are only capable of learning their first language between the age of two years and the early teens (Lenneberg, 1967). A variety of explanations have been put forward for the apparent decline in adults: physical factors such as the loss of "plasticity" in the brain and "lateralization" of the brain; social factors such as the different situations and relationships that children encounter compared to adults; and cognitive explanations such as the interference with natural language learning by the adult's more abstract mode of thinking (Cook, 1986). It has often been concluded that teachers should take advantage of this ease of learning by teaching a second language as early as possible (Cook, 2011).

Age and language teaching

How should a language teacher take the student's age into account? One question is when L2 teaching should start. This also involves how long the learners are going to be studying. If they are intending to spend many years learning the second language, they might as well start as children rather than as adults since they will probably end up better speakers. If they are going to learn the second language for a few years and then drop it, like the majority of learners perhaps, there is an advantage for adults, who would reach a higher standard during the same period.

A related question is whether the use of teaching methods should vary according to the age of the students. At particular ages students prefer particular methods. Teenagers may dislike any technique that exposes them in public; role play and simulation are in conflict with their adolescent anxieties. Adults can feel they are not learning properly in play-like situations and prefer a conventional, formal style of teaching. Adults learn better than children from the "childish" activities of total physical response—if you can get them to join in! Age is by no means crucial to L2 learning itself (Asher et al., 1969). Spolsky (1989) describes three conditions for L2 learning related to age:

1. "Formal" classroom learning requires "skills of abstraction and analysis." That is to say, if the teaching method entails sophisticated understanding and reasoning by the student, as for instance a traditional grammar-translation method, then it is better for the student to be older.
2. The child is more open to L2 learning in informal situations. Hence children are easier to teach through an informal approach.
3. The natural L2 situation may favor children. The teaching of adults requires the creation of language situations in the classroom that in some ways compensate for this lack. An important characteristic of language spoken to small children is that it is concerned with the "here and now," rather than with the absent objects or the abstract topics that are talked about in adult conversation—adults do not talk about the weather much to a 2-year-old! That is to say, ordinary speech spoken by adults to adults is too sophisticated for L2 learning. Restricting the language spoken to the beginning L2 learner to make it reflect the here and now could be of benefit. This is reminiscent of the audio-visual and situational teaching methods, which stress the provision of concrete visual information through physical objects or pictures in the early stages of L2 learning. But it may go against the idea that the content of teaching should be relevant and should not be trivial.

Most adaptation to the age of the learner in textbooks probably concerns the presentation of material and topics. But, as always with published materials, they have to aim at an "average" student; many teenagers may scorn soap operas, many adults have no interest in discussing holidays (Cook, 2011)[149-150].

Intelligence

Intelligence is the general set of cognitive abilities involved in performing a wide range of learning tasks. It constitutes "a general sort of aptitude that is not limited to a specific performance area but is transferable to many sorts of performance" (Dörnyei, 2005). Intelligence, working memory, and language aptitude are clearly all closely linked. They all refer to cognitive capacities and the difference between their conceptualizations lies largely in how broad and how language-specific the terms are (Ellis, 2013)[649].

In relating intelligence to second language learning, can we say simply that a "smart" person will be capable of learning a second language more successfully because of greater intelligence? After all, the greatest barrier to second language learning seems to boil down to a matter of memory, in the sense that if you could just remember everything you were ever taught, or you ever heard, you would be a very successful language learner. Or would you? It appears that our language-learning "IQs" are much more complicated than that (Brown, 2002)[93].

Multiple intelligences (MI)

Multiple Intelligences (MI) refers to a learner-based philosophy that characterizes human intelligence as having multiple dimensions that must be acknowledged and developed in education. Gardner posits eight native "intelligences," which are described as follows:

1. Linguistic: the ability to use language in special and creative ways, which is something lawyers, writers, editors, and interpreters are strong in.
2. Logical/mathematical: the ability to think rationally, often found with doctors, engineers, programmers, and scientists.
3. Spatial: the ability to form mental models of the world, something architects, decorators, sculptors, and painters are good at.
4. Musical: a good ear for music, as is strong in singers and composers.
5. Bodily/kinesthetic: having a well-coordinated body, something found in athletes and crafts persons.
6. Interpersonal: the ability to be able to work well with people, which is strong in salespeople, politicians, and teachers.
7. Intrapersonal: the ability to understand oneself and apply one's talent successfully, which leads to happy and well-adjusted people in all areas of life.
8. Naturalist: the ability to understand and organize the patterns of nature.

The idea of Multiple Intelligences has attracted the interest of many educators as well as the general public. Schools that use MI theory encourage learning that goes beyond traditional books, pens, and pencils. Teachers and parents who recognize their learners'/children's particular gifts and talents can provide learning activities that build on those inherent gifts. As a result of strengthening such differences, individuals are free to be intelligent in their own ways (Richards et al., 2008)[115-116].

Applications of MI in language teaching

Language learning and use are obviously closely linked to what MI theorists label "Linguistic Intelligence." However, MI proponents believe there is more to language than what is usually subsumed under the rubric linguistics. There are aspects of language such as rhythm, tone, volume, and pitch that are more closely linked, say, to a theory of music than to a theory of linguistics. Other intelligences enrich the tapestry of communication we call "language." In addition, language has its ties to life through the senses. The senses provide the accompaniment and context for the linguistic message that give it meaning and purpose. A multisensory view of language is necessary, it seems, to construct an adequate theory of language as well as an effective design for language learning (Richards et al., 2015)[117].

Campbell notes that MI theory "is not prescriptive. Rather, it gives teachers a complex mental model from which to construct curriculum and improve themselves as educators" (Campbell, 1997). Teachers then become curriculum developers, lesson designers and analysts, activity finders or inventors, and, most critically orchestrators of a rich array of multisensory activities within the realistic constraints of time, space, and resources of the classroom. Teachers are encouraged not to think of themselves merely as language teachers. They have a role that is not only to improve the second language abilities of their students but to become major "contributors to the overall development of students' intelligences" (Christison, 1999).

Like teachers, learners need to see themselves engaged in a process of personality development above and beyond that of being successful language learners. The MI classroom is one designed to support development of the "whole person," and the environment and its activities are intended to enable students to become more well-rounded individuals and more successful learners in general. Learners are encouraged to see their goals in these broader terms. Learners are typically expected to take an MI inventory and to develop their own MI profiles based on the inventory. "The more awareness students have of their own intelligences and how they work, the more they will know how to use that intelligence [*sic*] to access the necessary information and knowledge from a lesson" (Christison, 1997)[9]. All of this is to enable learners to benefit from instructional approaches by reflecting on their own learning (Richards et al., 2008)[120].

Christison describes a low-level language lesson dealing with description of physical objects as follows.

Stage 1: Awaken the Intelligence. The teacher brings many different objects to class. Students experience feeling things that are soft, rough, cold, smooth, and so on. They might taste things that are sweet, salty, sour, spicy, and so on. Experiences like this help activate and make learners aware of the sensory bases of experience.

Stage 2: Amplify the Intelligence. Students are asked to bring objects to class or to use something in their possession. Teams of students describe each object attending to the five physical senses.

Stage 3: Teach with/for the Intelligence. At this stage, the teacher structures larger sections of lesson(s) so as to reinforce and emphasize sensory experiences and the language that accompanies these experiences. Students work in groups.

Stage 4: Transfer of the Intelligence. This stage is concerned with application of the intelligence to daily living. Students are asked to reflect on both the content of the lesson and its operational procedures (working in groups, completing tables, etc.).

This particular lesson on describing objects is seen as giving students opportunities to "develop their linguistic intelligence (for example, describing objects), logical intelligence (for example, determining which object is being described), visual/ spatial intelligence (for example, determining how to describe things), interpersonal intelligence (for example, working in groups), and intrapersonal intelligence (for example, reflecting on one's own involvement in the lesson)."

Motivation

Motivation is one of the most important concepts in psychology as motivation theories attempt to explain nothing less than *why humans behave and think as they do*. The notion is also of great importance in language education as it is one of the most common terms teachers and students use to explain what causes success or failure in learning. Indeed, it provides the primary impetus to initiate second/foreign (L2) learning and later the driving force to sustain the long and often tedious learning process. Without sufficient motivation, even individuals with the most remarkable abilities cannot accomplish long-term goals, and neither are appropriate curricula and good teaching enough on their own to ensure student achievement (Dörnyei, 2012)[249].

Gardner and Lambert's ideas about motivation were largely shaped by Mowrer's (1950) view of L1 acquisition. Mowrer attributed a child's success in acquiring an Ll to the child's quest for identity, initially with members of the child's immediate family and then later with members of the larger speech community. Borrowing the concept of identification from Mowrer, Gardner and Lambert proposed a construct they called integrative motivation. A learner is said to be integratively motivated when the learner wishes to identify with another ethnolinguistic group. By way of contrast to integrative motivation, Gardner and Lambert introduced the concept of instrumental motivation, in which the learner is motivated to learn an L2 for utilitarian purposes, such as furthering a career, improving social status or meeting an educational requirement (Larsen-Freeman et al., 2000)[173].

L2 motivational self system theory

The L2 Motivational Self System suggests that there are three primary sources of the motivation to learn a foreign/second language:

1. the learner's vision of him/herself as an effective L2 speaker
2. the social pressure coming from the learner's environment
3. positive learning experiences.

In 2005, Dörnyei proposed that the "L2 Motivational Self System" was made up of the following three components:

1. Ideal L2 Self, which is the L2-specific facet of one's "ideal self": if the person we would like to become speaks an L2, the "ideal L2 self" is a powerful motivator to learn the L2 because of the desire to reduce the discrepancy between our actual and ideal selves. Traditional integrative and internalized instrumental motives would typically belong to this component.
2. Ought-to L2 Self, which concerns the attributes that one believes one ought to possess to meet expectations and to avoid possible negative outcomes. This dimension corresponds to Higgins's ought self and thus to the more extrinsic (i. e. less internalised) types of instrumental motives.
3. L2 Learning Experience, which concerns situated, "executive" motives related to the immediate learning environment and experience (e. g. the impact of the teacher, the curriculum, the peer group, the experience of success). This component is conceptualised at a different level from the two self-guides.

The central tenet of this theory has become students' ideal L2 selves, which led research into vision-related issues. Dörnyei and Kubanyiova (2014) devoted a volume to the use of vision in the classroom. The main point of their book is that by adding a vision as a part of teaching, students are better able to develop future self-guides, such as students' ideal L2 selves, and goals that will enhance their motivation and as a result, their achievement in language learning. Dörnyei and Kubanyiova (2014) also argue that their teachers' visions about themselves as language learners (i. e. , when teachers are, or used to be, L2 learners of the students' target language themselves) as well as language teachers contribute to the motivational dynamics of the L2 classroom. The role of ought-to L2 self has been seen as very complex because the diverse nature of outside expectations makes the operationalisation of the concept rather difficult (Kormos et al. , 2008). As for the third component of the model, language learning experiences (unspecified whether or not these experiences are related to instructed language learning) remain a somewhat neglected aspect of the model, with some studies measuring it as general positive attitudes to learning while others as positive attitudes to classroom learning (You et al. , 2016).

Demotivation

Demotivation is a process whereby initially motivated students lose their willingness to invest energy into language learning (Csizér, 2017). Dörnyei defines demotivation as "specific external forces that reduce or diminish the motivational basis of a behavioral intention or an ongoing action" (Dörnyei, 2001)[143]. What he means by this is that the positive motivations that were initially present when a choice was made to undertake some activity were diminished by some negative factor, very often some classroom experience, most notably a teacher (Gass, 2020)[526]. Ushioda (2003)[93-94] illustrate this point as follows:

> The inevitable problems in classroom motivation arise when there is not a happy fusion between internal and external forces but a negative tension, where the latter dominate at the expense of the former. In other words, individual motivation becomes controlled, suppressed or distorted by external forces. this may happen through negative influences in the classroom social dynamic, or through regulating forces in the educational system ...

Collective motivation can all too easily become collective demotivation, boredom, or at the far end of the spectrum, collective dissatisfaction or rebellion, often in the form of classroom counter-cultures defined by rejection of educational aims and values.

In Dörnyei's (1998) study teachers were identified to be the most "important" demotivating factors in students' motivation.

Motivation& dynamic system theory

The most recent development in L2 motivation research is the inclusion of dynamic system theory into the L2 motivation field. Dörnyei et al. 's (2015) volume on the applicability of and empirical evidence on dynamic system theory points toward the fact that a classroom can indeed be selected as a "domain of reality" to investigate L2 motivation because L2 motivation in the classroom "is nothing if not complex and dynamic". The volume indeed contains several classroom-related motivational studies.

Waninge (2015) looks into motivational and demotivational attractor states in classrooms, that is, states when motivation stops fluctuating for a time and how these relatively stable states are linked to language learning experience. This study concludes that there are four main characterising elements related to classroom experience: interest, boredom, neutral attention, and anxiety. Changes in motivation during a 14-week writing seminar are reported (Piniel et al. , 2015), in which it was mapped how the motivation, anxiety, and self-efficacy changed during a university writing course. Learners with different level of motivation are typified and investigated (Chan et al. , 2015) and it was pointed out that a limited number of learners' archetype existed in a class, which teachers were usually aware of. MacIntyre and Serroul's (2015) investigation delves into L2 motivation within a short period of time and looked at how it fluctuated second by second during a particular task. Because theoretical considerations of dynamic system theory take into account both change and interaction of various motivational variables in the classroom, dynamic system theory researchers could offer important contributions to L2 motivation research in ISLA settings (Dörnyei et al. , 2015).

Motivation and teaching

Students will find it difficult to learn a second language in the classroom if they have neither instrumental nor integrative motivation, as is probably often the case in school language teaching, or if they feel negatively about bilingualism or are too attached to monolingualism. Schoolchildren have no particular contact with the foreign culture and no particular interest in it, nor do their job prospects depend on it; their attitudes to L2 users may depend more on the stereotypes from their cultural situations than on any real contact.

Teachers may have to go along with the students' motivation, or at least be sufficiently aware of the students' motivation so that any problems can be smoothed over. They have to be aware of the reservations and preconceptions of their students. What they think of the teacher, the course and L2 users in general heavily affects their success. These are the factors that teachers can influence, rather than the learners' more deep-seated motivations.

Motivation also goes in both directions. High motivation is one factor that causes successful learning; in reverse, successful learning causes high motivation. The process of creating successful learning which can spur high motivation may be under the teacher's control, if not the original motivation. The choice of teaching materials and the information content of the lesson, for example, should correspond to the motivations of the students (Cook, 2011)[138-139].

Attitude

The roots of the motivations are deep within the students' minds and their cultural backgrounds. One issue is how the student's own cultural background relates to the background projected by the L2 culture.

Lambert (1981 & 1990) makes an important distinction between "additive" and "subtractive" bilingualism. In additive bilingualism, the learners feel they are adding something new to their skills and experience by learning a new language, without taking anything away from what they already know. In subtractive bilingualism, on the other hand, they feel that the learning of a new language threatens what they have already gained for themselves. Successful L2 learning takes place in additive situations; learners who see the second language as diminishing themselves will not succeed (Cook, 2011)[140-141].

Attitudes and language teaching

One crucial point coming out of this is how teaching reinforces unfavorable images of 12 users. Virtually all the L2 users represented in coursebooks, for example, are either students who are in the process of learning the second language or ignorant foreigners using tourist services. Students never see successful L2 users in action and so have no role model to emulate other than the native speaker, which they will very rarely match. The famous people whose photos proliferate in coursebooks tend to be people who are not known as anything other than monolingual, though a few sportspeople who give interviews in English are sometimes mentioned. Successful L2 users such as Gandhi, Einstein, Picasso, Marie Curie and Samuel Beckett, all taken from Francois Grosjean's list of bilinguals (1982), are never mentioned. It cannot do the students any harm to show them that the world is full of successful L2 users; indeed, as de Swaan (2001) argues, they are necessary for its functioning. The goals of language teaching include changing people's attitudes towards other cultures and using second languages effectively. These are hardly advanced by showing students either students like themselves or people who are unable to use more than one language (Cook, 2011)[143].

Aptitude

Some people have more aptitude for learning second languages than others. Aptitude has almost invariably been applied to students in classrooms. It does not refer to the knack that some people have for learning in real-life situations, but to the ability to learn from teaching. In the 1950s and 1960s, considerable effort went into establishing what successful students had in common. The Modern Languages Aptitude Test (MLAT) requires the student to carry out L2 learning on a small scale. It incorporates four main factors that predict a student's success in the classroom (Carroll, 1981). These are:

1. Phonemic coding ability: how well the student can use phonetic script to distinguish phonemes in the language.
2. Grammatical sensitivity: whether the student can pick out grammatical functions in the sentence.
3. Inductive language learning ability: whether the student can generalize patterns from one sentence to another.
4. Rote learning: whether the student can remember vocabulary lists of foreign words paired with translations.

MLAT predicts how well a student will do in a course that is predominantly audio-lingual in methodology rather than in a course taught by other methods.

Krashen (1981) suggests aptitude is important for "formal" situations such as classrooms, and attitude is important for informal real-world situations.

Aptitude and teaching

The problem for language teachers is what to do once the students have been tested for academic language learning aptitude. There are at least four possibilities:

1. *Select students who are likely to succeed in the classroom* and bar those who are likely to fail. This would, however, be unthinkable in most settings with open access to education.
2. *Stream students into different classes for levels of aptitude*, say high-flyers, average and below-average. The Graded Objectives Movement in England, for instance, set the same overall goals for all students at each stage, but allowed them different periods of time for getting there (Harding et al., 1981).

3. *Provide different teaching for different types of aptitude* with different teaching methods and final examinations. This might lead to varied exercises within the class, say, for those with and without phonemic coding ability, to parallel classes, or to self-directed learning. In most educational establishments this would be a luxury in terms of staffing and accommodation, however desirable.
4. *Excuse students with low aptitude from compulsory foreign language requirements.* In some educational systems the students may be required to pass a foreign language which is unrelated to the rest of their course, as I had to take French and Latin to order to read English at university. An extremely low aptitude for L2 learning may be grounds for exemption from this requirement if their other work passes.

The overall lesson is to see students in particular contexts. The student whose performance is dismal in one class may be gifted in another. Any class teaching is a compromise to suit the greatest number of students. Only in individualized or self- directed learning perhaps can this be overcome.

Personality

The theory of personality currently dominant in psychology is the "big five" model. This distinguishes five dimensions of personality:

1. Openness to experience
2. Conscientiousness
3. Extraversion versus introversion
4. Agreeableness
5. Neuroticism versus emotional stability

These higher order personality traits refer to consistent patterns in the way individuals behave, feel and think (Pervin et al., 2010). The Big Five bipolar higher order dimensions are situated at the summit of the hierarchy. Another higher order dimension used by some psychologists is Psychoticism, typified by aggressiveness and interpersonal hostility. Scores are normally distributed, meaning that a majority of people are situated in the middle of the dimension.

These higher order dimensions are correlated with facets beneath them. For example, people who score high on Openness to experience are typically creative, original, imaginative, curious, and flexible; those at the low end of the dimension are unartistic, conservative, conventional, practical, and down to earth. People who score high on Conscientiousness are typically meticulous, efficient, organized, reliable, hardworking, and persevering; low scorers are typically unreliable, careless, disorganized, lazy, and negligent. Extroverts are typically talkative, assertive, sociable, gregarious, active, and passionate; Introverts tend to be shy, passive, quiet, reserved, withdrawn, and sober. People who score high on Agreeableness are typically friendly, good-natured, kind, trusting, cooperative, modest, and generous; low scorers are typically cold, rude, unpleasant, critical, antagonistic, suspicious and uncooperative. People who score high on Neuroticism tend to worry, to be anxious, insecure, depressed, emotional, and unstable; people at the Emotional stability end of the scale are typically calm, relaxed, hardy, content, even-tempered, and self-satisfied (Dewaele, 2017)[438].

Self-esteem

Shavelson et al. (1976) proposed a ternary hierarchy to account for self-esteem, or the feeling of self-worth an individual possesses. At the highest level is global self-esteem, or the individual's overall self-assessment. At the medial level is specific self-esteem, or how individuals perceive themselves in various life contexts (education, work, etc.) and according to various characteristics (intelligence, attractiveness, etc.). At the lowest level is the evaluation one gives oneself on specific tasks (writing a paper, driving a car, etc.).

Heyde (1979) studied the effects of these three levels of self-esteem on performance on a French oral production task by American college students. She found that the students' performance correlated significantly with all three levels, the highest correlation existing for task self-esteem. One of the interesting side points of Heyde's research was her discovery that the task self-esteem scores fluctuated from one class to the next. Assuming that the students' distribution in the classes was random, it would appear that the instructors had some effect on the students' self-evaluations.

This finding (Brown, 2002)[138] suggests that teachers really can have a positive and influential effect on both the linguistic performance and the emotional well-being of the student. Perhaps those "good" teachers succeeded because they gave optimal attention to linguistic goals and to the personhood of their students.

Extroversion-introversion

Extroversion/introversion (Ellis, 2013)[673-674] represents a continuum (i. e. individuals can be more or less extroverted), but it is also possible to identify idealized types:

> Extroverts are sociable, like parties, have many friends and need excitement; they are sensation-seekers and risk-takers, like practical jokes and are lively and active. Conversely introverts are quiet, prefer reading to meeting people, have few but close friends and usually avoid excitement (Eysenck et al., 1982)[154].

The extent to which individuals verge towards one of these types is usually measured by analysing responses to self-report questions such as those in the Eysenck Personality Questionnaire or the Myers Briggs Type Indicator.

There are two major hypotheses regarding the relationship between extraversion/introversion and L2 learning. The first-which has been the most widely researched—is that extroverted learners will do better in acquiring basic interpersonal communication skills (BICS). The rationale for this hypothesis is that sociability (an essential feature of extraversion) will result in more opportunities to practise, more input, and more success in communicating in the L2. The second hypothesis is that introverted learners will do better at developing cognitive academic language proficiency (CALP). The rationale for this hypothesis comes from studies which show that introverted learners typically enjoy more academic success, perhaps because they spend more time reading and writing (See Griffiths, 1991b).

Anxiety

While all humans presumably experience anxiety at one time or other, it is thought that certain people might be anxious more often than others, or have a more severe reaction to anxiety-producing situations such that language learning would be impeded (Larsen-Freeman, 2000). Scovel (1978)[139] comments:

> Facilitating anxiety motivates the learner to "fight" the new learning task; it gears the learner emotionally for approval behavior. Debilitating anxiety, in contrast, motivates the learner to "flee" the new learning task; it stimulates the individual emotionally to adopt avoidance behavior.

A distinction can be made between Trait Anxiety, State Anxiety, and Situation-Specific Anxiety. Scovel (1978), drawing on work in general psychology, defined trait anxiety as "a more permanent predisposition to be anxious." It is perhaps best viewed as an aspect of personality. State anxiety can be defined as apprehension that is experienced at a particular moment in time as a response to a definite situation (Spielberger, 1983). It is a combination of trait and situation-specific anxiety. This latter type consists of the anxiety which is aroused by a specific type of situation or event such as public speaking, examinations, or class participation. "Language anxiety" is a particular type of situation anxiety—largely independent of other types of anxiety (Ellis, 2013)[691].

Horwitz et al. (1986) included descriptions of three specific anxieties: Communication Apprehension (anxiety about speaking or public speaking), Test Anxiety (anxiety experienced in testing situations or in anticipation of testing situations), and Fear of Negative Evaluation (the fear that people will judge the learner negatively) to illustrate concepts of specific anxieties (Dewaele, 2017)[435].

Figure 4. 1 shows relationship between the anxieties of foreign language learners and users: a nested design could be imagined with Communicative Anxiety as the outer ring, with gradually smaller inner rings starting with Language Anxiety, Foreign Language Anxiety (FLA), Foreign Language Classroom Anxiety (FLCA), and the anxieties linked to specific classroom activities such as speaking, listening, reading, and writing (Dewaele, 2017)[438-439].

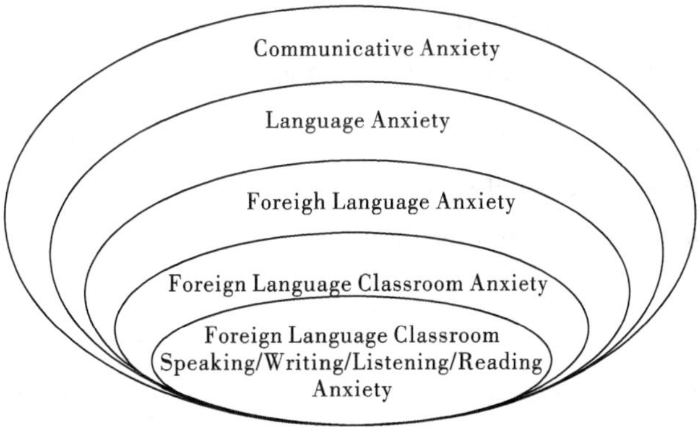

Figure 4. 1 Nested design of anxieties

Research has found that the effects of various psychological variables on levels of FLA/FLCA are not constant but dynamic and often language specific. On top of these complex interactions come other layers of sociobiographical, situational, and social variables, which could interact among themselves but also with a wide range of psychological variables(Dewaele, 2017)[443-444].

Risk-taking

Perhaps closely related to a high tolerance for anxiety-inducing situations is the willingness to take risks. Rubin (1975) characterized good language learners as willing to guess, willing to appear foolish in order to communicate, and willing to use what knowledge they do have of the TL in order to create novel utterances. All of these could be termed risk-taking behaviors (Beebe, 1983). However, just as too much anxiety can be debilitating, there might be an upper threshold to risk-taking beyond which further risk-taking could be detrimental. We say this in part due to the fact that people with a high motivation to achieve are moderate, not high, risk-takers (Kogan et al., 1967).

Beebe (1980) has studied the risk-taking behavior of Puerto Rican children learning ESL. Children who were experiencing difficulty with do insertion in WH-questions displayed significantly greater risk-taking behavior with an English- speaking interviewer than with a bilingual English-dominant Hispanic interviewer. Risk-taking was defined by both the amount of talk by the children and the amount of information they volunteered. Beebe looks for an explanation in Giles's Accommodation Theory, the central thesis of which is that people will unconsciously adjust their speech to their interlocutors. Thus, the bilingual children may have made their speech converge with that of the native speakers in order to gain the latter's approval (Larsen-Freeman, 2000)[188].

Ely (1986)[8] studied the risk-taking behavior of university students enrolled in Spanish courses during the first two quarters of the academic year. Ely operationalized risk-taking as being evidenced by four behaviors:

> a lack of hesitancy about using a newly encountered linguistic element; a willingness to use linguistic elements perceived to be complex or difficult; a tolerance of possible incorrectness or inexactitude in using the language; and an inclination to rehearse a new element silently before attempting to use it aloud.

Classroom participation was measured as the times a student said something in Spanish without being called onto do so. Ely found that the students 'risk-taking behavior was a positive predictor of students' voluntary classroom participation.

Empathy

In common terminology, empathy is the process of "putting yourself into someone else's shoes," of reaching beyond the self and understanding and feeling what another person is understanding or feeling. It is probably the major factor in the harmonious coexistence of individuals in society. Language is one of the primary means of empathizing, but nonverbal communication facilitates the process of empathizing and must not be overlooked (Brown, 2002).

In more sophisticated terms, empathy is usually described as the projection of one's own personality into the personality of another in order to understand him or her better. Empathy is not synonymous with *sympathy*. Empathy implies more possibility of detachment; sympathy connotes an agreement or harmony between individuals. Guiora et al. (1972) defined empathy as "a process of comprehending in which a temporary fusion of self-object boundaries permits an immediate emotional apprehension of the affective experience of another."

There are two necessary aspects to the development and exercising of empathy: first, an awareness and knowledge of one's own feelings, and second, identification with another person (Hogan, 1969). In other words, you cannot fully empathize—or know someone else—until you adequately know yourself.

Communication requires a sophisticated degree of empathy. In order to communicate effectively you need to be able to understand the other person's affective and cognitive states; communication breaks down when false presuppositions or assumptions are made about the other person's state, From the very mechanical, syntactic level of language to the most abstract, meaningful level, we assume certain structures of knowledge and certain emotional states in any communicative act. In order to make those assumptions correctly we need to transcend our own ego boundaries, or using Guiora's term, to "permeate" our ego boundaries so that we can send and receive messages clearly.

Guiora (1972b) has given the role of empathy in SL learning a decidedly psychoanalytic interpretation. Just as a child develops a general ego, so the child also acquires a language ego. When the child is young, the ego boundaries are relatively flexible, but they become more rigid with age. When the language ego boundaries are flexible, a new accent is more readily adopted than when the boundaries are more fixed. Some adults, presumably those who are more empathic, are likely to have more permeability of language ego boundaries, since they are able to temporarily suspend the separateness of their identity, and that should in turn result in their having an advantage in FL pronunciation (Larsen-Freeman, 2000)[190].

Inhibition

All human beings, in their understanding of themselves, build sets of defenses to protect the ego. The newborn baby has no concept of its own self; gradually it learns to identify a self that is distinct from others. Then in childhood, the growing degrees of awareness, responding, and valuing begin to create a system of affective traits that individuals identify with themselves. In adolescence, the physical, emotional, and cognitive changes of the preteenager and teenager bring on mounting defensive inhibitions to protect a fragile ego, to ward off ideas, experiences, and feelings that threaten to dismantle the organization of values and beliefs on which appraisals of self-esteem have been founded. The process of building defenses continues on into adulthood. Some persons—those with higher self-esteem and ego strength—are more able to withstand threats to their existence and thus their defenses are lower. Those with weaker self-esteem maintain walls of inhibition to protect what is self-perceived to be a weak or fragile ego, or a lack of self-confidence in a situation or task.

The human ego encompasses what Guiora called the language ego to refer to the very personal, egoistic nature of second language acquisition. Meaningful language acquisition involves some degree of identity conflict as language learners take on a new identity with their newly acquired competence. An adaptive language ego enables learners to lower the inhibitions that may impede success.

Guiora et al. (1972) produced one of the few studies on inhibition in relation to second language learning. In one study, some subjects who had been given one and a half ounces of alcohol scored significantly better on a Thai pronunciation test (Standard Thai Procedure or STP) than those who had a non-alcoholic placebo. However, the subjects given two and three ounces of alcohol scored significantly lower than the control group. Guiora et al. (1972) attribute the one and-a-half-ounce group's superior performance to the fact that the subjects' ego boundaries became more flexible (permeable) with a small ingestion of alcohol.

In another study (Schumann et al., 1978), subjects were hypnotized during an experiment. Earlier, Guiora had hypothesized that hypnosis would both lower inhibitions and make a person willing to modify a basic self-identification. No evidence, however, was found to indicate that hypnosis improved pronunciation, although subjects who rated themselves deeply hypnotized did perform significantly better than less well hypnotized subjects (Larsen-Freeman, 2000)[190].

In 1980, Guiora et al. tested the effect of benzodiazepine (Valium) on subjects' performance on the STP. No direct effects on the pronunciation score were found, although as the dosage of Valium increased, the effect of having been tested by a particular experimenter also increased. The researchers interpret this finding as suggesting that Valium does affect permeability of ego boundaries, but in a different way than they had anticipated (Larsen-Freeman, 2000)[190-191].

These findings have given rise to a number of steps that have been taken in foreign language teaching practices to create techniques that reduce inhibition in the classroom. Language teaching approaches in the last quarter of the twentieth century have been characterized by the creation of contexts for meaningful classroom communication such that the interpersonal ego barriers are lowered to pave the way for free, unfettered communication (Brown, 2002)[139].

Tolerance of ambiguity

This concerns the degree to which you are cognitively willing to tolerate ideas and propositions that run counter to your own belief system or structure of knowledge. Some people are, for example, relatively "open-minded" in accepting ideologies and events and facts that contradict their own views; they are more content than others to entertain and even internalize contradictory propositions. Others, more "closed-minded," more dogmatic, tend to reject items that are contradictory or slightly incongruent with their existing system; they wish to see every proposition fit into an acceptable place in their cognitive organization, and if it does not fit, it is rejected

(Brown, 2002)[111].

Advantages and disadvantages are present in each style. The person who is tolerant of ambiguity is free to entertain a number of innovative and creative possibilities and not be cognitively or affectively disturbed by ambiguity and uncertainty.

In second language learning a great amount of apparently contradictory information is encountered: words that differ from the native language, rules that not only differ but that are internally inconsistent because of certain "exceptions," and sometimes a whole cultural system that is distant from that of the native culture. Successful language learning necessitates tolerance of such ambiguities, at least for interim periods or stages, during which time ambiguous items are given a chance to become resolved.

On the other hand, too much tolerance of ambiguity can have a detrimental effect. People can become "wishy-washy," accepting virtually every proposition before them, not efficiently subsuming necessary facts into their cognitive organizational structure. Such excess tolerance has the effect of hampering or preventing meaningful subsumption of ideas. Linguistic rules, for example, might not be effectively integrated into a whole system; rather, they may be gulped down in meaningless chunks learned by rote (Brown, 2002)[111].

Intolerance of ambiguity also has its advantages and disadvantages. A certain intolerance at an optimal level enables one to guard against the wishy-washiness referred to above, to close off avenues of hopeless possibilities, to reject entirely contradictory material, and to deal with the reality of the system that one has built. But clearly intolerance can close the mind too soon, especially if ambiguity is perceived as a threat; the result is a rigid, dogmatic, brittle mind that is too narrow to be creative. This may be particularly harmful in second language learning.

A few research findings are available on this style in second language learning. Naiman et al. (1978) found that ambiguity tolerance was one of only two significant factors in predicting the success of their high school learners of French in Toronto. Chapele and Roberts (1986) measured tolerance of ambiguity in learners of English as a second language in Illinois. They found that learners with a high tolerance for ambiguity were slightly more successful in certain language tasks.

These findings suggest—though not strongly so that ambiguity tolerance may be an important factor in second language learning. The findings have intuitive appeal. It is hard to imagine a compartmentalizer—a person who sees everything in black and white with no shades of gray—ever being successful in the overwhelmingly ambiguous process of learning a second language (Brown, 2002)[111-112].

Learners' Beliefs

Language learners form "mini theories" of L2 learning (Hosenfeld, 1978) which shape the way they set about the learning task. These theories are made up of beliefs about language and language learning. Clearly "beliefs" constitute an individual difference variable notably different from the other variables we have examined in that they are neither an ability nor a trait-like propensity for language learning. For this reason, Dörnyei (2005) queried whether they constitute "a proper ID variable." However, this would seem a little obtuse as clearly learners do vary considerably in their beliefs about language and language learning and it is reasonable to assume that their beliefs influence both the process and product of learning. Also, as we have seen, many of the other variables examined are also not really stable and trait- like but rather dynamic and situated.

Three different approaches to investigating learners' beliefs can be distinguished (Barcelos, 2003). According to the normative approach, beliefs are seen as "preconceived notions, myths or misconceptions," which can be studied by means of Likert-style questionnaires such as the Beliefs About Language Learning Inventory —BALLI (Horwitz, 1987a). The metacognitive approach views learners' metacognitive knowledge about language learning as "theories in action" (Wenden, 1999); these are examined by means of the content analysis of learner self-reports in semi-structured interviews. Finally, the contextual approach views learner beliefs as varying according to context; it involves collecting a variety of data types and diverse means of data analysis. Barcelos argued that the contextual approach is superior because rather than viewing beliefs as a "mental trait," it takes into account the "experience-based nature of beliefs." A fourth approach can also be identified-metaphor analysis (Ellis, 2001; Kramsch, 2003). This entails analysing the metaphors used by learners to describe their learning and constitutes an indirect means of identifying beliefs.

Much of the research has been concerned with describing and classifying the types of beliefs learners hold (based on responses to questionnaires), the sources of beliefs, and the situated and dynamic nature of learners' belief systems. Somewhat disappointingly, very few studies have examined the relationship between beliefs and language learning (Ellis, 2013)[698-699].

Learner belief systems

Learners' belief systems cover a wide range of issues and can influence learners' motivation to learn, their expectations about language learning, their perceptions about what is easy or difficult about a language, as well as the kind of learning strategies they favor (Richards et al., 2000)[52-58].

1. Beliefs about the nature of English

Learners often have very focused perceptions about which aspects of English they find difficult, and about the status of English in comparison to other languages.

2. Beliefs about speakers of English

Learners often have specific views and attitudes about native speakers of English, based on their contacts with speakers of English or derived from other sources, such as the media.

3. Beliefs about the four language skills

Learners' beliefs about language may also be reflected in specific assumptions about the nature of listening, speaking, reading, and writing.

4. Beliefs about teaching

By the time a student completes secondary school, he or she has been exposed to thousands of hours of teaching from a variety of different teachers. As a result, the learner may have formed very definite views about what constitutes effective or ineffective teaching. This is reflected in the following statements by language learners.

Teachers should explain grammar rules.

You can't learn very much from other students in groups.

It's useful for the teacher 10 correct all the mistakes I make in my writing.

Differences between learners' and teachers' beliefs can lead to students undervaluing an activity assigned by the teacher. For example, a teacher working with intermediate-level students in a speaking class reported that she included a large number of group and pair work tasks in the course. However, her students gave her poor evaluations for the course. They commented that they could not see the point of such activities because they could not identify the teaching point.

Learners often have specific expectations as to how teachers teach and what their roles and responsibilities are. For example:

The teacher's responsibility is to provide information.

The teacher should follow the book.

The teacher should always set an example.

Learners from different cultures may have different beliefs about what constitutes good teaching.

5. Beliefs about language learning

Students bring to the classroom very specific assumptions about how to learn a language and about the kinds of activities and approaches they believe to be useful.

6. Beliefs about appropriate classroom behavior

Learners may have views about what constitutes appropriate forms of classroom interaction and classroom behavior. These beliefs may be culturally based and, at times, at odds with the teacher's beliefs.

7. Beliefs about self

Learners often have specific beliefs about their own abilities as language learners, as is seen in the following statements.

I'm not a good language learner. I can't pick up the language naturally.

Remembering vocabulary is easy for me.

I feel uncomfortable when I have to speak to a native speaker.

Learners' perceptions of their own strengths and weaknesses as language learners can influence the use they make of opportunities available for language learning and the priorities they set for themselves.

8. Beliefs about goals

Learners may have very different goals for language learning.

I just want to be able to make myself understood.

I'd like to be able to write well in English.

I'm not interested in learning to read, only to speak.

Just as teachers' belief systems influence how they go about teaching, so learners' belief systems influence how they conceptualize learning and the way they interpret learning within the classroom context.

Types of learner beliefs

In an early attempt to identify the types of beliefs held by language learners, Horwitz (1987) administered the BALLI to groups of learners. Five general areas of beliefs emerged from the analysis of the responses relating to

1. the difficulty of language learning
2. aptitude for language learning
3. the nature of language learning
4. learning and communication strategies
5. motivation and expectations

Wenden (1986 & 1987) grouped the beliefs she identified in 25 adults enrolled in a part-time advanced-level class at an American university into three general categories:

1. use of the language (for example, the importance of "learning in a natural way")
2. beliefs relating to learning about the language (for example, the importance of learning grammar and vocabulary)
3. the importance of personal factors (i. e. beliefs about the feelings that facilitate or inhibit learning, self-concept, and aptitude for learning)

Both of these early studies identified a very similar set of learner beliefs.

The sources of learners' beliefs

An interesting question is what determines learners' beliefs about language learning. Little et al. (1984) surveyed random samples of undergraduate and postgraduate students of foreign languages at Trinity College, Dublin. They found that "past experience, both of education in general and of language learning in particular, played a major role in shaping attitudes to language learning." For example, the students stated that they preferred to learn by production activities (repeating orally and writing) rather than through receptive activities involving listening and reading. Little and Singleton claimed that this belief reflected the general nature of the instruction they had experienced (i. e. was shaped by their instructional experiences).

Another possibility is that beliefs are culturally determined. However, Horwitz (1999) in her review of the research into L2 beliefs, concluded that there was insufficient evidence to show that learners' beliefs varied systematically according to cultural background. It is possible, however, that learners' beliefs are more substantially influenced by general factors such as personality and cognitive style but this remains to be shown (Ellis, 2013)[701].

The situated and dynamic nature of learner beliefs

Learner beliefs are situation specific and dynamic. Kern (1995), for example, reported changes in the beliefs of 180 students studying first-year level French at a university in the US over the course of one semester (15 weeks). He administered Horwitz's BALLI to the students during the first and last week of the semester. Analysing the responses of 180 students, Kern reported that 35 per cent to 59 per cent of the responses changed over the 15-week period. A significant change was observed in the response to the statement "If you are allowed to make mistakes in the beginning, it will be hard to get rid of them later on," with 37 per cent of the students reporting greater agreement and 15 per cent lesser agreement. This suggests that many students had become increasingly conscious of their mistakes and were having difficulty in avoiding them. The learners also changed their responses to the statement "Learning a foreign language is mostly a matter of learning a lot of grammar rules," with 32 per cent showing greater agreement and 20 per cent lesser agreement (Ellis, 2013)[701].

The relationship between beliefs and learning

There have to date been very few studies of the relationship between learner beliefs and learning outcomes.

Abraham and Vann (1987) found some evidence that beliefs might affect learning outcomes in a case study of two learners, Gerardo and Pedro. Both learners believed that it was important to create situations for using English outside the classroom, to practise as much as possible, and to have errors corrected. Both also believed it important to participate actively in class. Gerardo, however, believed that paying conscious attention to grammar was important, while Pedro did not and expressed a strong dislike of meta-language. Also, Gerardo thought that it was important to persevere in communicating or understanding an idea, while Pedro considered topic abandonment the best strategy in some cases. Abraham and Vann characterized Gerardo's philosophy of language learning as "broad" and Pedro's as "narrow." They suggested that this might have contributed to Gerardo's better TOEFL score (523 versus 473) at the end of a course of instruction. Pedro, however, did better on a test of spoken English, which might suggest that different views about language learning result in different kinds of success.

Overall, these studies do not show a strong relationship between beliefs and learning/proficiency. However, it is perhaps not surprising that the relationship between beliefs and proficiency is weak, as the fact that learners hold a particular belief is no guarantee they will act on it; conflicts with other strongly held beliefs, situational constraints, or personal reasons may prevent them. If beliefs do impact on learning it is likely that they do so indirectly by influencing the kinds of learning strategies learners employ (Ellis, 2013)[702-703].

Cognitive Styles

Suppose you are visiting a foreign country whose language you don't speak or read. You have landed in the airport and your contact person, whose name you don't know, is not there to meet you. To top it off, your luggage is missing. It's 3:00 A.M. and no one in the sparsely staffed airport speaks English. What will you do?

There is obviously no single solution to this multifaceted problem. Your solution will be based to a great extent on the styles you happen to bring to bear. For example, if you are tolerant of ambiguity, you will not get easily flustered by your unfortunate circumstances. If you are reflective, you will exercise patience, and not jump quickly to a conclusion about how to approach the situation; if you are field- independent you will focus on the necessary and relevant details and not be distracted by surrounding but irrelevant details.

The way we learn things in general and the particular attack we make on a problem seem to hinge on a rather amorphous link between personality and cognition; this link is referred to as cognitive style (Brown, 2002).

The term "cognitive style" refers to a technical psychological distinction between typical ways of thinking. Imagine standing in a room that is slowly leaning to one side without the people inside it knowing. Some people attempt to stand upright, others lean so that they are parallel to the walls. Those who lean have a field-dependent (FD) cognitive style; that is, their thinking relates to their surroundings. Those who stand upright have a field-independent (FI) style; they think independently of their surroundings. The usual test for cognitive style is less dramatic, relying on distinguishing shapes in pictures and is thus called the embedded figures test. Those who can pick out shapes despite confusing backgrounds are field-independent, those who cannot are field-dependent.

A difference in cognitive style might well make a difference to success in L2 learning—another aspect of aptitude. Most researchers have found that a tendency towards FI (field independence) helps the student with conventional classroom learning (Alptekin et al., 1990). This seems obvious in a sense, in that formal education in the West successively pushes students up the rungs of a ladder of abstraction, away from the concrete (Donaldson, 1978). Hansen and Stansfield (1981) used three tests with L2 learners: those that measured the ability to communicate, those that measured linguistic knowledge, and those that measured both together. FI learners had slight advantages for communicative tasks, greater advantages for academic tasks, and the greatest advantages for the combined tasks. However, Bacon (1987) later found no differences between FD and FI students in terms of how much they spoke and how well they spoke. This illustrates again the interaction between student and teaching method; not all methods suit all students.

Cognitive style varies to some extent from one culture to another. There are variations between learners on different islands in the Pacific and between different sexes, though field independence tends to go with good scores on a cloze test (Hansen, 1984). Indeed, there are massive cross-cultural differences in these measures. To take Chinese as an example, first of all there is a general cultural difference between East and West as to the importance of foreground versus background, which affects the issue; second, the embedded figures test does not work, since people who are users of character-based scripts find it much easier to see embedded figures, and other tests have to be used (Nisbett, 2003).

There is no general reason why FI people in general should be better or worse at cognitive functioning than those who are FD. FIand FD are simply two styles of thinking. A challenge has been posed to the use of FI/FD in second language acquisition by Griffiths et al. (1992), who argue that the concept has not been sufficiently well defined in the research and is no longer of much interest within the discipline of psychology, from which it came.

Learning Styles

When cognitive styles are specifically related to an educational context, where affective and physiological factors are intermingled, they are usually more generally referred to as learning styles (Brown, 2002).

Learning styles might be thought of as "cognitive, affective, and physiological traits that are relatively stable indicators of how learners perceive, interact with, and respond to the learning environment" (Keefe, 1979). Or, more simply, perhaps, as "a general predisposition, voluntary or not, toward processing information in a particular way" (Skehan, 1991). In the enormous task of learning a second language, one that so deeply involves affective factors, a study of learning style brings very important variables to the forefront. Such styles can contribute significantly to the construction of a unified theory of second language acquisition.

Learning styles mediate between emotion and cognition, as you will soon discover. For example, a reflective style invariably grows out of a reflective personality or a reflective mood. An impulsive style, on the other hand, usually arises out of an impulsive emotional state. People's styles are determined by the way they internalize their total environment, and since that internalization process is not strictly cognitive, we find that physical, affective, and cognitive domains merge in learning styles. Some would claim that styles are stable traits in adults. This is a questionable view. It would appear that individuals show general tendencies toward one style or another, but that differing contexts will evoke differing styles in one individual. Perhaps an "intelligent" and "successful" person is one who is "bicognitive"—one who can manipulate both ends of a style continuum.

Reid's perceptual learning styles

If it were to enumerate all the learning styles that educators and psychologists have identified, a very long list would emerge. However, only a few of the possible number of styles have received the attention of second language researchers in recent years (Brown, 2005).

Reid (1987) distinguished four perceptual learning modalities:

1. visual learning: reading, studying charts;
2. auditory learning: listening to lectures, audio tapes;
3. kinesthetic learning: experiential learning that is, total physical involvement with a learning situation;
4. tactile learning: "hands-on" learning, such as building models or doing laboratory experiments.

In addition, she distinguished two social learning styles:

1. group preference: learning with other learners;
2. individual preference: learning by oneself.

Generally speaking, the results of Raid's (1987) study showed that ESL (English as a second language) students strongly preferred kinesthetic and tactile learning styles. Most groups showed a negative preference for group learning.

Chinese Cultural Learning Styles

Individuals are most likely not born with a genetic predisposition to learn analytically or relationally, visually or kinesthetically. They "learn how to learn" through the socialization processes that occur in families and friendship groups.

The Confucian tradition places a high value on education, and particularly on educating the members of society in the ways humans should relate and interact with each other. Hsu (1981) contends that the "Chinese child learns to see the world in terms of a network of relationships." The structuring of these relationships is presented in one of the Confucian classics, the Mencius, which gives the earliest full formulation concerning the "Five Relationships":

> According to the way of men, if they are well fed, warmly clothed and comfortably lodged but without instruction, they will become almost like animals. The Sage [emperor Shun] was concerned with this and appointed Hsieh to be Minister of Instruction and teach human relations: that between father and son there should be affection, between ruler and minister there should be righteousness, between husband and wife there should be proper distinction, between elder and younger there should be proper order, and between friends there should be faithfulness (Kalton, 1991)[3-4].

This doctrine of the Five Relationships is the cornerstone of Confucian moral and social teaching "in which the individual should be concerned first and foremost with his place in the scheme of human relations" (Hsu, 1981). Confucianism stresses the benefits of fixed hierarchical relationships in which respect is shown for age, seniority, rank, and family background.

In China, the teacher is an authority figure. Confucius and his disciples modeled a close teacher-student relationship in which teachers, like parents, help students develop as complete well-adjusted human beings (Herbert, 1988). An ancient Chinese saying goes: "If a teacher for a day, a father for life."

In addition to specifying the proper nature of relationships, Confucianism set forth four principles as guides to proper human behavior: humanism, faithfulness, propriety, and wisdom. The principles of humanism, faithfulness, and propriety are operationalized in the learning-style dimensions of cooperation and field-sensitivity. The cardinal principle of Confucianism is humanism, defined as "warm human feelings between people" (Yum, 1988). The second principle, faithfulness, refers to social relationships. Yum defines faithfulness through its antithesis, "which is personal or individual interest and profit." Faithfulness, then, is "that part of human nature which allows us to look beyond personal, immediate profit and to elevate ourselves to the original goodness of human nature." The third principle, propriety, is the outward form of humanism and faithfulness, the "fundamental regulatory etiquette of human behavior."

Classroom dynamics& learning styles

Learning styles are one of many variables in the process of learning. Keefe (1979) diagrams the school learning process as a triangle of interaction between the learning environment, the teaching style, and the learning style of the students. Grasha (1984) adds the dynamic of content, since people with certain learning styles may prefer different content areas, and since some content areas seem to be better understood across learning styles. Other researchers have found that students' learning styles may vary from subject to subject (Dixon, 1985).

The role of the instructor cannot be underestimated in a classroom that purports to promote diversity. The classroom environment hinges on the attitude of the instructor; instructors must be willing to look at their own learning/teaching styles objectively before they can be non-judgmental with their students. Teachers who are unaware of learning/teaching style dynamics may unconsciously watch for thinking patterns similar to their own, and penalize students who use processes that are dissimilar (Claxton et al., 1978). A study by James (1973) showed that teachers gave higher course grades to students with learning styles most similar to their own teaching style, and they believed these students understood the material better, when in fact the differences were not significant.

School systems themselves are not without bias. To empower students as much as possible, instructors need to continually and actively explore learning-style processes with their students (Eliason, 2012)[31-32].

Implications for ESL/EFL classroom teachers

Teachers can enhance their students' learning by adjusting their teaching styles to match their students' learning styles.

The first classroom implication relates to the dimension of competition versus cooperation. Teachers should not repeatedly praise any one student. They might try treating the entire class as a whole, as one group. For instance, the teacher could explicitly state at the beginning of the course that the students should work together to help each other so that the whole class passes the course.

A related implication concerns the use of groups in the ESL/EFL (English as a second language/English as a foreign language) classroom. In making decisions about whether or not to use groups, teachers should consider the group's purpose. If the purpose can be achieved in another way, it may be better not to use groups.

A third implication relates to the dimension of impulsivity versus reflectivity. At times the teacher's goal may be for students to talk; it does not much matter what they say because the value is in the talking. At other times the teacher may be looking for particular responses. ESL/EFL teachers can structure classroom activities to give reflective learners more time to think about responses. If the teacher wants students to talk about what they have written, it is better to call on them by name rather than to issue an open invitation to the class and expect someone to volunteer a response.

The next implication relates to the learning style of modeling. Chinese students memorize model texts as exemplars of good writing. They also learn information by memorizing pages or chapters of textbooks. They write this memorized material on examinations to show the examiner that they have learned the course content. However, this practice of producing memorized material is often perceived by U. S. teachers as cheating and/or plagiarism.

Finally, in considering cultural variation in learning, maybe our most important task as ESL/EFL teachers is to learn about the particular pedagogy of our students' home cultures. There is a great deal of pedagogical variation even among cultures that share the same learning-style dimension. It is not enough to know that a culture's learning style is, for example, cooperative. Classroom implementation of a cooperative learning-style varies from one culture to another, and so ESL/EFL teachers should learn the particular variations for the cultures of their students.

Exercises, Questions and Tasks

1. Multiple Choices.

(1) Which of the following might not be a feature of individual differences?

A. They are an intricate set of interconnected components.

B. In everyday parlance, they show some salient temporal variation.

C. The overall of the system is stable.

D. The different variables interact with the environment synchronically and diachronically.

(2) Adult language learners might be at an advantage for ________.

A. loss of "plasticity" in the brain and "lateralization" of the brain

B. the natural language situations

C. the interference with natural language learning

D. sophisticated understanding and reasoning

(3) Which one is not a primary source of the motivation to learn a foreign/second language in

terms of the L2 Motivational Self System?

A. the learner's vision of him/herself as an effective L2 speaker

B. the social pressure coming from the learner's environment

C. positive learning experiences

D. repeated failures as a language learner

(4) L2 Motivational Self System was made up of the following three components except ________.

A. Ideal L2 Self B. Ought-to L2 Self

C. L2 self-esteem D. L2 Learning Experience

(5) Which of the following might not be a factor that predicts a student's success in the classroom in terms of the Modern Languages Aptitude Test (MLAT)?

A. Deductive language learning ability B. Phonemic coding ability

C. Grammatical sensitivity D. Rote learning

(6) Which one is not a dimension in "Big Five" model of the personality theory?

A. openness to experience B. conscientiousness

C. neuroticism versus emotional stability D. FI versus FD

(7) According to Horwitz et al, which of the following descriptions might not be an example of specific anxieties?

A. Communication Apprehension B. Test Anxiety

C. learner's competitive nature D. Fear of negative Evaluation

(8) Which of the following couldn't be termed as risk-taking behaviors?

A. willing to guess

B. willing to get corrected

C. willing to appear foolish in order to communicate

D. willing to use what knowledge they do have of the TL

(9) Which of the following language learning does not necessitate a certain tolerance of ambiguities?

A. words that differ from the native language

B. rules that differ from the native language

C. a whole cultural system that is distant from that of the native culture

D. propositions that are internally consistent with the native language

(10) Which of the following might not be a perceptual learning modality?

A. cooperative learning B. auditory learning

C. kinaesthetic learning D. visual learning

2. Fill in each blank with an appropriate word.

(1) Motivation in L2 learning refers to long-term stable attitudes in the students' minds, in particular ________ and instrumental motivation.

(2) In ________ bilingualism, the learners feel that the learning of a new language threatens what they have already gained for themselves.

(3) In the embedded figures test for cognitive style, those who can pick out shapes despite confusing backgrounds are ________.

(4) The ________ period hypothesis claims that human beings are only capable of learning their first language between the age of two years and the early teens.

(5) Learners' ________ systems influence how they conceptualize learning and the way they interpret learning within the classroom context.

(6) Teachers can become most critically ________ of a rich array of multisensory activities within the realistic constraints of resources of the classroom.

(7) Some adults, presumably those who are more empathic, are likely to have more ________ of language ego boundaries.

(8) When cognitive styles are specifically related to an educational context, where affective and ________ factors are intermingled, they are usually more generally referred to as learning styles.

(9) The apparent decline in adults' foreign language learning might be contributed to the ________ of the brain.

(10) Teachers who are unaware of learning style dynamics may ________ watch for thinking patterns similar to their own.

3. Mark "True" or "False" for the following statements and explain why.

(1) Both internal and external individual internal factors moderate and influence the effectiveness of instruction.

(2) Individual differences are stable and monolithic learner attributes.

(3) If learners are intending to spend many years learning the second language, they might as well start as adults.

(4) The greatest barrier to second language learning seems to boil down to a matter of memory.

(5) MI theory gives teachers a complex mental model from which to construct curriculum and improve themselves as educators.

(6) You cannot fully know yourself until you adequately empathize—or know someone else.

(7) Learner beliefs are situation specific and dynamic.

(8) Learning styles might be thought of as cognitive, affective, and physiological traits that are quite dynamic indicators of how learners perceive, interact with, and respond to the learning environment.

(9) Teachers might not believe that students with learning styles most similar to their own teaching style understand the material better.

(10) The way we learn things in general seem to hinge on a rather amorphous link between personality and cognition; this link is referred to as cognitive style.

4. Short answer questions.

(1) What do you think is the best age for learning a new language? Why?

(2) How would your teaching of, say, the present tense, differ according to whether you were teaching children or adults?

(3) Does intelligence relate to FL learning? Why?

(4) Is it really possible to change the students' underlying motivation, as opposed to simply increasing it?

(5) What should be done with students who have a low aptitude for L2 learning?

(6) Why does learning English require a sophisticated degree of empathy?

(7) How does a language teacher reduce inhibition in the classroom?

(8) How does tolerance of ambiguity relate to language learning?

(9) How can you interpret the following statements?

It's not polite to ask the teacher a question during class time.

You shouldn't leave the classroom until the teacher has dismissed the class.

(10) How can you interpret school learning process?

5. Evaluate and mark how much you agree with the following statements.

strongly agree	slightly agree	neither agree nor disagree	slightly disagree	strongly disagree

(1) Studying a foreign language is important to my students because they will be able to participate more freely in the activities of other cultural groups.

(2) Studying a foreign language can be important for my students because it will some day be useful in getting a good job.

(3) What do you think are people's typical reactions to foreigners? To bilinguals? To monolinguals?

(4) It is important to be able to speak two languages.

(5) I will always feel more myself in my first language than in my second.

Suggested Readings

BROWN H D, 2002. Principles of language learning and teaching[M]. Beijing: Foreign Language Teaching and Research Press.

COOK V, 2011. Second language learning and language teaching[M]. 4th ed. Beijing: Foreign Language Teaching and Research Press.

CSIZÉR K, 2017. Motivation in the L2 classroom[M]// LOEWEN S, SATO M. The Routledge handbook of instructed second language acquisition. New York: Routledge, 418 – 432.

DEWAELE J M, 2017. Psychological dimensions and foreign language anxiety[M]// LOEWEN S, SATO M. The Routledge handbook of instructed second language acquisition. New York: Routledge, 433 – 450.

DÖRNYEI Z, 2012. Motivation in language learning[M]. Shanghai: Shanghai Foreign Language Education Press.

ELIASON P A, 2012. Difficulties with cross-cultural learning-styles[M]// Learning styles in the ESL/EFL classroom. Beijing: Foreign Language Teaching and Research Press, 19 - 33.

ELLIS R, 2013. The study of second language acquisition[M]. 2nd ed. Shanghai: Shanghai Foreign Language Education Press.

GASS S M, 2020. Second language acquisition: An introductory course[M]. 4th ed. Beijing: Tsinghua University Press.

JOHNSON K, 2002. An introduction to foreign language learning and teaching[M]. Beijing: Foreign Language Teaching and Research Press.

LARSEN-FREEMAN D L, LONG M H, 2000. An introduction to second language acquisition research[M]. Beijing: Foreign Language Teaching and Research Press.

LI S F, HIVER P, PAPI M, 2022. Individual differences in second language acquisition: Theory, research, and practice[J]. The Routledge Handbook of Second Language Acquisition and Individual Differences, 3 - 34.

LOEWEN S, SATO M, 2017. Instructed second language acquisition (ISLA): An overview [M]// LOEWEN S, SATO M. The Routledge handbook of instructed second language acquisition[M]. New York: Routledge, 1 - 12.

NELSONA L, 2012. Cultural differences in learning styles[M]// Learning styles in the ESL/EFL classroom. Beijing: Foreign Language Teaching and Research Press, 3 - 18.

REID J M, 1987. The learning style preferences of ESL students[J]. TESOL Quarterly, 21(1): 87 - 111.

REID J M, 2012. Learning styles in the ESL/EFL classroom[M]. Beijing: Foreign Language Teaching and Research Press.

RICHARDS J C, LOCKHARTC, 2000. Reflective teaching in second language classrooms[M]. Beijing: People's Education Press.

RICHARDS J C, RODGERS T S, 2008. Approaches and methods in language teaching[M]. 2nd ed. Beijing: Foreign Language Teaching and Research Press.

CHAPTER 5

Learning Strategies

Focusing Question

- How would you deal with some problems in a language learning task?
- What would you do when you do not know the words to talk about things?
- When you are learning English, what special means do you use for:
  - pronunciation?
  - getting meanings from contexts?
  - making oral presentations?
  - using the language socially outside the classroom?

Introduction

Most of the time teachers think they know best: they make the students carry out various activities; they select the language they are going to hear or read; they prescribe the language they should produce, all hopefully in their best interests. But as human beings students have minds of their own; ultimately they decide how they are going to tackle the tasks of the classroom and the aims of their learning. Sometimes their choices are visible to us—they put electronic dictionaries on their desks; sometimes they are invisible decisions in their privacy of their own heads—they work out translations in their minds. This independence from the teacher has been recognized by the tradition of strategies research, which tries to discover the choices that students are making and to recognize them in language teaching.

Measuring the invisible contents of the mind has always been difficult. One way is to ask people what they think they are doing—"how do you try to remember new vocabulary?" The answer may not accurately reflect what you actually do, since so much of our language behavior is subconscious and not available to our conscious minds. Introspection is a potentially suspect source of evidence.

Another way of investigating strategies is to look for outward signs of behavior: Does a student sit at the back of the class or are they always the first to ask a question? The problem with this observational evidence is interpretation; we have to connect what the student appears to be doing with some process in their minds—an extremely difficult feat scientifically: Is a silent student someone who is bored, deep in concentration or naturally shy? We have to observe their behavior in a consistent way so that someone else would make the same deduction from it.

A third way is to get the students to carry out a specific task and to see what language they produce: "Describe this picture to someone over the phone." While this should yield clear linguistic evidence, the technique is limited to strategies visible from language production; many powerful strategies may have no obvious linguistic consequences. Furthermore, it is open to the objection that it is essentially the technique of the psychological laboratory; do the results tell us anything about the real learning or use situations that the students encounter?

Exploring the private world of people's minds is a problem for any research. Nevertheless, potentially, strategies research leads to interesting results for language teaching (Cook, 2011)[105-106].

Strategies

The word *strategy* comes from the ancient Greek term *strategia* meaning generalship or the art of war. More specifically, strategy involves the optimal management of troops, ships, or aircraft in a planned campaign. A different, but related, word is tactics, which are tools to achieve the success of strategies. Many people use these two terms interchangeably. The two expressions share some basic implied characteristics: planning, competition, conscious manipulation, and movement toward a goal. In nonmilitary settings, the strategy concept has been applied to clearly non-adversarial situations, where it has come to mean a plan, step, or conscious action toward achievement of an objective (Oxford, 2008)[7-8].

Learning Strategies

One commonly used technical definition says that learning strategies are operations employed by the learner to aid the acquisition, storage, retrieval, and use of information. To fully convey the excitement or richness of learning strategies, it is useful to expand this definition by saying that learning strategies are specific actions taken by the learner to make learning easier, faster, more enjoyable, more self-directed, more effective, and more transferrable to new situations (Oxford, 2008)[8].

A given strategy is neither good nor bad; it is neutral until the context of its use is thoroughly considered. It is useful if the following conditions are present (Oxford, 2006)[362]:

1. the strategy relates well to the L2 task at hand;
2. the strategy fits the particular student's learning style preferences to one degree or another;
3. the student employs the strategy effectively and links it with other relevant strategies.

Learning strategies can enable students to become more independent, autonomous, lifelong learners

(Allwright, 1990; Little, 1991). Yet students are not always aware of the power of consciously using L2 learning strategies to make learning quicker and more effective (Nyikos et al., 1993).

Language Learning Strategies

Scarcella and Oxford (1992) define language learning strategies as "specific actions, behaviors, steps, or techniques—such as seeking out conversation partners, or giving oneself encouragement to tackle a difficult language task—used by students to enhance their own learning".

Oxford (2008)[9] summarizes key features of language learning strategies:

1. Contribute to the main goal, communicative competence.
2. Allow learners to become more self-directed.
3. Expand the role of teachers.
4. Are problem-oriented.
5. Are specific actions taken by the learner.
6. Involve many aspects of the learner and indirectly.
7. Are not always observable.
8. Are often conscious.
9. Can be taught.
10. Are flexible.
11. Are influenced by a variety of factors.

Three categories

Typically, strategies are divided into three main categories, as noted in Table 5 - 1.

Table 5 - 1 Learning strategy definitions (O'Malley et al., 1985b)[582-584]

Learning Strategy	Description
Metacognitive Strategies	
Advance Organizers	Making a general but comprehensive preview of the organizing concept or principle in an anticipated learning activity
Directed Attention	Deciding in advance to attend in general to a learning task and to ignore irrelevant distractors
Selective Attention	Deciding in advance to attend to specific aspects of language input or situational details that will cue the retention of language input
Self-Management	Understanding the conditions that help one learn and arranging for the presence of those conditions
Functional Planning	Planning for and rehearsing linguistic components necessary to carry out an upcoming language task
Self-Monitoring	Correcting one's speech for accuracy in pronunciation, grammar, vocabulary, or for appropriateness related to the setting or to the people who are present

Continued

Learning Strategy	Description
Delayed Production	Consciously deciding to postpone speaking in order to learn initially through listening comprehension
Self-Evaluation	Checking the outcomes of one's own language learning against an internal measure of completeness and accuracy
Cognitive Strategies	
Repetition	Imitating a language model, including overt practice and silent rehearsal
Resourcing	Using target language reference materials
Translation	Using the first language as a base for understanding and/or producing the second language
Grouping	Reordering or reclassifying, and perhaps labeling, the material to be learned based on common attributes
Note Taking	Writing down the main idea, important points, outline, or summary of information presented orally or in writing
Deduction	Consciously applying rules to produce or understand the second language
Recombination	Constructing a meaningful sentence or larger language sequence by combining known elements in a new way
Imagery	Relating new information to visual concepts in memory via familiar, easily retrievable visualizations, phrases, or locations
Auditory Representation	Retention of the sound or a similar sound for a word, phrase, or longer language sequence
Keyword	Remembering a new word in the second language by (1) identifying a familiar word in the first language that sounds like or otherwise resembles the new word and (2) generating easily recalled images of some relationship between the new word and the familiar word
Contextualization	Placing a word or phrase in a meaningful language sequence
Elaboration	Relating new information to other concepts in memory
Transfer	Using previously acquired linguistic and/or conceptual knowledge to facilitate a new language learning task
Inferencing	Using available information to guess meanings of new items, predict outcomes, or fill in missing information
Socio-affective Strategies	
Cooperation	Working with one or more peers to obtain feedback, pool information, or model a language activity
Question for Clarification	Asking a teacher or other native speaker for repetition, paraphrasing, explanation, and/or examples

"Metacognitive" is a term used in information-processing theory to indicate an "executive" function, strategies that involve planning for learning, thinking about the learning process as it is taking place, monitoring of one's production or comprehension, and evaluating learning after an activity is completed.

"Cognitive" strategies are more limited to specific learning tasks and involve more direct manipulation of the learning material itself.

"Socio-affective" strategies have to do with social-mediating activity and transacting with others.

Goh (1998) notes that learners who have a high degree of metacognitive awareness seem better able to control and manage their learning in terms of understanding and storing new information as well as finding the best ways to practise and reinforce what they have learned. Students without metacognitive approaches are essentially learners without direction or opportunity to plan their learning, monitor their progress, or review their accomplishments and future learning directions (O'Malley et al., 2001)[8].

Six-factor model

Rebecca Oxford (1990) published a method for finding out the strategies used by learners called the Strategy Inventory for Language Learning (SILL). It includes between 6 and 18 items for six broad classes of strategies, divided into "Direct" and "Indirect" (Figure 5 – 1).

Direct strategies deal with the new language, working with the language itself in a variety of specific tasks and situations. These are specific procedures that learners can use to internalize the language.

1. *Memory strategies*: remembering more effectively, say by visualizing the spelling of a new word in your mind.
2. *Cognitive strategies*: using all your mental processes, for instance by looking for patterns in the new language.
3. *Compensation strategies*: compensating for missing knowledge, for example by trying to anticipate what the other person is going to say next.

Indirect strategies for general management of learning include things such as evaluating one's learning, taking steps to power one's anxiety, and cooperating with others.

1. *Metacognitive strategies*: organizing and evaluating knowledge, for example, by preparing in advance what is going to come up in the next class.
2. *Affective strategies*: managing your emotions, say, by trying to relax when speaking.
3. *Social strategies*: learning with others, for instance, by asking the other person to slow down.

Figure 5.1 Oxford's strategy classification system

The two classes support each other, and that each strategy group is capable of connecting with and assisting every other strategy group. This strategy system is more comprehensive and detailed; it is more systematic in linking individual strategies, as well as strategy groups, with each of the four language skills (listening, reading, speaking, and writing). Visual and verbal cues are used for understanding and remembering the system (Oxford, 2008)[14].

Oxford explains direct and indirect strategies by an analogy from the theatre. When using direct strategies, the language learner is like the performer in a play. An actor's task is to come to grips with the play itself. Similarly, the language learner's direct strategies help him to come to grips with the language. They deal with things memorizing vocabulary, and for getting to understand new grammar rules. The language learner's indirect strategies are more akin to the role of the play's director. They deal with regulation and control. In the case of language learner, this would include planning issues (like how many hours you spend on learning, and what you do in preparation for each lesson), as well as issues to do with affective demands-coping with the 'stain on the nerves' that speaking and learning a foreign language can involve (Johnson, 2002)[153].

We have to exercise caution in applying strategies research: it can show some benefits, but there is great variation between learners in the strategies they use and in the extent to which teaching them is of benefit (Cook, 2011)[116].

Language Use Strategies

Language learning strategies are strategies for the learning of language material for the first time while language use strategies are those for using the material that has already been learned, at least to some degree (Cohen et al., 2006).

Language learning strategies (Cohen, 2000)[5] include strategies for:

1. identifying the material that needs to be learned;
2. distinguishing it from other material if need be;
3. grouping it for easier learning (e.g., grouping vocabulary by category into nouns, verbs, adjectives, adverbs, and so forth);
4. having repeated contact with the material (e.g. through classroom tasks or the completion of homework assignments);
5. formally committing to memory when it does not seem to be acquired naturally (whether through rote memory techniques such as repetition, the use of mnemonics or some other memory technique).

Note that repeated contact with material could be seen as a form of rehearsal, although rehearsal usually implies that the material is at least partially learned already and can therefore be rehearsed.

Using the material at whatever the current level of mastery involves at least the following four subsets of strategies (Cohen, 2014)[13-16].

Retrieval strategies

Retrieval strategies are used to call up language material from storage by means of whatever memory searching strategies the learner can muster. In the above example with the subjunctive, retrieval strategies would be those strategies used to help remember when to use the subjunctive and how to form the present subjunctive. Likewise, a language use strategy could entail using a keyword mnemonic in order to retrieve the meaning of a given vocabulary word.

Rehearsal strategies

Rehearsal strategies are strategies for rehearsing target language structures. An example of rehearsal would be form-focused practice, such as practicing the subjunctive forms so as to be able to use them correctly in a midterm exam. Some rehearsal strategies could be part of language learning as well as part of language use. First, you commit the structures to memory through rehearsal, and then once you have learned them, you use them in an actual communicative exchange.

Coping strategies

Coping strategies are of two kinds—those that learners use to allow them to compensate for a lack of some specific language knowledge, and those for creating the impression that they have control over material when they do not. The former has been referred to as *compensatory strategies* and the latter as *cover strategies*.

Compensatory strategies would include, for example, lexical avoidance, simplification, and approximation when the exact word escapes you under pressure or possibly because you simply do not know the word that well or at all. Consequently, you may engage in a form of paraphrase or word invention.

The cover strategies involve creating an appearance of language ability so as not to look unprepared, foolish, or even stupid. A learner's primary intention in using such strategies is not to learn any language material, nor even necessarily to engage in genuine communication. An example of a cover strategy would be using a memorized and perhaps only partially understood phrase in an utterance in, say, a classroom drill in order to keep the action going. In some cases, the result is the production of an utterance where the learners use only that part of a phrase that they can deal with. In other cases, the learners' output may reflect an elaborate and complex circumlocution in order to avoid the use of finely-tuned vocabulary or in order to avoid using the subjunctive.

Communication strategies

Communication strategies focus on approaches to conveying a message that is both meaningful and informative for the listener or reader. They have primarily been viewed as the verbal (or nonverbal) first aid devices which may be used to deal with problems or breakdowns in communication. These devices enable learners to remain active partners in communication, even when things do not go well. They may, for example, use communication strategies to steer the conversation away from problematic areas, to express their meaning in creative ways (for example, by paraphrasing a word or concept), or to create more time to think and to negotiate the difficult parts of their communication with their conversation partner until everything is clear. Thus, these strategies extend the learners' communicative means beyond the constraints of LT proficiency and consequently help to increase their linguistic confidence as well.

Communication strategies also include conversational strategies, such as strategies for maintaining the floor. Examples would be in asking for help, seeking clarification or confirmation, and using fillers (such as *uh* and *uhm*) when pausing while speaking, along with other hesitation devices such as repeating keywords.

During the early years of language learner research, communication strategies were seen to include the following:

1. intralingual strategies. E. g., overgeneralizing a grammar rule or vocabulary meaning from one context to another where it does not apply.
2. interlingual strategies.
   a) negative transfer (i. e. applying the patterns of the native or another language in the target language where those patterns do not apply);
   b) topic avoidance or abandonment;
   c) message reduction;
   d) code switching;
   e) paraphrasing (i. e., using synonymous words or phrases, or using circumlocution).

When learners experience problems or breakdowns in communication, they may use communication strategies to avoid the problematic areas and express their meaning in some other way. For example, learners may paraphrase words or concepts (e. g., "I'd like something to dry my hands with" when they don't know the word for "towel"), coin words ("air maker" when they don't know "bicycle pump"), or use facial expressions or gestures in an effort to communicate and to create more time to think (e. g., hoping that a frown will signal that they do not approve of the other person's behavior). At times, learners also compensate for gaps by using literal translation from their L1 or switching to the L1 altogether.

We note that communication strategies may or may not have any impact on learning. For example, learners may use a vocabulary item encountered for the first time in a given lesson to communicate a thought, without any intention of trying to learn the word. In contrast, they may insert the new vocabulary item into their communication expressly in order to help commit it to memory.

Whereas a distinction has been made here between language learning and use strategies, the distinction can be fuzzy at times. In her new book, Oxford (2011) would contend that the distinction is inappropriate given that learning can only be accomplished through use, such as through meaningful communication. But I would contend that for many language learners much of what they "learn," especially in language classes, never makes it to real-world communication.

Good Language Learner Strategies

Certain people appeared to be endowed with abilities to succeed, others lacked those abilities. This observation led Rubin (1975) and Stern (1975) to describe "good" language learners in terms of personal characteristics, styles, and strategies. Rubin et al. (1982) summarized fourteen characteristics. Good language learners:

1. find their own way, taking charge of their learning;
2. organize information about language;
3. are creative, developing a "feel" for the language by experimenting with its grammar and words;
4. make their own opportunities for practice in using the language inside and outside the classroom;
5. learn to live with uncertainty by not getting flustered and by continuing to talk or listen without understanding every word;
6. use mnemonics and other memory strategies to recall what has been learned;
7. make errors work for them and not against them;
8. use linguistic knowledge, including knowledge of their first language, in learning a second language;
9. use contextual cues to help them in comprehension;
10. learn to make intelligent guesses;
11. learn chunks of language as wholes and formalized routines to help them perform "beyond their competence";
12. learn certain tricks that help to keep conversations going;
13. learn certain production strategies to fill in gaps in their own competence;
14. learn different styles of speech and writing and learn to vary their language according to the formality of the situation.

Such lists, speculative as they were in the mid 70s, inspired a group of collaborators in Toronto to undertake a study of good language learning traits (Naiman et al. 1978). Such research has led some to offer advice to would-be students of foreign language on how to become better learners.

Learner Strategy Training

Building Strategic Techniques

Overt admonition or calling students' conscious attention to principles need not be the major approach; instead, teachers can encourage successful subconscious strategy employment through their choice, among several options, of classroom techniques that enhance strategy building. Suggestions for building strategic competence are shown as follows (Brown, 2002)[130-131]:

1. **to lower inhibitions**: play guessing games and communication games; do role plays and skits; sing songs; use plenty of group work; laugh with your students; have them share their fears in small groups.
2. **to encourage risk taking**: praise students for making sincere efforts to try out language; use fluency exercises where errors are not corrected at that time; give outside-of- class assignments to speak or write or otherwise try out the language.
3. **to build students' self-confidence**: tell students explicitly (verbally and nonverbally) that you do indeed believe in them; have them make lists of their strengths, of what they know or have accomplished so far in the course.
4. **to help them to develop intrinsic motivation**: remind them explicitly about the rewards for learning English; describe (or have students look up) jobs that require English; play down the final examination in favor of helping students to see rewards for themselves beyond the final exam.
5. **to promote cooperative learning**: direct students to share their knowledge; play down competition among students; get your class to think of themselves as a team; do a considerable amount of small group work.
6. **to encourage them to use right-brain processing**: use movies and tapes in class; have them read passages rapidly; do skimming exercises; do rapid "free writes," do oral fluency exercises where the object is to get students to talk (or write) a lot without being corrected.
7. **to promote ambiguity tolerance**: encourage students to ask you, and each other, questions when they don't understand something; keep your theoretical explanations very simple and brief; deal with just a few rules at a time; occasionally you can resort to translation into a native language to clarify a word or meaning.
8. **to help them use their intuition**: praise students for good guesses; do not always give explanations of errors—let a correction suffice; correct only selected errors, preferably just those that interfere with learning.
9. **to get students to make their mistakes work FOR them**: tape record students' oral production and get them to identify errors; let students catch and correct each other's errors; do not always give them the correct form; encourage students to make lists of their common errors and to work on them on their own.
10. **to get students to set their own goals**: explicitly encourage or direct students to go beyond the classroom goals; have them make lists of what they will accomplish on their own in a particular week; get students to make specific time commitments at home to study the language; give "extra credit" work.

Oxford (1990)[1] argues that strategies are important for two reasons. In the first place, strategies "are tools for active, self-directed involvement which is essential for developing communicative competence". Secondly, learners who have developed appropriate learning strategies have greater self-confidence and learn more effectively. Perhaps a more subtle but no less effective way to manifest learner strategy training in a classroom is to make sure that techniques are directed as much as possible toward good language learning behaviors.

A framework for training learning strategies

The research shows that learners who are taught the strategies underlying their learning are more highly motivated than those who are not and not all learners automatically know which strategies work best for them. For this reason, explicit strategy training, coupled with thinking about how one goes about learning, and experimenting with different strategies, can lead to more effective learning (Nunan, 2001)[172].

The following is a framework of strategy training from Chamot et al. (1999)[45].

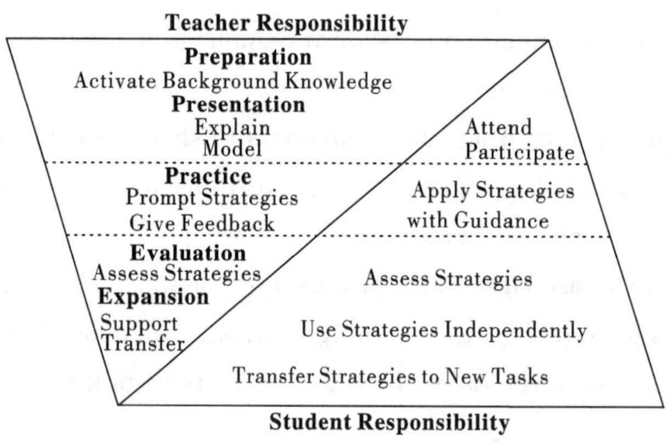

Figure 5 - 2 A framework of strategy training

The idea of learner training leads on to autonomous, self-directed learning, in which the students take on responsibility for their own learning. They choose their goals; they control the teaching methods and materials; they assess how well they are doing themselves (Cook, 2011)[118].

Learning Strategies and Tasks

When teachers identify the strategies underlying the tasks they typically use in the classroom, they are sometimes surprised to find that they are based on a rather limited repertoire of strategies. Some of them will be used more frequently than others, depending on the age and proficiency of the students, the skills being focused on, and the individual learner needs (Nunan, 2001)[182-183].

A typology of learning strategies

Nunan(2001)[183-188] has developed a typology of strategies for his own teaching and textbook writing (Table 5. 2).

Table 5. 2 A typology of learning strategies

Strategy	Description
Cognitive	
Classifying	Putting things that are similar together in groups Example: Study a list of names and classify them into male and female.
Predicting	Predicting what is to come in the learning process Example: Look at unit title and objectives and predict what will be learned.
Inducing	Looking for patterns and regularities Example: Study a conversation and discover the rule for forming the simple past tense.
Taking Notes	Writing down the important information in a text in your own words
Concept Mapping	Showing the main ideas in a text in the form of a map
Inferencing	Using what you know to learn something new
Discriminating	Distinguishing between the main idea and supporting information
Diagramming	Using information from a text to label a diagram
Interpersonal	
Cooperating	Sharing ideas and learning with other students Example: Work in small groups to read a text and complete a table.
Role-Playing	Pretending to be somebody else and using the language for the situation you are in Example: You are a reporter. Use the information from the reading to interview the writer.
Linguistic	
Conversational Patterns	Using expressions to start conversations and keep them going Example: Match formulaic expressions to situations.
Practicing	Doing controlled exercises to improve knowledge and skills Exercise: Listen to a conversation, and practice it with a partner
Using Context	Using the surrounding context to guess the meaning of unknown words, phrases, and concepts.
Summarizing	Picking out and presenting the major points in a text in summary form
Selective Listening	Listening for key information without trying to understand every word Example: Listen to a conversation and identity the number of speakers.
Skimming	Reading quickly to get a general idea of a text Example: Decide if a text is a newspaper article, a letter, or an advertisement.
Personalizing	Learners share their own opinions, feeling and ideas about a subject Example: Read a letter from a friend in need and give advice.
Self-Evaluating	Thinking about how well you did on a learning task, and rating yourself on a scale.
Reflecting	Thinking about ways you learn best
Creative	
Brainstorming	Thinking of as many new words and ideas as you can Example: Work in a group and think of as many occupations as you can.

Classifying

Classifying helps learners because it is easier to memorize items that are grouped together in meaningful ways than trying to remember isolated items.

Inductive reasoning

In an inductive approach to learning, students are given access to data, and are provided with structured opportunities to work out rules, principles, and so on for themselves rather than simply being told. The idea here is that information will be more deeply processed and stored.

Inferencing

Inferencing involves using what you know to learn something new. Because learning is basically making links between what is new and what is already known, inferencing is an extremely important strategy.

Discriminating

Discriminating means distinguishing between the main idea and supporting information. Learners who are skilled at identifying the most important information in a text can process language more quickly, and are able to identify and remember the speaker or reader's central message more effectively.

Cooperating

When we cooperate, we share ideas and learn with other students. This principle exploits the old saying that "two heads are better than one."

Selective listening

A key strategy for learners is listening for key information without trying to understand every word. This strategy is essential if learners are to cope effectively in genuine communicative situations outside the classroom. It is unnecessary to process every single word in most listening situations.

Strategies-Based Instruction

According to MacIntyre and Noels (1996), almost any tactic or plan that the learner believes will help in learning some part of the language or in managing the language learning process can be considered a strategy.

Strategies-Based Instruction (SBI) is a learner-centered approach to teaching that extends classroom strategy training to include both explicit and implicit integration of strategies into the course content. In a typical classroom strategy instruction situation, the teachers (Cohen, 2000[81]):

1. describe, model, and give examples of potentially useful strategies;
2. elicit additional examples from students based on the students' own learning experiences;
3. lead small-group/whole-class discussions about strategies (e. g., reflecting rationale behind strategy use, planning an approach to a specific activity, and evaluating the effectiveness of chosen strategies);

4. encourage their students to experiment with a broad range of strategies;
5. integrate strategies into everyday class materials, explicitly and implicitly embedding them into the language tasks to provide for contextualized strategy practice.

Teachers have at least three options for how to conduct strategy instruction (Cohen, 2000[82]):

1. start with the established course materials and then determine which strategies to insert and where;
2. start with a set of strategies that they wish to focus on and design activities around them;
3. insert strategies spontaneously into the lessons whenever it seems appropriate (e. g. to help students overcome problems with difficult material or to speed up the lesson).

In addition, they can have students choose their own strategies and do so spontaneously, without prompting from the teacher. In all likelihood, teachers will be engaged in strategy instruction with an explicit focus on strategies only part of the time, while the rest of the time the strategies will be implicitly embedded into the language tasks. The goal is to help L2 students become more aware of:

1. how they learn most effectively;
2. how they can enhance their own comprehension and production of the target language;
3. how they can continue to learn on their own and communicate in the target language after they leave the language classroom.

Strategy instruction aims to assist learners in becoming more responsible for their efforts in learning and using the target language. It also aims to assist them in becoming more effective learners by allowing them to individualize their L2 experience. For example, strategies such as "rehearsing structures" are gone over in class and practiced so that in real speaking situations, the learners would select the strategies as a regular part of their functioning (Cohen, 2000)[82].

In principle, strategy instruction is not specific to any given teaching methodology or culture. A given teaching method might favor certain strategies over others. For example, not translating material or, to the contrary, putting an emphasis on translation. Also, certain cultures may favor or refrain from certain practices such as public correction of spoken errors in class. SBI is not prescriptive, but rather provides a panoply of strategies, and students must determine which to use, when, for what purposes, and how to use them (Cohen, 2000)[83].

Although in-class strategy instruction takes valuable time away from teaching the language content, students become more efficient in completing classroom language tasks, take more responsibility for self-directing their learning outside of class, and gain more confidence in their ability to learn and use the target language (Cohen, 2000)[83].

Exercises, Questions and Tasks

1. Multiple Choices

(1) Learners who have a high degree of ________ awareness seem better able to control and manage their learning in terms of finding the best ways to practice.

A. metacognitive B. cognitive

C. social D. affective

(2) Which of the following is not a strategy for good language learners?

A. learning certain tricks that help to keep conversations going

B. making their own opportunities to use the language

C. avoiding taking risks

D. using contextual cues to help them in comprehension

(3) Which of the following classroom technique cannot enhance strategy building?

A. Cooperative learning

B. Always giving explanations of errors

C. Directing students to go beyond the classroom goals

D. Playing down the final examination

(4) To build strategic competence, classroom teachers can ________.

A. encourage fierce competition among students

B. do oral fluency exercises where the object is to get students to talk a lot

C. resort to translation into a native language to clarify a word or meaning

D. have them avoid their fears in small groups

(5) Which of the following strategies is not interlingual?

A. code switching B. topic avoidance or abandonment

C. negative transfer D. overgeneralizing a grammar rule

(6) Li Ming is practicing the subjunctive forms so as to be able to use them correctly in an exam. He is using ________ strategy.

A. compensatory B. cover

C. retrieval D. rehearsal

(7) Strategy training in class helps learners to have greater ________ at activating these strategies and having them enhance their performance in real speaking situations.

A. awareness B. facility

C. responsibility D. inertia

(8) Cognitive strategies mean using all your mental processes including ________.

A. resourcing B. recombination

C. self-monitoring D. elaboration

(9) Compensation strategies involve ________.

A. semantic mapping B. analyzing contrastively

C. getting help D. adjusting or approximating the message

(10) Language learning strategies include strategies for ________.

A. repeated contact with material

B. grouping it for easier learning

C. identifying the material that needs to be learned

D. creating an appearance of language ability so as not to look unprepared

2. Fill in each blank with an appropriate word.

(1) Strategy involves the ________ management of troops, ships, or aircraft in a planned campaign.

(2) Learning strategies are ________ actions taken by the learner to make learning easier, faster, more enjoyable, more self-directed, more effective, and more transferrable to new situations.

(3) Learning strategies can enable students to become more independent, ________, lifelong learners.

(4) There is great ________ between learners in the strategies they use and in the extent to which teaching them is of benefit.

(5) ________ strategy training, coupled with thinking about how one goes about learning, and experimenting with different strategies, can lead to more effective learning.

3. Mark "True" or "False" for the following statements and explain why.

(1) A given strategy is neither good nor bad; it is neutral until the context of its use is thoroughly considered.

(2) Students without cognitive approaches are essentially learners without direction or opportunity to plan their learning, monitor their progress.

(3) Direct and indirect strategies support each other, and that each strategy group is capable of connecting with and assisting every other strategy group.

(4) In a deductive approach to learning, students are given access to data, and are provided with structured opportunities to work out rules.

(5) Strategies-Based Instruction is a learner-centered approach to teaching that explicitly integrates strategies into the course content.

4. Short answer questions.

(1) Why is knowledge of strategies important for learners?

(2) In what ways are direct strategies different from indirect ones?

(3) How useful are metacognitive strategies to the learner?

Suggested Readings

BROWN H D, 2002. Principles of language learning and teaching[M]. 3rd ed. Beijing: Foreign Language Teaching and Research Press.

CHAMOT A U, BARNHARDT S, E1-DINARY P B, et al., 1999. The learning strategies handbook[M]. White Plains, NY: Longman.

COHEN A D, 2000. Strategies in learning and using second language[M]. Beijing: Foreign Language Teaching and Research Press.

COHEN A D, 2014. Strategies in learning and using second language[M]. 2nd ed. New York: Routledge.

COOK V, 2011. Second language learning and language teaching[M]. Beijing: Foreign Language Teaching and Research Press.

JOHNSONK, 2002. An introduction to language learning and teaching[M]. Beijing: Foreign Language Teaching and Research Press.

NUNAN D, 2001. Second language teaching and learning[M]. Beijing: Foreign Language Teaching and Research Press.

O'MALLEY J, CHAMOT M, ANNA U, et al., 1985b. Learning strategy applications with students of English as a second language[J]. TESOL Quarterly, 19(3): 557-584.

O'MALLEY J M, CHAMOT A U, 2001. Learning strategies in second language acquisition [M]. Shanghai: Shanghai Foreign Language Education Press.

OXFORD R L, 2006. Language learning styles and strategies[M]// CELCE-MURCIA M. Teaching English as a second or foreign language[M]. Beijing: Foreign Language Teaching and Research Press, 359-366.

OXFORD R L, 2008. Language learning strategies: What every teacher should know[M]. Beijing: Beijing World Publishing Corporation.

SHRUM J L, GLISAN E W, 2016. Teacher's handbook: Contextualized language instruction [M]. Beijing: Foreign Language Teaching and Research Press.

CHAPTER 6

Context Theory

Focusing Question

- Why should we attach importance to context?
- How is context shaped?
- What does teaching a language mean in terms of contextual shaping?

Introduction: Context and Convention

No matter how natural our language facilities or how convention-bound their use, as language users, we always operate in contexts. Therefore, the context looms large, and has to be taken into account whenever we formulate our thoughts about language. Language is conventional. Thus, one and the same utterance can obtain completely different, even diametrically opposed effects, depending on convention and context. Consider the following conversation (Levinson, 1983):

(*A and B are on the telephone, talking over arrangements for the next couple of days.*)

A: So can you please come over here again right now?

B: Well, I have to go to Edinburgh today sir.

A: Hmm. How about this Thursday?

It does not take us long to realize how many presuppositions, implicatures, references and other factual and contextual conditions have to be drawn upon in this exchange in order for it to make sense. All of this cannot be accounted for by semantics or syntax, let alone by reference to "bare facts." For instance, the time of the conversation ("today") is understood as being different from "this Thursday", but not only that: "this Thursday" (time reference) only makes sense if uttered on a day between "last Thursday" and the "Tuesday preceding this Thursday"—otherwise the speaker would probably have said "tomorrow" or "the day after tomorrow" (conversational implicature). Further, the place from which A is speaking is obviously not Edinburgh but neither is it a place that is too far removed from either Edinburgh or the speaker's location (presupposition). In addition, A (being addressed as "sir") seems to be in a position that allows him to give orders to B (presupposition and implicature). And so on.

All these facts are dealt with nor as "bare facts," on their face value, but as elements forming part of a context that they pragmatically determine and presuppose, and which "reflect our ability to compute out of utterances in sequence the contextual assumptions they imply: ... the spatial, temporal and social relationships between participants, and their requisite beliefs and intentions in undertaking certain verbal exchanges" (Levinson, 1983)[49].

Pragmatically speaking, the decisive importance of context is that it allows us to use our linguistic resources to the utmost, without having to spell out all the tedious details every time we use a particular construction. However, the observation that language operates in force of contextually implied conditions and assumptions is by no means restricted to the above case (Mey, 2001).

Definitions

Halliday (1978) defined context as "the total environment in which a text unfolds." This definition is part of a view of language as social semiotic, in which context always includes and is in a dialectic relationship with a text. As Halliday (1990) pointed out, "language is at the same time a part of reality, a shaper of reality, and a metaphor for reality." This definition puts into question purely structuralist views of language and context (Becker, 1984).

Context is more than just reference. Context is action. Context is about understanding what things are for; it is also what gives our utterances their true pragmatic meaning and allows them to be counted as true pragmatic acts (Mey, 2001)[41].

Theoretical Perspectives of Context

Context in relevance theory

The set of premises used in interpreting an utterance (apart from the premise that the utterance in question has been produced) constitutes what is generally known as the context. A context is a psychological construct, a subset of the hearer's assumptions about the world. It is these assumptions rather than the actual state of the world that affect the interpretation of an utterance. A context in this sense is not limited to information about the immediate physical environment or the immediately preceding utterances: expectations about the future, scientific hypotheses or religious beliefs. Anecdotal memories, general cultural assumptions, beliefs about the mental state of the speaker, may all play a role in interpretation.

In much of the pragmatic literature, events are assumed to take place in the following order: first the context is determined, then the interpretation process takes place, then relevance is assessed. In other words, relevance is seen as a variable to be assessed in function of a predetermined context. However, from a psychological point of view, this is a highly implausible model of comprehension. Humans are not in the business of simply assessing the relevance of new information. They try to process information as productively as possible; that is, they try to obtain from each new item of information as great a contextual effect as possible for as small as possible a processing effort. The assessment of relevance is not the goal of the comprehension process, but only a means to an end, the end being to maximize the relevance of any information being processed (Sperber et al., 2001)[132-142].

Context in adaptation theory

Any ingredient of a communicative event is a potential contextual correlate of adaptability. Contextual correlates may be found in the mental, social (or cultural), and physical worlds, and that they also include properties of the linguistic channel that is used and the linguistic context in which the event takes place.

Language use is always situated against a complex background with which it is related in a variety of ways. The contextual aspects of the physical, social, and mental worlds do not usually start to play a role in language use until they have somehow been activated by the language users' cognitive processes.

Verbal interaction is communication from mind to mind—though we should never forget that minds are "minds in society." The mental world activated in language use contains cognitive and emotive elements. Mental states have always been central to certain endeavors in linguistic pragmatics such as personality, emotions, beliefs, desires or wishes, motivations or intentions, etc. Beliefs, for instance, are at the core of the "background assumptions" that verbal behavior is anchored into and that are implicitly communicated. Similarly, a variety of mental states has been relied upon for the definition of speech act types, as ingredients of felicity conditions.

The adaptability of language to the social world is truly pervasive. Phenomena of the utmost importance in the relationship between linguistic choices and the social world are the setting, institution, or community-specific communicative norms that have to be observed. Culture, with its invocation of norms and values, has indeed been a favorite social-world correlate to linguistic choices in the pragmatic literature. "Cultural" dimensions include the contrast between oral and literate societies, rural versus urban patterns of life, or a mainstream versus a subcultural environment. Other social dimensions of variability with which linguistic choice-making is interadaptable include social class, ethnicity and race, nationality, linguistic group, age, level of education, profession, kinship, gender, sexual preference, and so on.

Temporal deixis and spatial deixis are the most visible ways of anchoring language choices into a physical world. "Time" is a relative notion rather than an absolute value in relation to language, and that it interferes with a lot of other considerations. In many ways, spatial concepts are central to human thinking, as they form the basis of standard metaphors in numerous areas of experience: *before the end of the year* (time), *close friends* (social relations), *high voice* (sounds), *high society* (status), *high amount* (quantity), *ups and downs* (moods, etc.), *the rising tide of pluralism*, *a narrow mind*, *go downhill*, etc. Hence, the relevance of space as a contextual correlate of adaptability stretches beyond mere spatial reference. The relativity of temporal and spatial reference is primarily a function of the positioning of language users in the "world."

Linguistic choices are contextually anchored, for instance by referring back to earlier discourse, by being self-referential, or by projecting towards a future linguistic context. The study of such phenomena often goes under the label of cohesion. Other features of linguistic context are intertextuality and sequencing (Verschueren, 2000)[75-112].

Characteristics of Context

Multidisciplinarity/interdisciplinarity

No definition of pragmatics would be complete in the absence of some mention of context. The notion of context extends beyond its obvious manifestation as the physical setting within which an utterance is produced to include linguistic, social and epistemic factors. How these various factors interrelate with language to generate meaning is studied by a range of disciplines (Cummings, 2007).

Dynamics

Whether a linguistic form is properly learned and whether it can be put to correct use depend largely on concomitant variables. Accordingly, all the variables within the system can be conceived of as the background against which the form is learned and can be broadly defined as the context of learning. Among the myriad variables that may be relevant in any given context are the relationship between interlocutors, their psychological states, their proficiency in the target language and their sociocultural background and values, along with factors such as the time and location of a conversation, bodily activities, discourse type, non-verbal reactions and, of course, the linguistic forms and meanings. Any change in the combination of the component variables of a context may indeed affect the context, including changes in the meaning (Yu et al., 2018).

Contexts can be subcategorized according to the characteristics of the contextual variables involved in the use and learning of a linguistic form. For example, variables characteristic of a social situation constitute the social context. Likewise, we have the cognitive context, the psychological context, the linguistic context and so on, each of which can be still further specified. Within the linguistic context, for example, there is a phonetic context, a phrasal context, a sentential context, etc. In the dynamic process of a speech event, an incoming utterance is also capable of shaping a new context for subsequent linguistic action. Contexts and utterances thus interact in multiple dimensions (Duranti et al., 1992).

Five Dimensions

Foreign language pedagogy has been increasingly aware of the need to teach language in context—for example, by contextualizing grammatical exercises and situating them in socially appropriate verbal exchanges. Yet as the professional rhetoric focuses on context, it is not always clear what teachers mean when they purport to teach language "in its social context." So we may ask: What is really at stake when we relate language and context?

There are different ways of looking at a situation of communication. Each of them highlights a different dimension of the communicative event (Kramsch, 1999).

Linguistic context

The first dimension is linguistic. The choice of one linguistic form over another is determined by the co-text—that is, those linguistic elements that precede or follow and that ensure the text's cohesion. If a speaker starts an argument with "on the one hand," the logic of the spoken text—that is, its cohesive structure—leads the listener to expect "on the other hand" to turn up somewhat later on. Cohesion is established by a host of textual features such as pronouns, substitutions, deictics.

The choice of a linguistic form is also determined by the internal context of utterance, constituted by all the factors which, by virtue of their influence upon the participants in a language event, systematically determine the form, the appropriacy and the meaning of utterances (Lyons, 1977). Context here refers to the intentions, assumptions, and presuppositions of speakers and hearers, which ensure that their discourse is perceived as coherent and therefore makes sense for the participants. Intended meanings depend on the speech acts that preceded as well as on those that will follow them. The coherence of a text relies on the illocutionary force of its component parts and their perlocutionary effect on the hearer/reader.

Within the linguistic context, for example, there is a phonetic context, a phrasal context, a sentential context, etc. In the dynamic process of a speech event, an incoming utterance is also capable of shaping a new context for subsequent linguistic action. Context and utterances thus interact in multiple dimensions (Yu et al., 2018)[263].

Situational context

Meanings also depend on the external context of communication, or situational context of the speech event. The most well-known definitions of the situational context are those by Roman Jakobson (1960) and Dell Hymes (1974). Among the six factors that Jakobson sees as constituting the speech event (addresser, addressee, context, message, contact, code), context is that which the message refers to, "seizable by the addressee, and either verbal or capable of being verbalized;" it is, in other words, the topic or propositional content of utterance (Jakobson, 1960). The language function associated with context is the referential function.

The refinement of our way of viewing context has been well described recently by sociolinguists. Firth, inspired by the work of the anthropologist Malinowski, was the first to include in the context not only spoken words, but facial expression, gestures, bodily activities, the whole group of people present during an exchange of utterances, and the part of the environment in which these people are engaged, and to call the totality of these factors "context of situation" (Berns, 1990). Hymes (1974), picking up on Malinowski and Firth, and expanding Jakobson's notion of context, devised his own set of factors to describe the situational context of the speech event. He lists these under the acronym SPEAKING, which Kramsch (1999) explains below with reference to the language classroom. According to Hymes:

> **Setting** refers to the time and place—that is, the physical setup of the class. Place includes: the space occupied by teacher and students; the movements of participants within that space; the seating arrangement; the temperature, background noise, place, size, and quality of the blackboard, etc. Time includes: the time devoted to each activity, its timing within the whole lesson, its relative length, its pace, the presence or absence of concurrent activities.
>
> **Participants** include combinations of speakers and listeners in various roles, that are either given to them or taken on during the lesson.
>
> **Ends** refers to the purposes of the activities and what participants seek to accomplish. These can be short-term learning goals such as the linguistic, cognitive, or affective outcomes of a particular activity, or they can be long-term goals such as motivations or attitudes or specific professional outcomes.
>
> **Act** sequence refers both to the form and the content of utterances, both to what is said and what is meant by the way it is said.
>
> **Key** refers to the tone, manner, or spirit in which a particular message is conveyed: serious or ironical, matter-of-fact or playful. The key can be conveyed verbally and nonverbally and the two may sometimes contradict one another.
>
> **Instrumentalities** refers to the choice of channel (for example, oral or written), and of code (mother tongue, foreign language, or a mix of codes or code-switching).
>
> **Norms of interaction and interpretation** refers to the way participants in the lesson interact and interpret what is said or what they are reading.
>
> **Genre** refers to the type of oral or written activity students and teacher are engaged in: casual conversation, drill, lecture, discussion, role-play; grammatical exercise, written summary, report, essay, written dialogue.

The work of Goffman enables us to detail Hymes' characterization further by diversifying the notion of setting and participants. In particular, we can distinguish between various orientations or "footings" that speakers and hearers take toward each other and toward various audiences in the classroom. Goffman (1981) defines footing as "the alignment we take up to ourselves and the others present as expressed in the way we manage the production or reception of an utterance." It represents the way we frame events and the stance we take toward these events and the participants in the social encounter.

Interactional context

The third dimension of context is that which is created by the interaction itself, through the beliefs and presuppositions that the interlocutors bring to the encounter. Ellis and Roberts (1987) define this interactional context as follows:

> Context is created in interaction partly on the basis of particular and individual choices by speakers at a local level and partly by those speakers being able to make inferences about each other on the basis of shared knowledge and assumptions about the world and about how to accomplish things interactionally.

Goodwin (1981), studying the social organization of conversation, shows how the perception by the speaker of the extent to which the information conveyed is shared or not by the other participants can affect the "recipient design" of the speaker's utterance. Topics are introduced not only because of participants' intentions, but also because of perceived local interactional needs and the constraints imposed by multiple audiences. For example, as in Allwright's famous Igor case, a student may ask a question, not because he is seeking information, but because he wants to show the rest of the class that he knows something the others do not know, or because his interaction with the teacher develops its own dynamic of which both become prisoners without having intended it (Edmondson, 1983).

In the last ten years, research on interaction in language classrooms has made great strides. It has shown how non-native speakers of a language negotiate with other nonnative speakers (their peers in the classroom) or with native or near-native speakers (e. g. the teacher) to clarify the meaning of each other's utterances in the performance of classroom tasks.

For example, Pica et al. (1994) found that the tasks that fostered the most negotiation of meaning, and thus, interaction, were the jigsaw and information-gap tasks, in which participants had to share information in order for the group to solve a problem or arrive at one decision. The open-ended opinion-exchange tasks offered the least interactional "pull." Yule et al. (1991) found that pairing a low-proficiency learner and a high-proficiency learner in an information-gap task, but giving the low-proficiency learner the greater information to share—that is, putting him or her in a position of expertise—increased the amount of participation of the low-proficiency learner.

We have seen how individual choices in the shaping of the context are constrained by the intratextual linguistic demands of cohesion and coherence, the situational demands of, e. g., the physical setting and the participants, and the interactional demands of exchanging utterances both for display and for communication.

Cultural context

Context of culture is a term originally coined by Malinowski to describe the institutional and ideological background knowledge shared by participants in speech events. This context, called by Fowler (1986) "the community's store of established knowledge," consists of "structures of expectation" that allow people to make sense of the world around them. Tannen describes these structures as follows:

> People approach the world not as naive, blank-slate receptacles who take in stimuli as

> they exist in some independent and objective way, but rather as experienced and sophisticated veterans of perception who have stored their prior experiences as an organized mass, and who see events and objects in the world in relation to each other and in relation to their prior experience. This prior experience… then takes the form of expectations about the world, and in the vast majority of cases, the world, being a systematic place, confirms these expectations.

Native speakers of a language speak not only with their own individual voices, but through them speak also the established knowledge of their native community and society, the stock of metaphors this community lives by, and the categories they use to represent their experience. This is what makes it so difficult for non-native speakers to communicate with native speakers, because they do not share the native-speaking community's memory and knowledge. And all the more so if they are fully socialized adults who carry with them twenty or thirty years of their own speech community's ways of talking. Even if they have mastered the forms of the new language, they might still have difficulty in meeting the social expectations of speakers from the new speech community.

In a foreign language classroom, the problem is, beyond the structures of the language they use, teachers and learners are often not aware of the cultural nature of their discourse. Furthermore, the increasingly multicultural nature of foreign language classrooms and the hesitations of many teachers to recognize deeper misunderstandings due to social and cultural factors, are making the foreign language class as complex as the traditional ESL class.

By teaching a foreign language we should objectivize the learner's native discourse patterns and help them adopt those of the new language. The question is, however, to what extent can and should we teach foreign forms of discourse and insist on their production by foreign language learners? The sociolinguist Saville-Troike gives (1992) the example of the Japanese learner of English who bows a lot to her professors:

> One of her professors told her that she shouldn't bow to English or to American professors, because that wasn't considered appropriate. This professor was trying to teach her a sociolinguistic rule in English. She was crushed. "I know Americans don't bow," she said, "but that's my culture, and if I don't do that, I'm not being respectful and I won't be a good person" (Kramsch et al., 1992b).

Saville-Troike (1992) concludes from this event that "the sociolinguistic rules can be talked about, but it should be left to the learners' own decision to adopt them or not for productive use." The foreign language educator Jorden (1992) agrees with Saville-Troike, but points to the dilemma:

> Without forcing the person to change her ways, I think it's extremely important to explain to her how the average American reads that particular signal. The person can then make her own decision. In one ESL class, for example, Japanese students were asked to introduce themselves by their first name. So they said: "My name is Taro" and so on, but then suddenly one man, the oldest in the class, said: "I will be called Mr.

Tanaka." The teacher was very upset and asked me what to do about it. And I told her, of course it's all right for him to be called Mr. Tanaka, but he must know how Americans are going to react to someone in this culture who says: "Don't call me by my first name, call me only Mr. Tanaka."

This teacher probably felt it was her responsibility to socialize the student into American society so that he could function appropriately outside the classroom. Would she be abdicating her responsibility if she left him free to flout the conventions of that society? Or was she overestimating the amount of consensus about the use of first names in American society? This is a very difficult question, and one that is ultimately a matter of judgment on the part of the teacher.

The two examples above point to the ambivalence of social roles and to the teacher's pedagogical responsibility to make that ambivalence explicit. But, given the traditionally normative nature of everything that is taught in classrooms, it is difficult for teachers to present a type of knowledge that does not automatically translate into normative behavior. The teacher in the example above was building on a series of prior texts in the educational culture she was trained in: conversations, textbooks, interviews, model lessons, and so on. These texts were part of a teacher-training pattern that views the teacher as the expert knower, who represents a native-speaking host speech community, and whose role is to impart a certain body of knowledge to non-native speaking non-knowers in order to facilitate their integration into the speech community.

Intertextual context

Halliday (1989) introduces intertextual context that arises from the friction between the texts that people generate and the contexts that are thereby shaped by them, that is, the relation of a text with other texts, assumptions, and expectations. Halliday writes:

> Every lesson is built on the assumption of earlier lessons in which topics have been explored, concepts agreed upon and defined... At a deeper level, the entire school learning experience is linked by a pervading "intertextuality" that embodies the theory and practice of education as institutionalized in our culture.

The American ESL teacher may believe that by teaching Mr. Tanaka the proper American uses of the English language she is helping him get the "equal opportunity" promised to any immigrant to the United States. She is therefore not only echoing mainstream ways of speaking (i. e. use of the first name in informal situations), she is also echoing texts from well-established American educational philo-sophy. Her distress at the student's lack of compliance has much deeper roots than the local fear of losing authority or of having her student use improper American English. Its causes are to be found to a large extent in the many other educational texts she is implicitly citing.

The reverse example is equally illustrative of the complexity of intertextual context. Like many native English speakers teaching ESL, native speakers of Japanese who teach Japanese in American schools often use pedagogical methods typical of their native culture: teacher-centered classes, emphasis on the written language, discipline, academic hierarchy. However, as Jorden (1992) points out, in addition to replicating, sometimes unconsciously, the context of their own educational culture, they also replicate the views of many Japanese educators who believe that it is impossible for foreigners to learn perfect Japanese, so what they should teach is a watered-down form of Japanese for foreigners. Thus the context that is slowly built-up from one text to the next across the syllabus reflects the larger cultural assumptions about the role of foreigners in Japanese society.

In our exploration of the notion of context we have seen that contexts are alignments of reality along five different axes: linguistic, situational, interactional, cultural, and intertextual. Context is shaped by persons in dialogue with one another, saying things about the world and thus making statements about themselves and their relationship to one another. Through this dialogue, they exchange and negotiate meanings that belong to a community's stock of common knowledge and that draw on a variety of past and present "texts." Context is the matrix created by language as discourse and as a form of social practice.

In sum, the notion of context is a relational one. In each of its five dimensions: linguistic, situational, interactional, as well as cultural and intertextual, it is shaped by people in dialogue with one another in a variety of roles and statuses. Because language is at the intersection of the individual and the social, of text and discourse, it both reflects and construes the social reality called "context."

High & Low Context

Hall (1977) proposed the notion of low context and high context to differentiate between two ends of a continuum. On one end are low-context messages, where the context or situation plays a minimal role in the communication. Low-context messages are explicit, direct, and conveyed primarily through spoken language. ("It's cold in here. Would you please turn the thermostat up to 74?") High-context messages are on the opposite end of the continuum. They are implicit, indirect, conveyed primarily through the context or the social situation. (In silence, one person shivers slightly and glances quickly at an underling, who immediately turns up the thermostat to an understood setting.) Hall (1977) cites numerous examples that illustrate these two extremes. Low-context messages include communication between two U. S. trial lawyers in the courtroom or two politicians drafting legislation. High-context messages are the unspoken messages expressed and understood by twins, or by people who have extensive networks with others, where the circumstances of the social situation carry the messages.

Another way of looking at the low/high-context distinction is to see messages in degrees of explicitness, from explicit to tacit, direct to indirect. Seen this way, some practices require greater explicitness or visibility in the messages, meanings, or understandings, whereas others call for less. In other words, low-context practices like courtroom exchanges or air-traffic control tower communications require explicitness. High-context practices like folk dancing, buying and selling at a cattle auction, or learning through apprenticeship may call for more tacit messages.

The following diagram illustrates how perspectives, underlying meanings, and messages are more tacit in high-context situations and more explicit in low-context situations.

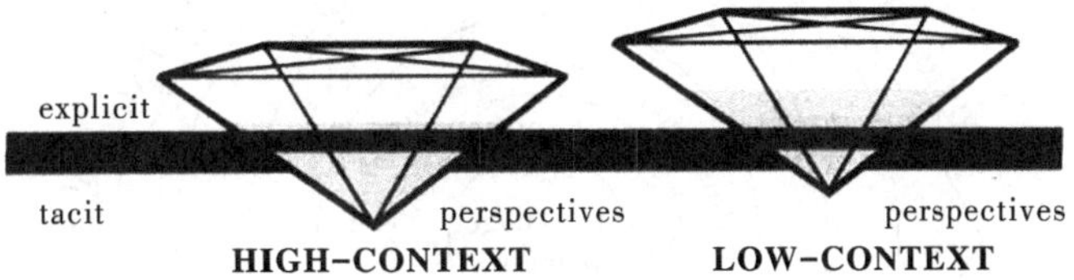

Figure 6. 1 Context in practices

Looking exclusively at the linguistic dimension in terms of high/low context leads us to degree of directness in language, an important feature of practices. In direct communications, people tend to say what is on their minds and to mean what they say, to "tell it like it is." In indirect communications, people tend to not say what is on their minds and to rely more on suggestion and inference. Craig Storti (1999) offers a useful comparison of interpretations of the same language items by speakers from direct and indirect cultures. When direct communicators say "yes", for example, they are conveying agreement, approval, acceptance, or understanding. When indirect communicators say "yes", however, they are expressing politeness and respect and acknowledgment of having heard what the other has said (Moran, 2009).

The Context of Language Teaching

Context can be addressed at multiple levels: from the micro-level contexts of intrapersonal narratives and interpersonal interactions, to the physical and social contexts of individual classrooms in which instructional contextual features (such as the teacher, learning tasks, pedagogical method, and so on) are embedded, right through and up to the broader sweep of macro-level sociocultural and national contexts (King, 2016).

Foreign language planners—and the teachers who put their plans into action—need to know a lot about the context in which the teaching takes place. Context is all important, and applied linguists who try to make lists of the factors that are relevant to language teaching always include a set called "contextual" (Johnson, 2002)[202].

Stern's framework for describing these factors is shown in figure 6. 2. They are sociocultural, historical/political, educational, economic/technological, linguistic and geographic.

Any subject, whether English, history, music, or religion, enters the educational domain when it is found to be relevant to the demands and needs of a society. It is the task of educational and curriculum planners to examine these needs to determine what goals may be relevant to its educational system. The decision as to what the status of English will be within a society is a question of language policy. Language-policy decisions are made at the highest levels of national and educational planning. Such policies may specify the aims or goals that serve as justifications for the teaching of English and the circumstances under which English will be taught (Richards, 2001).

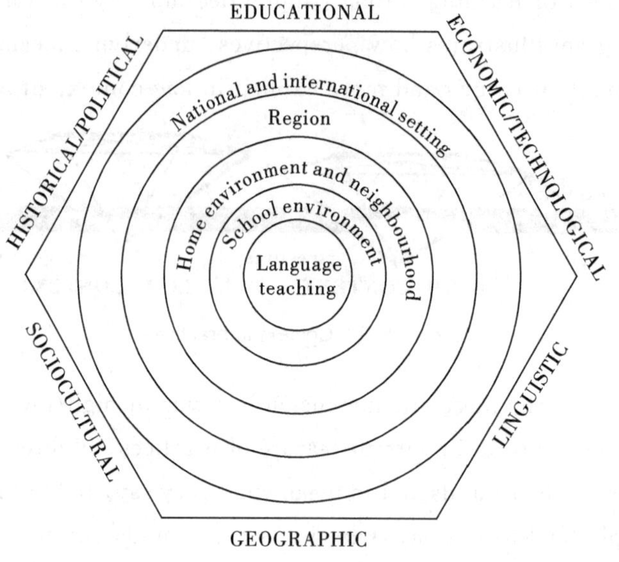

Figure 6.2 Contextual factors in language teaching from Stern (1983)

Examples of educational aims for the teaching of English might be:

- for appreciation of foreign cultures;
- for reasons of higher education;
- for scientific and technological advancement;
- for international commerce, trade, and communication.

Policy concerning the circumstances under which English will be taught may affect whether it will be taught in primary or in secondary school, the number of hours per week devoted to teaching it, and whether it will be made available to all or only certain students in the school system.

Language-policy decisions have repercussions across a wide spectrum of the educational system and ultimately determine how English is learned or taught (Richards, 2001).

Stern mentions a number of language-teaching situations that can illustrate the relevance of the factors in his model. They are: an English class for adult immigrants, French in a comprehensive school in Great Britain, English in a German primary school, Spanish in a US high school. Each of these situations occurs within a school environment, and teachers as well as administrators therefore need to know something about the school's policy on language teaching—how much importance is given to it, how it fits into the curriculum and so on. The school is located within a "home environment and neighborhood" and once again the teacher needs to know something about this.

An oft-quoted example of how home and neighborhood background can affect language teaching comes from Burstall's Report. Here is one finding from her study of French teaching in Britain: "for pupils of both sexes in each group of primary schools, high mean scores on the Listening, Reading and Writing tests coincide with high-status parental occupation and low mean scores with low-status parental occupation" (Burstall et al. 1974). And again: "children with parents in higher-status occupations receive greater parental support when they approach new learning experiences than do those with parents in lower-status occupations" (both these quotes are cited in Stern, 1983).

Region affects language teaching. Burstall provides some interesting information. In her study it was consistently found that a high level of achievement in French was found in small rural schools, not large city ones (Johnson, 2002)[203].

Context and Complex Sub-Systems within the Learner

CDST and learner context

According to Complex Dynamic Systems Theory (CDST), processes of learner intentionality, reflexivity, awareness, agency, engagement and action may be said to constitute interacting components within their own internal complex system. We might conceptualize this complex system as the "language learner," comprising a dynamic constellation of cognitive, affective, motivational and behavioural characteristics in constant evolving interaction with one another, such as described by Dörnyei (2009b).

CDST posits that individuals are intrinsically joined to their environment and context does not therefore represent a static external variable but is in reality part of the individual, meaning learners are influenced by context and they in turn help shape the context itself as time progresses (de Bot et al., 2007; Dörnyei, 2009a & 2009b; Larsen-Freeman, 2015; Larsen-Freeman et al., 2008). Using the example of language input, Ushioda (2016) provides us with a good illustration of this dynamically evolving, bi-directional relationship and explains "the ways in which language learners orient and respond to language input will affect the content, quantity and quality of further input in the developing context of the interaction." Building upon this example, Ushioda argues that learners co-adapt with their environments to become part of the "physical, historical, social and cultural context within which the interaction is taking place ... In short, learners are not simply located in particular contexts, but inseparably constitute part of these contexts" (King, 2016)[1].

Learner internal contexts

We might think of interconnecting complex sub-systems within the language learner, such as a "cognitive ecosystem" as characterized by de Bot et al. (2007), or the complex adaptive systems of L2 development and use (e. g. Beckner et al, 2009; Ellis et al., 2009), or of possible selves. In other words, having highlighted earlier the problem of how to deal with psychological and historical elements of context that are internal to the learner, such as memories and experiences, we find we must also contend with the complexity of interacting dynamic sub-systems that are located within the learner, and consider what might be meant by context within, and in relation, to these multiple internal ecosystems.

At one level, of course, from the perspective of complex sub-systems within the learner, context may refer simply to features of the environment that are external to the learner. For example, these might be features of the linguistic and social environment, such as L2 input, classroom instruction or peer group relations. Such features will be in dynamic interaction with various components within the learner's cognitive, language development or self-and-identity complex systems.

Learner external contexts

Broadly speaking, this is no different from the concept of "external" context already considered in relation to learner-context ecosystems. This concept of external context brings the same complications concerning how to define and delimit relevant contextual characteristics in this surrounding environment, and how to distinguish between contextual and learner-internal elements when these are interconnected and mutually constitutive. In this latter respect, for example, we might think of the learner's multiple social identities evolving within a self-and-identity complex system. While theoretically located within (or attributed to) the learner, these varying social identities are defined, negotiated or contested (e. g. Norton et al., 2011) relationally in interaction with other people's social identities in the surrounding context. In the case of social identity, there is a mutually constitutive and co-adaptive relationship between internal and social-environmental processes. Identity both moulds and is moulded by shifting relations and social networks.

Learner context ecosystems

Whereas social identity is a good example of a learner characteristic that is organically connected to the external surrounding context, it clearly also interplays with many other cognitive and affective sub-systems within the learner, such as processes of motivation, agency or self-esteem. Learner characteristics and systems constitute an internal ecology or co-adaptive environment with which social identity processes interact. In short, at this internal micro level, when our attention turns to specific components of complex sub-systems within the learner, the notion of what we mean by context or environment seems to transform in scale.

As Larsen-Freeman and Cameron (2008) explain, when we focus on a particular aspect of a complex system, "other aspects or systems are taken as the environment in which the focal aspect or system changes." This means that, depending on where we point our lens (e. g. willingness to communicate in the L2, such as in MacIntyre et al., 2011), context may come to refer to various background systemic elements within the language learner (e. g. cognitive, affective and linguistic characteristics, such as motivation, self-confidence, anxiety, need, intentionality, linguistic competence, agency) with which the focal elements interact and co-adapt.

As our analytical lens shifts (e. g. to speaking anxiety or linguistic competence), originally foregrounded elements may merge with contextual background systemic elements in this internal ecology. At the same time, if we broaden the focus of our lens, context will refer also to the wider ecology of external social and environmental conditions (e. g. social setting, communication topic, task difficulty, relationship with interlocutors), which are in organic interaction with these learner-internal systemic processes (Ushioda, 2016).

Teaching Language in Contexts

Networked individualism

In today's language learning landscape, learners are often active members within a range of communities and cultures—real, virtual and imagined—and thus the learner's personal culture can be thought of as being composed of a myriad of individual cultural connections.

The term "networked individualism" coined by Rainie and Wellman (2012) captures well this new understanding of personal cultures. It highlights how individuals connect to other individuals and groups beyond and across spatial or community boundaries in uniquely personal ways. Instead of being understood as embedded in cultures, Rainie and Wellman see individuals as being connected to multiple cultures and subcultures simultaneously generating a personally meaningful and unique individual cultural frame (Mercer, 2016b).

An ecological perspective of learning context

Learning takes place in particular contexts of use, which in turn influence the language used and its appropriateness; learning the socially informed constraints and opportunities of particular situations is seen as fundamental to successful acquisition (Handford, 2016)[152].

One highly influential, more complexified understanding of contexts can be found in ecological perspectives on SLA. Any individual or process is considered within the ecological systems in which they function.

An ecological perspective on language learning offers an alternative way of looking at the contexts in which language use and language learning are situated. The concept of ecology embraces not only the context of classroom learning but, more fundamentally, the very definitions of language, of development, and of mind. The learning environment is viewed as a complex adaptive system, of the mind as the totality of relationships between a developing person and the surrounding world, and of learning as the result of meaningful activity in an accessible environment. The language observed in a sociolinguistic (or semiotic) ecology is not seen as input directed at the learner for the purposes of intake and eventual output, but rather as potential affordances, that is, as signs that acquire meaning and relevance as a result of purposeful activity and participation by the learner and the perceptual, cognitive, and emotional engagement that such activity stimulates (Van Lier, 1997).

The hallmark of ecological research is a focus on action, perception, and language within the context, however broadly or narrowly drawn for the purposes of research in which they occur (Van Lier, 1997).

Individual nested systems

A key feature of ecological approaches is a nested systems perspective as proposed by Bronfenbrenner (1979). This sees the individual person as nested within a hierarchical set of different levels of context stretching from more micro to more macro levels of contexts, such as from the immediate family context to the attitudes and beliefs represented at the larger societal cultural level (Mercer, 2016b).

Running across all the nested context systems is what is termed the chronosystem, which refers to all the experiences an individual has across their lifespan and the continual development of contexts across time. One key implication of this perspective is that we cannot meaningfully understand one level of context without fully appreciating its relationship to the other levels of contexts and cultures within the overall ecological system as they are all interconnected with one another. The second especially important implication is the understanding that context cannot just be conceived of in spatial or social terms, but it inherently involves a temporal dimension too. As such, ecological systems draw attention to the fact that we are situated within multiple layers of interconnected contexts as well as our own personal history, all of which are continually undergoing change across time at different paces (Mercer, 2016b).

Contextual affordances

Language learning begins with learning to perceive while engaging in language-related activity. What we perceive are affordances, relationships of possibility between us and something in the environment (Gibson, 1979; Greeno, 1994; Neisser, 1987). Perceiving these affordances and acting upon them must be learned. Sometimes affordances may be directly and easily perceived, other times they may require much practice. Teachers, parents and caregivers direct the learner's attention to affordances in the environment, and at the same time the learner also perceives certain affordances directly.

Activity (including specifically joint activity) guides the perception of affordances, and the affordances themselves guide (facilitate, direct, change) further activity. Activity involves motive, purpose, planning and emotional engagement, thus on the one hand combining affect and intellect in the ways that Vygotsky considered essential for the development of consciousness and the higher mental functions, and on the other hand including past-present-future orientations that, in the perspective of the semiotic self, lead to the establishment of healthy identities that can connect the self to the new languaculture (Van Lier, 2010).

Contextual shaping

In the foreign language class, culture is created and enacted through the dialogue between students and between teacher and students. Through this dialogue, participants not only replicate a given context of culture, but, because it takes place in a foreign language, it also has the potential of shaping a new culture (Kramsch, 1999)[47].

As foreign language classrooms are composed of students from an increasingly diverse background, language teachers can no longer count on a stock of common knowledge against which to teach the foreign language and culture; they cannot build on common schooling habits, common conversational styles; they cannot even count on shared levels of knowledge of a common native tongue. The notion of a generic native speaker has become so diversified that it has lost its meaning.

Attention to this diversity forces teachers to take into consideration differences in class, gender, race, and ethnicity in the design of classroom activities. For example, cultural differences in the distribution of silences may force them to rethink their communicative language teaching practices (e. g. Philips, 1972); and gender differences in conversational style may prompt them to diversify the discussion format in their classrooms (Treichler et al., 1983). Thus teachers themselves become instrumental in creating alternative contexts of culture. The consensus they used to take for granted, the fixed point from which to view the foreign culture has become an illusion that demands to be looked at with the same critical distance as the foreign culture itself. In the classroom, teachers can learn to "read" their students' attempts to define and make sense of its various contexts (Kramsch, 1999)[49].

In the classroom, the success of any communicative activity is heavily determined by the way the participants perceive the context of situation and shape it accordingly through their verbal and non-verbal behavior. Learners and teachers shape the context of learning through the way they define each of Hymes' (1974) eight aspects of the speech situation:

1. the speech genre the participants think they are engaged in;
2. the norms of interaction and interpretation they think are called for;
3. the code and register they view as appropriate;
4. the key they believe they share;
5. the type and level of act sequence they believe they should attend to;
6. the ends or purpose they attribute to the exchange;
7. the role they think they should play as participants;
8. the meaning they attribute to the whole setting or scene.

Several of these factors can contribute to the success or failure, the pleasure or frustration, of the intended communication (Kramsch, 1999)[49-50].

Teaching a language is teaching how to shape the context of the "lesson" as an individual learning event and as a social encounter with regard to its setting, its participant roles, the purpose of its activities, its topics of conversation, its tone, modalities, norms of interaction, and the genre of its tasks. The way context is shaped through the foreign language determines the types of meanings the students will be allowed to explore, discover, and exchange. The more potential meanings they are encouraged to discover, the richer the opportunities for learning (Kramsch, 1999)[67].

Exercises, Questions and Tasks

1. Multiple Choices.

(1) The contextual aspects of the physical, social, and mental worlds do not usually start to play a role in language use until they have somehow been activated by the language users' ________ processes.

A. physical　　B. social　　C. metacognitive　　D. cognitive

(2) The selection of a particular context is determined by the search for ________.

A. adaptability B. relevance C. information D. implicature

(3) Context is a ________ concept: it is to be understood as the continually changing surroundings.

A. static B. physical C. dynamic D. objective

(4) The notion of context extends beyond its obvious manifestation as the physical setting within which an utterance is produced to include ________ factors.

A. linguistic B. social C. epistemic D. cultural

(5) Contextual correlates may be found in the ________ worlds.

A. mental B. social C. cultural D. physical

2. Fill in each blank with an appropriate word.

(1) The ________ of a text relies on the illocutionary force of its component parts and their perlocutionary effect on the hearer/reader.

(2) In the foreign language class, culture is created and enacted through the ________ between students and between teacher and students.

(3) The language function associated with context is the ________ function.

(4) In an interactional context, topics are introduced not only because of participants' intentions, but also because of ________ local interactional needs and the constraints imposed by multiple audiences.

(5) In the classroom, teachers can learn to "read" their students' ________ to define and make sense of its various contexts.

3. Mark "True" or "False" for the following statements and explain why.

(1) In understanding an exchange we have to make a great detailed inferences about the nature of the context in which it is assumed to be taking place.

(2) The more vocabulary and grammar students are encouraged to learn, the richer the opportunities for learning.

(3) Low-context messages are implicit, indirect, and conveyed primarily through the context or the social situation.

(4) A common cultural misunderstanding in language classes involves conflicts between direct and indirect communication style.

(5) The entire school learning experience is linked by a pervading "intertextuality" that embodies the theory and practice of education as institutionalized in our culture.

4. Short answer questions.

(1) How is context important?

(2) What determines the choice of one linguistic form over another?

(3) What makes it difficult for non-native speakers to communicate with native speakers?

(4) How can you interpret some variables in the context of language teaching?

(5) What does teaching a language mean?

5. Discuss the following questions.

(1) What do you know about pedagogical methods typical of Chinese culture?

(2) If you had a chance to teach Chinese to a British, which pedagogical methods would you

likely to use? Typical of English or Chinese? Why?

Suggested Readings

CUMMINGS L, 2007. Pragmatics: A multidisciplinary perspective[M]. Beijing: Peking University Press.

JOHNSON K, 2002. An Introduction to language learning and teaching[M]. Beijing: Foreign Language Teaching and Research Press.

KING J, 2016. Introduction to the dynamic interplay between context and the language learner [M]// KING J. The dynamic interplay between context and the language learner. London: Palgrave MacMillan, 1 - 10.

KRAMSCH C, 1999. Context and culture in language teaching[M]. Shanghai: Shanghai Foreign Language Education Press.

LEVINSON S C, 1983. Pragmatics[M]. Cambridge: Cambridge University Press.

MERCER S, 2016a. Social network analysis and complex dynamic systems[M]// DÖRNYEI Z, MACLNTYRE P D, HENRY A. Motivational dynamics in language learning. Shanghai: Shanghai Foreign Language Education Press, 73 - 82.

MERCER S, 2016b. The Contexts within me: L2 self as a complex dynamic system// KING J. The dynamic interplay between context and the language learner. London: Palgrave MacMillan, 11 - 28.

MEY J, 2001. Pragmatics: An introduction[M]. Beijing: Foreign Language Teaching and Research Press.

MORAN P R, 2009. Teaching Culture: Perspectives in practice[M]. Beijing: Foreign Language Teaching and Research Press.

RICHARDS J C, 2001. The Context of Language Teaching[M]. Beijing: Foreign Language Teaching and Research Press.

SPERBER D, WILSON D, 2001. Relevance: Communication and cognition[M]. 2nd ed. Beijing: Foreign Language Teaching and Research Press.

USHIODA E, 2016. Context and complex dynamic systems theory [M]// DÖRNYEI Z, MACLNTYRE P D, HENRY A. Motivational dynamics in language learning. Shanghai: Shanghai Foreign Language Education Press, 47 - 54.

VAN LIER L, 1997. Approaches to observation in classroom research: Observation from an ecological perspective[J]. TESOL Quarterly, 31(4): 783 - 787.

VAN LIER L, 2010. The ecology of language learning: Practice to theory, theory to practice [J]. Procedia-Social and Behavioral Sciences, 3: 2-6.

VERSCHUEREN J, 2000. Understanding pragmatics[M]. Beijing: Foreign Language Teaching and Research Press.

YU L M, ODLIN T, 2018. New perspectives on transfer in second language learning[M]. Beijing: Foreign Language Teaching and Research Press.

CHAPTER 7

Schema Theory

Focusing Question

- Why are some texts more difficult to understand than others?
- Do conventional teaching techniques strain students' memory? If so, what can we do about it?
- How can teachers go about supplying the background information students would need for a particular text?

Introduction

Most second-language educators would agree, at least in theory, with the idea that learning and practicing language in meaningful contexts is more appealing to both students and teachers than learning isolated bits of language through extensive memorization and drilling. Yet the rationale for contextualizing and personalizing classroom activities should not rest solely upon intuition. When one examines various theories of language comprehension and learning, it becomes clear that additional support can be found for the use of authentic or simulated authentic input in listening and reading, as well as meaningful and contextualized materials for encouraging language production (Hadley, 2009)[144].

It is well established that words can have different meanings in different contexts, even when the words are being used in the same sense (Anderson et al., 1976; Anderson et al., 1980). This fact poses a grave problem for any theory along the lines that the meaning of a compound is the product of the general meanings of the constituent words. This conventional theory does work in some cases. For instance, it seems to work in the case of the compound, red dress. The dress can be construed as having a typical shade of red (Anderson et al., 2006)[52].

Definition

The term "schema" was introduced by Bartlett (1932) in his very influential book, *Remem-*

bering: A Study in Experimental and Social Psychology, in which he demonstrated the role that one's previous experience and knowledge has on perception and memory. The previously acquired knowledge structures accessed in the comprehension process are called schemata (the plural of schema).

Rumelhart (1977) defines a schema as "an abstract representation of a generic concept for an object, event, or situation". For example, each of us has an abstract representation for the concept house, which may be altered considerably depending upon whether one adds adjectives such as elegant or enormous, as opposed to ramshackle or squalid. Cultural differences may also alter the abstract representation for a given concept: house may have many of the same attributes as maison, yet there will undoubtedly be different mental images associated with the two terms because of cultural factors. According to Rumelhart, "misunderstanding" happens when we have found the wrong schema for a given concept or event.

When a schema represents a whole situation (such as going to a movie, repairing a car, going on a picnic, buying groceries, doing laundry, etc.) a chain of stereotypic events or features is called up in an individual's mind in association with the situation. Schank et al. (1977) explain this phenomenon using the term script, defined as a structure that describes in a predetermined, stereotypic fashion appropriate sequences of events in a particular context. For example, a generic script for the situation "going to a restaurant" might be as follows:

One may call for a reservation, depending on the restaurant, get in the car, arrive at the restaurant, sit at a table, order from the menu, eat the meal in a stereotypic sequence, ask for the check, pay the cashier, and leave (Hadley, 2009)[147].

Background Knowledge

How does what learners know impact specifically on second-language acquisition? It might first be helpful to think about the kinds of knowledge learners can bring to comprehension tasks. In the second-language comprehension process, at least three types of background knowledge are potentially activated:

1. *linguistic information*, or one's knowledge of the target-language code;
2. *knowledge of the world*, including one's store of concepts and expectations based on prior experience;
3. *knowledge of discourse structure*, or the understanding of how various kinds or types of discourse (such as conversations, radio broadcasts, literary texts, political speeches, newspaper and magazine stories, and the like) are generally organized.

When language practice is limited to the manipulation or processing of linguistic form, only the first type of background knowledge is involved. By contrast, language learning activities that provide relevant context should be helpful in activating students' knowledge of the world and of familiar discourse structure. One might hypothesize that the need for activating knowledge beyond that of the linguistic code is greatest for learners at lower levels of proficiency, whose imperfect control of the language can be a serious hindrance to comprehension (Hadley, 2009)[145].

Characteristics of Schemata

Instantiation

Hudson (1982) refers to the selection of a particular form of a schema as instantiation, a term used by Anderson et al. in the year of 1976. In the case of the "restaurant schema," one instantiation might involve a quick trip to a drive-up window for a hamburger, while another might involve an elegant evening of fine dining at a restaurant downtown. Comprehending someone's story about going to a restaurant depends, in part, on the schema that is instantiated as one listens. The listener would need to construct a correspondence between the schema he or she had activated and the actual information in the message itself. When both sources of information match sufficiently, the message is said to be understood. Comprehension, therefore, is not a matter of simply processing the words of the message, but involves fitting the meaning of the message to the schema that one has in mind.

Any one individual's interpretation of a message will be heavily influenced by his or her personal history, interests, preconceived ideas, and cultural background. For second-language learners, distortions in comprehension may be due not only to misunderstandings of the linguistic aspects of the message, but also to misreadings of the script or schema due to cultural differences (Hadley, 2009)[148].

Structure

A schema is an abstract knowledge structure. It is abstract in the sense that it summarizes what is known about a variety of cases that differ in many particulars. An important theoretical puzzle is to determine just how much and what sort of knowledge is abstracted and how much remains tied to knowledge of specific instances. A schema is structured in the sense that it represents the relationships among its component parts. The theoretical issue is to specify the set of relationships needed for a general analysis of knowledge. The overriding challenge for the theorist is to specify the form and substance of schemata and the processes by which the knowledge embodied in schemata is used.

An adequate account of the structure of schemata includes information about the relationships among components; a complete theory of schema activation includes a major role for inference; during language comprehension, people probably rely on knowledge of particular cases as well as abstract and general schemata (O'Malley et al., 2001)[23].

Types of Schemata

Carrell and Eisterhold (1983) explain that there are two basic kinds of schemata used in understanding messages:

1. Content schemata: relating to one's background knowledge and expectations about objects, events and situations;
2. Formal schemata: relating to one's knowledge of the rhetorical or discourse structures of different types of texts.

Research findings suggest not only that background knowledge of the first two type can enhance comprehension, but also that attitudes and emotional reactions may have a role in the activation of schemata and ultimately in the comprehension process (Hadley, 2009)[14].

Functions of Schema Theory

Enabling to make predictions

Schema theory suggests that the knowledge we carry around in our heads is organized into interrelated patterns. These are constructed from all our previous experiences of a given aspect of the experiential world, and they enable us to make predictions about future experience. Given the fact that making sense of discourse is a process of using both our linguistic knowledge and our content knowledge, these schemata or "mental film scripts" are extremely important.

The central insight provided by researchers using mental models such as frame and schema theory is that meaning does not come neatly prepackaged in aural and written texts. Widdowson (1978) has suggested that texts are little more than elaborate "signposts" to the speaker or writer's original meanings, and that the reader or listener must use their linguistic and content knowledge to reconstruct the original meanings of the creator of the discourse (Nunan, 2001)[133-134].

Providing direction

Any given text does not carry meaning in and of itself. Rather, it provides direction for listeners or readers so that they can construct meaning from their own cognitive structure (previously acquired or background knowledge) (Hadley, 2009)[147].

Facilitating making inferences

The schema for an object consists of the specific values that it has for these and perhaps other attributes.

The principal value of schemata is that they facilitate making inferences about concepts. If we hear the concept wheel, and the reference clearly is to the tires on a car, we understand that the wheel is round, is made of rubber, and has other features specified in the hierarchical organization. This inferential process is based on probabilities in that the wheel size may be substantially different if the car is a gocart or a grand prix racer. Stated differently, the value of schemata is that they enable us to organize and understand new information. Upon hearing the word wheel, we can juxtapose the concept relative to other important and related concepts and thereby develop a broader understanding than is evident from the information supplied by any particular sentence (O'Malley et al., 2001)[23-24].

Interactive Model of Comprehension

Schema theorists describe an interactive model of comprehension. They posit two separate but interrelated modes of information processing: bottom-up processing and top-down processing (Rumelhart, 1980).

Bottom-up processing and top-down processing

Carrell and Eisterhold (1983) explain the difference between these two operations in terms of the type of information that is used in comprehending the message and the way in which that information enters the system. When a message is interpreted principally by paying attention to the specific details (including the decoding of individual words or other linguistic cues) and the listener or reader attempts to instantiate the best fitting lower-level schema for the incoming data, bottom-up processing is taking place. This type of processing is considered data-driven, moving from the parts to the whole concept (Rumelhart, 1980). If, on the other hand, the listener/reader begins with a more general higher-order schema, makes predictions based on background knowledge, and then searches the input for information to fit into the "slots," top-down processing is occurring. This latter type of processing is considered to be conceptually driven, moving from the whole to the parts (Rumelhart, 1980; Carrell et al., 1983).

Schema theorists point out that bottom-up processing and top-down processing occur at the same time. Details are attended to in order to instantiate the appropriate schema while conceptual understanding of a more general nature allows the listener or reader to anticipate and predict. "Bottom-up processing ensures that the listeners/readers will be sensitive to information that is novel or that does not fit their ongoing hypotheses about the content or structure of the text; top-down processing helps the listeners/ readers to resolve ambiguities or to select between alternative possible interpretations of the incoming data" (Hadley, 2009)[148].

Unidirectional processing

Carrell (1988) maintains that skilled readers constantly shift from one processing mode to the other as they accommodate to the demands of the task, while lower-proficiency readers tend to rely too much on one or the other mode of processing, resulting in problems with comprehension. Lower-proficiency readers may be too text-bound—relying too heavily on bottom-up decoding of the words and morpho-syntactic features, or conversely too dependent upon their background knowledge, making unwarranted assumptions and missing relevant features of the input. She attributes this unidirectional processing to five possible causes (Carrell, 1988)[103]:

1. lack of relevant background knowledge to help readers use top-down processing;
2. failure to activate available schemata;
3. linguistic or reading skill deficiencies;
4. misconceptions about reading, especially in a foreign language;
5. individual differences in cognitive style.

The problems alluded to in 4 may include those induced by inefficient approaches to the teaching of reading, where teachers have students read a text in order to answer questions on numerous details that may have little to do with the overall meaning. Test questions that place heavy emphasis on details and fail to encourage inferencing or global processing may promote decoding and one-way (bottom-up) processing, which in turn may result in lack of comprehension of the main ideas. Teachers need to be careful, therefore, to devise questions and activities that encourage the *bidirectional processing* that skilled readers use (Hadley, 2009)[149].

Discourse Comprehension

Widdowson (1984) provides a novel reinterpretation of schema theory from the perspective of discourse comprehension. He argues that there are two dimensions or levels to any given discourse, a systemic level and a schematic level. The systemic level includes the reader or listener's linguistic knowledge, while the schematic level relates to background content knowledge.

It is likely that you used at least six types of knowledge to help you make sense of the text (Hedge, 2002):

- Syntactic knowledge
- Morphological knowledge
- General world knowledge
- Sociocultural knowledge
- Topic knowledge
- Genre knowledge

Syntactic and morphological knowledge are to do with the language itself. These kinds of knowledge help a reader to decode the language of a text and can together be called linguistic, or systemic, knowledge. At the same time, general world knowledge, sociocultural, topic, and genre knowledge, together often referred to as schematic knowledge, enable a reader to work with the language of the text in order to interpret its meaning (Hedge, 2002)[189].

In making sense of a given piece of discourse, we try and match up our own schematic knowledge to that of the writer or speaker. In doing so, we have to interpret what we read or hear.

Widdowson (1984) has shown how these interpretative procedures might work in making sense of discourse. He argues that a major task for someone listening to or reading a piece of discourse is to keep track of the various things and events that are referred to within the discourse.

In doing so, they can make use of the various cohesive devices. It is often assumed that the ability to track cohesive relationships through a text is a fairly straightforward business. Consider the following text:

I saw John yesterday. He gave me his hat.

Most people would assume that the hat belongs to John. However, Widdowson demonstrates that the ability to establish and track such relationships often involves more than simple identification. There are cases in which we need to interpret what we see or hear. Widdowson illustrates this point through a number of rather bizarre texts, the first of which is as follows (as you read it consider what the underlined reference items refer to).

Statistical probability was discovered in a teapot. A postman saw it there and connected it to a petrol pump. He was wearing silk pajamas at the time. They were old and dusty.

As Widdowson rightly points out, while the reader might be surprised by this surrealistic piece of prose, there is no difficulty in identifying it with statistical probability, he with postman, and there with teapot. Other cases are more difficult. What, for instance, does it refer to in the following text?

Statistical probability was discovered in a teapot. A postman saw it and connected it to a petrol pump. It was old and dusty.

Determining what "*it*" refers to now becomes more difficult as there are two possible antecedents for the first "*it*" (*statistical probability* and *a teapot*), and three for the third (*statistical probability*, *a teapot*, and *a petrol pump*). Because we cannot use our background knowledge to help us, we are unable to say what it refers to.

Consider now a third text:

Statistical probability was discovered, in a teapot. A postman rinsed it out. He had no idea what it was of course.

In this text we can appeal to our knowledge of the world to determine what it refers to. We know that teapots are occasionally rinsed out, and therefore assume that the first it refers to teapot. As we also assume that postmen are familiar with teapots, we would assign the second it to statistical probability. The point of all this is that in many cases discourse processing depends, not only on the identification of cohesive relationships, but also on our knowledge of the world.

We engage in these interpretative procedures more frequently than might be imagined. Consider the following textual fragment from a popular magazine.

I believe all children have a mystical empathy with nature. We come into this world "trailing clouds of glory" as the poet Wordsworth put it.

Here, there are no direct links between the first sentence and the second, and so we need to use our background knowledge to create the links and establish a relationship between the metaphorical phrase "clouds of glory," and the mystical empathy that children are claimed to have with nature. Most native speakers have little difficulty in identifying the relationship (Nunan, 2001)[134-135].

A Schema-Based Approach to Reading and Listening

Many language students have experienced at one time or another the difficulties and frustrations that can arise when attempting to understand a spoken or written text in the foreign language, especially when one is in the earliest stages of language study.

What are some of the causes of difficulties in comprehension?

Why are some texts more difficult to understand than others?

How might language students approach listening or reading tasks differently to enhance comprehension?

How can teachers prepare students so that listening and reading materials become more comprehensible to them?

Answers to these questions can be found as we look at various comprehension theories that have been proposed over the years and examine available research about the comprehension process (Hadley, 2009)[144].

Meaningful learning theory

A common thread running through various perspectives on language acquisition is the view that the meaningfulness and familiarity of second-language materials play a crucial role as learners begin to develop their second-language skills. Beginning in the 1960s, the role of meaningfulness and organization of background knowledge was particularly emphasized by cognitive psychologists. Educators such as Ausubel (1968; 1978) believed that learning must be meaningful to be effective and permanent. For material to be meaningful, it must be clearly relatable to existing knowledge that the learner already possesses. Furthermore, this existing knowledge base must be organized in such a way that the new information is easily assimilated, or "attached," to the learner's cognitive structure (Hadley, 2009)[144].

Advance organizers

Ausubel stressed that teachers need to provide "advance organizers"—pedagogical devices that activate relevant background knowledge—to facilitate the learning and retention of new material. Hanley et al. (1995) point out that, although Ausubel was referring to textual organizers, many researchers and practitioners have used the term "advance organizer" in recent years to refer to an array of pedagogical aids, including pictures, titles, topic summaries, preposed questions, and the like (Hadley, 2009)[144-145].

Visual organizers

Since the early 1970s, there have been a number of experiments looking at the role that visual and other kinds of organizers might play in both listening and reading comprehension. Some of the subsequent studies have shown that visual materials, be they still pictures, video, or graphic organizers, also generally enhance comprehension of a target-language text, particularly when learners are at a fairly low level of proficiency. Results such as these make intuitive sense, since second-language learners are often faced with input (both in listening and reading tasks) that is by nature unfamiliar, difficult, and therefore unpredictable because of the learner's lack of familiarity with the linguistic code. The provision of additional contextual information in the form of a visual should make the comprehension task easier by providing an organizational schema for the passage as a whole.

Certain kinds of visual materials presented to language learners in advance of a listening or reading task can enhance their comprehension and memory for the new material, especially if learners are at lower levels of proficiency. Not all pictures are equally effective at enhancing comprehension, and that several pictures used together are not necessarily better than using just one (Hadley, 2009)[150-151].

Visual organizers compared to other prereading and prelistening activities

Studies indicate that nonpictorial prereading/prelistening activities such as studying vocabulary or answering or coming up with questions can have significantly positive effects on comprehension. Several studies indicate that pictorial organizers are particularly helpful to students at the lower levels of proficiency and may enhance comprehension most for beginning and intermediate learners, whereas nonpictorial aids can be as or more effective for learners at higher levels.

1. Titles and topic cues

   The provision of the title or topic in a brief sentence or two before reading or listening may "activate a script" and thus enhance comprehension of the passage.

2. Summaries, questions and captions

   Advance organizers such as brief summaries and prequestions can have very positive effects on learners' comprehension of listening materials; however, the effects of these various kinds of organizers may be different for learners depending on their proficiency level, with lower-proficiency learners generally benefitting the most from these sorts of comprehension supports. The use of captions while viewing video material can be beneficial to learners even at advanced levels of language study.

3. Reader's background knowledge and topic interest

   Students comprehend texts more successfully when the topic is familiar to them than when it is unfamiliar. When students' own schemata do not correspond on given points with the passage content, some problems may occur. They would overextend or distort schemata due to individual differences or cultural influences.

   Readers do not always activate the knowledge they have. The significance of factors such as prior knowledge and interest in the topic can differ with different populations and different proficiency levels. Teachers should avoid low-interest, low prior knowledge topics for readings, or allow students to self-select readings when possible.

4. Cultural background cues

   Attitudes and emotional reactions may have a role in the activation of schemata and ultimately in the comprehension process.

5. Rhetorical structure and comprehension

The research on the effects of rhetorical (as opposed to content) schemata shows that comprehension suffers when the structure of a story violates the expected norm. Most simple stories, such as fables, tales, and short narratives, use generic problem-solving motif as their essential rhetorical structure. Violations of this stereotypic structure might cause the reader to fail to comprehend. Second-language readers can benefit from instruction about the rhetorical structure of texts before reading.

Research into schema-based understanding supports the view that learning language in context (i. e. , larger discourse frameworks) may be easier than processing language in "bits and pieces" or in isolated sentence frames. "By dealing with related units of information rather than isolated bits, more efficient processing becomes possible" (McLaughlin et al. , 1983)[138].

Exercises, Questions and Tasks

1. Multiple Choices.

(1) Distortions in comprehension may be due not only to misunderstandings of the ________ aspects of the message, but also to misreadings of the script or schema due to cultural differences.

A. grammar B. lexical C. linguistic D. pragmatic

(2) A schema can be defined as "an abstract representation of a ________ concept for an object, event, or situation."

A. generic B. general C. specific D. special

(3) Any given text provides ________ for listeners or readers so that they can construct meaning from their own cognitive structure.

A. direction B. meaning C. information D. knowledge

(4) If the listener makes predictions based on background knowledge, and then searches the input for information to fit into the "slots," ________ processing is occurring.

A. text-bound B. decoding C. bottom-up D. top-down

(5) In making sense of a given piece of discourse, we try and match up our own ________ knowledge to that of the writer or speaker.

A. linguistic B. systemic C. schematic D. lexical

2. Fill in each blank with an appropriate word.

(1) The schema for an object consists of the specific values that it has for these and perhaps other ________.

(2) Teachers need to be careful to devise questions and activities that encourage the ________ processing.

(3) Widdowson argues that there are two dimensions or levels to any given discourse, a ________ level and a ________ level.

(4) The principal value of schemata is that they facilitate making about ________ concepts.

(5) Schema theorists describe a(n) ________ model of comprehension.

3. Mark "True" or "False" for the following statements and explain why.

(1) Schema theorists point out that bottom-up processing and top-down processing occur at the same time.

(2) According to Omaggio, several pictures used together are better than using just one.

(3) Several studies indicate that pictorial organizers are particularly helpful to students at the lower levels of proficiency and may enhance comprehension most for beginning and intermediate learners.

(4) The use of captions while viewing video material is helpless to learners at advanced levels of language study.

(5) Students would overextend or distort schemata of a topic due to one's limited knowledge of the target-language code.

4. Short answer questions.

(1) What kinds of knowledge can learners bring to comprehension tasks?

(2) Why is schema-based understanding necessary in language teaching?

(3) What are possible causes for unidirectional processing?

(4) How can teachers prepare students so that listening and reading materials become more comprehensible to them?

(5) Why is schema-based approach preferable in reading and listening tasks?

Suggested Readings

ANDERSON R C, PEARSON P D, 2006. A schema-theoretic view of basic processes in reading comprehension[M]// CARRELL P L, DEVINE J E, ESKEY D. Interactive approaches to second language reading[M]. Beijing: Beijing World Publishing Corporation, 37 – 55.

CARRELL P L, DEVINE J E, ESKEY D, 2006. Interactive approaches to second language reading[M]. Beijing: Beijing World Publishing Corporation.

HADLEY A O, 2009. Teaching language in context[M]. Beijing: Foreign Language Teaching and Research Press.

HEDGE T, 2002. Teaching and learning in the language classroom[M]. Shanghai: Shanghai Foreign Language Education Press.

NUNAN D, 2001. Second language teaching and learning[M]. Beijing: Foreign Language Teaching and Research Press.

O'MALLEY J, CHAMOT A, 2001. Learning strategies in second language acquisition[M]. Shanghai: Shanghai Foreign Language Education Press.

CHAPTER 8

Pragmatic Failure and Foreign Language Teaching

Focusing Question

- What are possible negative consequences of pragmatic failures?
- How can a language teachers help students to avoid pragmatic failures?
- Why are pragmatic principles needed?

Introduction

People do not always or even usually say what they mean. Speakers frequently mean much more than their words actually say. For example, I might say: "*It's hot in here*!" but what I mean is:

Please open the window!

or *Is it all right if I open the window*?

or *You're wasting electricity*!

People can mean something quite different from what their words say, or even just the opposite. For instance, to someone who has borrowed my car for the weekend and returned it with no petrol in the tank, I might say:

It was nice of you to fill the car up!

or *What a shame you couldn't find the petrol tank*!

Several interesting questions arise from these observations: if speakers regularly mean something other than what they say, how is it that people manage (as on the whole they do) to understand one another? If a single group of words such as "*It's hot in here*!" could mean so many different things at different times, how do we work out what it actually does mean on one specific occasion? And why don't people just say what they mean? These, and many other issues, are addressed within the area of linguistics known as pragmatics (Thomas, 2010)[1].

Speaker Meaning

Levels of Meaning

The first level is that of abstract meaning; we move from **abstract meaning** to **contextual meaning** (also called **utterance meaning**) by assigning sense and/or reference to a word, phrase or sentence. The third level of meaning is reached when we consider the speaker's intention, known as the *force* of an utterance (Thomas, 2010)[2].

Abstract meaning is concerned with what a word, phrase, sentence, etc. *could* mean (for example, the dictionary meanings of words or phrases). The term does not apply only to single words. It can apply equally well to phrases or even to whole sentences. Supposing at a party you heard someone saying:

The Pearsons are on coke.

Taken in the abstract (by consulting a dictionary of contemporary spoken English, for example) the word "coke" could (at least in theory) refer to "*Coca-Cola*," "*cocaine*," or "*a coal derivative*." And, accordingly, the whole expression "*to be on coke*" could have one of (at least) three abstract meanings: "*to be drinking Coca-Cola*," "*to use cocaine*," or "*to have solid-fuel heating*." What the words actually meant on the occasion in question could only be determined in context (Thomas, 2010)[2-4].

Levels of Speaker Meaning

There are two components of speaker meaning: utterance meaning and force.

Utterance meaning: the first level of speaker meaning

When in interaction we have resolved all the ambiguities of sense, reference and structure—when we have moved from abstract meaning (what a particular sentence could mean in theory) to what the speaker actually does mean by these words on this particular occasion—we have arrived at contextual meaning or **utterance meaning.** Utterance meaning can be defined as "a sentence-context pairing" (Gazdar, 1979) and is the first component of speaker meaning (Thomas, 2010)[16].

Force: the second level of speaker meaning

In pragmatics we use the term force to refer to the speaker's communicative intention. Force, a concept introduced by the philosopher, J. L. Austin, is the second component of speaker meaning. The psychologist, Miller, writing in 1974, was one of the first people to point out the significance of this level of analysis:

> Most of our misunderstandings of other people are not due to any inability to hear them or parse their sentences or understand their words... A far more important source of difficulty in communication is that we often fail to understand a speaker's intention.

Interrelationship of utterance and force

It is frequently (but not invariably) the case that we derive **force** from utterance meaning but we can, for example, use paralinguistic features (such as intonation and tone of voice) or non-linguistic features (such as gesture) in order to work out the intended force. Or we may rely mainly or entirely on context. On the other hand, if we fail to understand the utterance meaning, we may well fail to understand the force or if we cannot agree on utterance meaning, we are unlikely to be able to agree as to the intended force. The two components of speaker meaning are closely related, but not inseparable.

Pragmatics: Different Perspectives

Pragmatics as meaning in interaction

Pragmatics is the study of speaker(S) and hearer(H) meaning created in their joint actions that include both linguistic and non-linguistic signals in the context of socio-culturally organized activities (Lo Castro, 2003)[15].

Meaning is not something which is inherent in the words alone, nor is it produced by the speaker alone, nor by the hearer alone. Making meaning is a dynamic process, involving the negotiation of meaning between speaker and hearer, the context of utterance (physical, social and linguistic) and the meaning potential of an utterance (Thomas, 2010)[22].

Pragmatics as interpersonal rhetoric

It is the way speakers and writers accomplish goals as social actors who do not just need to get things done but must attend to their interpersonal relationships with participants at the same time.

As a means of mapping out the relevant territory for the study of how people accomplish their goals and attend to interpersonal relationships while using language, Leech (1983) and Thoms (1983) divided pragmatics into two components: pragmalinguistics—the resources for conveying communicative acts and relational or interpersonal meanings and sociopragmatics—the social perceptions underlying participants' interpretation and performance of communicative action (Kasper et al. , 2006)[2].

A Problem-solving View of Pragmatics

Whether we take the speaker's or the addressee's point of view, pragmatics is about problem solving. Suppose S as the speaker and H as the hearer. From S's point of view, the problem to be solved is: "Given that I want to communicate something to H, what is a good way of doing so?" From H's point of view, the problem to be solved is: "Given that S said such-and-such, what did S mean (i. e. , intend to communicate) by that?" The two types of problem solving are logically quite different, and yet they are closely related, in that the goal of H is to reconstruct the meaning that it was the goal of S to convey (Leech, 2018)[56].

Pragmatics in ISLA

The study of pragmatics in ISLA is the study of instructional and learner variables involved in facilitating the classroom learning of how to say what to whom, when, in a second or foreign language (Bardovi-Harlig, 2013).

Pragmatic Failure

Pragmatic competence refers to one's knowledge of linguistics, norms, and social conventions, and one's ability to use these knowledge bases in a socially-bound interaction (Taguchi, 2015).

The term "pragmatic failure" refers to the inability to understand "what is meant by what is said." One area of pragmatic failure—pragmalinguistic failure is fairly easy to overcome. It is simply a question of highly conventionalized usage which can be taught quite straightforwardly as "part of the grammar." The second area —sociopragmatic failure is much more difficult to deal with, since it involves the student's system of beliefs as much as his/her knowledge of the language. It is essential to avoid prescriptivism in this very sensitive area of language in use. To do so we must draw on insights from theoretical pragmatics and develop ways of heightening and refining students' metapragmatic awareness, so that they are able to express themselves as they choose (Thomas, 1983)[91].

Pragmatic Ambivalence

According to Leech (1983), pragmatics is the use of language in a goal-oriented speech situation in which S is using language in order to produce a particular effect in the mind of H.

Pragmatic failure has occurred on any occasion on which H perceives the force of S's utterance as other than S intended he/she should perceive it. For example, if:

a. H perceives the force of S's utterance as stronger or weaker than S intended he/she should perceive it;

b. H perceives as an order an utterance which S intended he/she should perceive as a request;

c. H perceives S's utterance as ambivalent where S intended no ambivalence;

d. S expects H to be able to infer the force of his/her utterance, but is relying on a system of knowledge or beliefs which S and H do not, in fact, share.

Thomas (1983)[94] uses the term "pragmatic failure" rather than "pragmatic error" advisedly. It is legitimate to speak of grammatical error, since grammaticality can be judged according to prescriptive rules (prescriptive for language-teaching purposes, at least), whereas pragmatic competence, as Candlin (1976) has observed, "entails probable rather than categorical rules." The nature of pragmatic ambivalence is such that it is not possible to say that the pragmatic force of an utterance is "wrong." All we can say is that it failed to achieve the speaker's goal.

Flout

As people become better acquainted, they seem to become increasingly tolerant of each other's "pragmalects," just as they become more tolerant of other forms of idiosyncratic behavior. Nevertheless, in order to be considered pragmatically competent, one must be able to behave linguistically in such a manner as to avoid being unintentionally offensive, for most of the time, to strangers who speak the same language or variety of language as oneself.

Pragmatic principles are normative rather than prescriptive. Whereas a grammatical error puts one outside the grammatical system of English, one can, as Leech (1980) points out, flout pragmatic principles and yet remain within the pragmatic system of English. It is possible, in other words, to be extremely impolite, untruthful, and uninformative and at the same time "speak perfect English."

All too often, however, language teachers and linguists fail to admit the possibility of a foreign student's flouting conventions, in the same way as they fail to allow her/him to innovate linguistically. In fact, the foreign learner is usually expected to be "hypercorrect," both grammatically and pragmatically. Schmidt et al. (1977) have pleaded the cause of the foreign learner, obliged to speak a "superstandard English" which native speakers rarely use:

> Superstandard English, however admired and perhaps admirable, is simply not functional in all situations.

Learners are rarely permitted the luxury of a flout (of being either "overpolite" or "impolite"), but are condemned to the "reduced personality," allowed only banal and conventional opinions. As one foreign colleague put it:

When I speak English, I feel I always have to occupy the middle ground.

It is the teacher's job to equip the student to express him/herself in exactly the way he/she chooses to do so—rudely, tactfully, or in an elaborately polite manner. What we want to prevent is his/her being *unintentionally* rude or subservient. It may behove the teacher to point out the likely consequences of certain types of linguistic behaviour (Thomas, 1983)[95-96].

Grammatical Error & Pragmatic Failure

Grammatical errors may be irritating and impede communication, but at least, as a rule, they are apparent in the surface structure, so that H is aware that an error has occurred. Once alerted to the fact that S is not fully grammatically competent, native speakers seem to have little difficulty in making allowances for it. Pragmatic failure, on the other hand, is rarely recognized as such by non-linguists. If a non-native speaker appears to speak fluently (i. e. is grammatically competent), a native speaker is likely to attribute his/her apparent impoliteness or unfriendliness, not to any linguistic deficiency, but to boorishness or ill-will. While grammatical error may reveal a speaker to be a less than proficient language-user, pragmatic failure reflects badly on him/her as a person. Misunderstandings of this nature are almost certainty at the root of unhelpful and offensive national stereotyping: "the abrasive Russian/German," "the obsequious Indian/Japanese," "the insincere American," and "the standoffish Briton."

Pragmatic failure is an important source of cross-cultural communication breakdown, but in spite of this, teacher and textbook writers alike have almost completely ignored it. It is not difficult to understand why this should be so, and why they should prefer to remain on the more solid ground of grammar. Firstly, as Widdowson (1979) has pointed out, pragmatic description has not yet reached the level of precision which grammar has attained in describing linguistic competence. Secondly, pragmatics—language in use—is a delicate area and it is not immediately obvious how it can be taught (Thomas, 1983)[96-97].

Pragmalinguistic Failure

Pragmalinguistic failure occurs when the pragmatic force mapped on to a linguistic token or structure is systematically different from that normally assigned to it by native speakers. Pragmalinguistic failure may arise from two identifiable sources: "teaching-induced errors" and "pragmalinguistic transfer"—the inappropriate transfer of speech act strategies from one language to another, or the transferring from the mother tongue to the target language of utterances which are semantically/syntactically equivalent, but which, because of different "interpretive bias," tend to convey a different pragmatic force in the target language.

Pragmalinguistic transfer

Psycholinguistic research has shown that in interpreting grammatical ambiguity there is almost always"bias" (by which they mean that one meaning is usually seen first by most people), and it seems that this is equally true in processing pragmatic ambiguity. Native speakers fairly predictably assign certain pragmatic force to certain utterances. Thus "*can you X?*" is a highly conventionalized politeness form in British English, likely to be interpreted by native speakers as a request to do X, rather than a question as to one's ability to do X. In other languages, French and Russian, for example, the opposite is true. Similarly, the utterance X, "*would you like to read?*" which in an English classroom would be a highly conventionalized polite request/directive to do so, in a Russian classroom often elicited the response "*no, I wouldn't*" (from students who had no intention of being rude, but who genuinely thought that their preferences were being consulted). Notice that theirs was not an impossible interpretation, but simply a less likely one.

Examples of the pragmatically inappropriate transfer of semantically/ syntactically equivalent structures would be:

In Russian "*конечно*" (meaning *of course*) is often used instead of "*da*" (yes) to convey an enthusiastic affirmative (cf. "*Yes, indeed,*" "*Yes, certainly,*" in English). "*Of course*" can be used in this way in English:

A: *Are you coming to my party?*

B: *Of course.* [Gloss: Yes, indeed/it goes without saying/I wouldn't miss it for the world!]

Often, however, "*of course*" implies that the speaker has asked about something which is self-evident, so that "*конечно*," transferred from Russian to English in answer to a "genuine" question, can sound at best peremptory and at worst insulting:

A: *Is it a good restaurant?*

B: *Of course.* [Gloss (for Russian S): Yes, (indeed) it is. (For English H): What a stupid question!]

A: *Is it open on Sundays?*

B: *Of course.* [Gloss (for Russian S): Yes, (indeed) it is. (For English H): Only an idiotic foreigner would ask!]

The inappropriate transference of speech act strategies from LI to L2 is a frequent cause of pragmalinguistic failure (e. g. using a direct speech act where a native speaker would use an indirect speech act or "off-record" politeness strategy) (cf. Brown et al., 1978). Thus, polite usage in Russian permits many more direct imperatives than does English. The usual way to ask directions, for example, is simply to say (in Russian!), "*Tell me (please) how to get to* …," and to use a more elaborate strategy, such as "*Excuse me, please, could you tell me* …?" is completely counterproductive, as it often means that your interlocutor is half way down the street before you finish speaking. Transferred into English, such direct imperatives seem brusque and discourteous.

Teaching-induced pragmalinguistic failure

Some teaching techniques may actually increase the likelihood of pragmalinguistic failure. Kasper (1982) has identified many examples of what she terms "teaching-induced errors," some of which might fall into category of pragmalinguistic failure. Some she attributes to teaching materials (inappropriate use of modals), others to classroom discourse (lack of marking for modality, complete sentence responses and inappropriate pre-positional explicitness). Complete sentence responses violate the textual pragmatic "principle of economy" (see Leech, 1983) and it is easy to see how they can create an unfortunate impression. To answer the question "*Have you brought your coat?*" with "*Yes, I have brought my coat!*" sounds petulant or positively testy! The same is true of inappropriate propositional explicitness. To say: "*I was sorry to hear about your Grandma*" sounds suitably sympathetic, whereas: "*I was sorry to hear that your Grandma killed herself*" is rather less tactful, and: "*I was very sorry to hear your Grandma tripped over the cat, cartwheeled down the stairs and brained herself on the electricity meter*" seems downright unfeeling.

Candlin (1979), Rutherford (1980), Clyne (1981) and Sharwood-Smith (1981) have all pointed out that it is a mistake to place too much emphasis on metalinguistic knowledge. It frequently leads the student to assume that there exists, for example, an isomorphism between the grammatical category "the imperative" and the speech act "ordering." As Ervin-Tripp (1976) and Brown et al. (1978) have pointed out, imperatives are scarcely ever used to command or request in formal spoken English.

There are doubtlessly other sources of pragmalinguistic failure, and certainly there is a great deal of overlap between the categories. It is not possible, for example, to say whether "pragmatic overgeneralization" (Schmidt et al., 1980) stems from "teaching-induced error" or pragmalinguistic transfer. Pragmatic overgeneralization is particularly likely to occur where a narrow range of structures in the mother tongue has a wider range of possible "translations" in the target language.

In general, the foreign learner is not noticeably more sensitive about having pragmalinguistic failure pointed out to him/her, than about having grammatical errors corrected. Insofar as he/she is prepared to learn the language at all, he/she is usually willing, if not able, to try to conform to the pragmalinguistic norms of the target language.

Sociopragmatic Failure

While the ability to make judgements according to the social scales of value is part of the speaker's "social competence," the ability to apply these judgements to linguistic utterances—knowing how, when, and why to speak—comes within the field of pragmatics. It is cross-cultural mismatches in the assessment of social distance, of what constitutes an imposition, of when an attempt at a face-threatening act should be abandoned, and in evaluating relative power, rights, and obligations, etc., which cause sociopragmatic failure.

Size of imposition

Goffman's (1967) notion of "free" and "non-free" goods provides a useful framework within which to discuss the concept of "size of imposition." "Free goods" are those which, in a given situation, anyone can use without seeking permission, for example, salt in a restaurant (providing, of course, that you are having a meal in that restaurant and have not simply wandered in off the street). Generally speaking, what an individual regards as free goods/services varies according to the relationships and the situation within which the interaction occurs (Thomas, 2010)[130].

Lakoff (1974) has pointed out that "free" and "non-free" goods are not necessarily material—the concept can be extended to information. Clearly there are some topics that one may ask about freely and others that are "none of your business"— that is, non-free goods.

Cultures differ greatly as to what is considered "freely available." The British bourgeois(e) considers it intrusive to inquire directly about a stranger's income, politics, religion, marital status, etc., whereas in other countries such information may be sought freely and without circumlocution (Thomas, 1983)[105].

Mobile impoliteness occurs when people mark their impatience in social context ('me first') or try to secure the biggest patty at a barbeque ('me most'). The practice is often masked by "pseudo-polite" behavior, as when we say "I'm sure you don't mind me going first," or "Wouldn't you be more comfortable in a smaller office?" These practices, when successfully deployed, often contribute to enhancing one's status as a clever negotiator or a useful go-getter (Mey, 2018).

Taboos

Typically, sexual or religious, taboos are by no means universal, and a second source of serious sociopragmatic failure is making reference in L2 to something which is taboo in that culture, although it may be capable of being discussed perfectly politely in L1.

Consider, for example, the furore accompanying the recent royal wedding. It was noticeable that the only details the British press spared us were the time, place, and manner of the actual consummation. It was not a question of the delicacy or otherwise of the language used (itself a pragmatic decision)—it would have been considered prurient and distasteful, a sociopragmatic miscalculation of gigantic proportions, to have alluded to it at all. Other cultures, in contrast, consider the ceremonial rupturing of the royal hymen a legitimate topic for public comment, providing, of course, that it is done in suitably, reverential, deferential, and pragmatically appropriate tones.

Cross-culturally different assessments of relative power or social distance

One final illustration of sociopragmatic failure may be provided by the not infrequent phenomenon of a foreign speaker's judging relative power or social distance differently from a native speaker. In a student's own culture, for example, teachers may have a rather higher status than they do here (a social judgement), leading the student to behave more deferentially than would normally be expected.

Sociopragmatic failure and value judgments

Without doubt, the most difficult type of pragmatic failure the language teacher has to deal with occurs when pragmatic principles, such as politeness, conflict with other, deeply held values, such as truthfulness or sincerity.

Cross-culturally different "pragmatic ground rules"

Every competent native speaker knows that there are times when what is said cannot be taken at face value but must be interpreted according to different "ground rules." Thus, when S says, "Have you heard the one about...?" H knows that what follows must be interpreted as a joke. Just as children have to learn not to interpret everything as the literal truth, so people need to be taught that pragmatic ground rules do not necessarily operate in the same way in other languages.

While a speaker who is not operating according to the standard grammatical code is at worse condemned as "speaking badly," the person who operates according to differently formulated pragmatic principles may well be censured as *behaving* badly; as being an untruthful, deceitful, or insincere person.

One task of the pragmaticist, then, should be to make explicit the "deep level rules of the game." Once the non-native speaker understands the "pragmatic ground rules," something which at first appeared to be a cross-cultural conflict of values may be shown not to be so (Thomas,

1983)[10 6-108].

For example, Japanese students and immigrants living in the United States, report that they find it strange and rather offensive when Americans extend an invitation to a social gathering by indicating when and where it will take place and then adding some sort of phrase like "Come if you want to." Since Japanese rules of speaking require that a potential guest be urged to accept an invitation, while American rules impose a constraint on pinning people down to accepting possibly unwanted invitations, and since neither group is likely to be aware of the other's rules, it is difficult to avoid misunderstandings. In a case like this, the Japanese feels hurt and uncertain whether the invitation is really sincerely meant (Wolfson, 1989)[17].

Cross-culturally different assessments of the relative importance of pragmatic principles

Pragmatic principles, as Leech (1980) has observed, "can conflict with other coexisting principles." This is as much a reflection of the human condition as of language: just as we must sometimes make moral choices between justice and mercy, so we must navigate linguistically between the Scylla of tactlessness and the Charybdis of dishonesty. In general, when two maxims or principles conflict, circumstances (such as urgency, the vulnerability of H) and the personality of the speaker dictate which principle prevails.

It may be, however, that in some cultures, certain relative values ("relative" in the sense of how polite is "polite" and how prolix is "prolixity"?) may systematically prevail over others. Thus, in culture X "generosity" may be systematically valued above "succinctness;" in culture Y "approbation" may outweigh "truthfulness."

We are not concerned here with spiritual or moral values, but with communicative values. When we speak of one society's observing the "generosity" principle to a greater degree than another, we are not suggesting that its members are necessarily in fact more open-handed than those of another. In the Ukraine, it may happen that a guest is pressed as many as seven or eight times to take more food, whereas in the UK it would be unusual to do so more than twice. For a Ukrainian, the "generosity" maxim systematically overrides the "quantity" maxim; for a British person it does not. Indeed, British recipients of such hospitality sometimes feel that their host is behaving impolitely by forcing them into a bind, since they run out of polite refusal strategies long before the Ukrainian host has exhausted his/her repertoire of polite insistence strategies.

Pragmatic Instruction

Using technology-mediated tasks

The main benefit of TBLT for L2 pragmatic instruction is that it provides students with goal-oriented meaningful activities that address their real-world needs and promote authentic communication in the classroom (Kim et al., 2015 & 2016; Taguchi et al., 2018). Because tasks are both contextually and socially situated, their implementation allows students to practice their pragmatic knowledge to interact with different interlocutors in a variety of simulated contexts

(González-Lloret, 2019). Since a large part of today's interactions take place in the digital era, technology-mediated tasks allow learners to engage in pragmalinguistic and socio-pragmatic practice in digital communication platforms such as emails, chat rooms or instant messaging. Technology-mediated TBLT would ultimately guide learners into being better prepared for an increasingly digital professional career (Sánchez-Hernández et al., 2021)[165].

The use of technology allows students to go beyond authentic language use in the classroom and immerse themselves in out-of-class real-world contexts where they can develop their L2 pragmatic ability. Emergent technologies such as simulated immersive environments (Sykes, 2012, 2014; Taguchi et al., 2013; Taguchi et al., 2017), place-based augmented reality (Holden et al., 2011, 2013), and social networking sites (Belz et al., 2005; Gonzales, 2013) offer students the opportunity to engage in authentic use of the language in a wide range of situations. Language students need to learn how to be pragmatically appropriate in contexts that have emerged in the current era of globalization, such as Computer-Mediated Communication (CMC) (e.g. emails, online forums, social networks), text messaging, online learning platforms, or virtual games (González-Lloret, 2018; Sykes, 2021). As González-Lloret (2018), students nowadays need to be exposed to the cyberpragmatics of such new communicative contexts (Sánchez-Hernández et al., 2021)[165].

Providing authentic pragmatic input

The teaching of L2 pragmatics in the current era of globalization also involves the challenge of how to obtain authentic pragmatic input that may be used to enhance implicit instruction (Bardovi-Harlig, 2020).

Authentic pragmatic input may come from a variety of speakers in a variety of contexts from speech communities that are relevant to one's learners. The target language variety, as well as the setting, register, and pragmatic features to be focused on, will determine the potential sources of the input (Bardovi-Harlig, 2020)[51].

The material on email and internet conversations opens up a new field of research on a global, and yet easily accessible scale. It uses authentic data which is available in written form in vast quantities, thus solving some methodological difficulties in obtaining live conversations, and in some formats, such as message boards and blog posts, it also shows how people deal with the consequences of pragmatic failure (Mcgee, 2019).

In a time in which people have access to online streaming of TV series and films in the original language, it seems relevant to explore how such input affects pragmatic learning and how it can be implemented in the language classroom (Sánchez-Hernández et al., 2021)[165].

The use of authentic input has been the front line of pedagogical revolution in pragmatics. One potential resource for teachers (and for pedagogical pragmatics) are free, online, readily accessible corpora. Most importantly for pragmatics, the corpora offer very different types of spoken language interaction which cannot be interchanged; but even this variety can be turned into an asset (Bardovi-Harlig, 2020)[53-54].

Foreign learners, bewildered by the large number of possible ways of expressing obligation in English (*must*, *ought*, *should*, *have to*, etc.), often select one which they then use in all contexts. For no very obvious reason, Russian speakers seem to favor "*to be to*"(*you are to be here by eight)*, an unfortunate overgeneralization, since pragmatically "*to be to*" is largely restricted to very unequal power relationships, such as military commands, directives from parents to small children, etc. Computer corpora of English readily reveal these pragmatic restrictions, and should enable teachers and textbook writers to help students make more informed generalizations (Thomas, 1983)[103].

Teaching Pragmatics Appropriateness

Linguistic and non-linguistic means to perform social functions, as well as norms and conventions behind these practices, are often uniquely defined in a given culture, and so it is often difficult for one to notice how people project appropriate levels of politeness or how they communicate meaning indirectly (Wolfson, 1989).

Appropriateness refers to a social judgment of the acceptability of some instance of language in context. Crystal (1997) defines appropriate language as "any use of language considered to be compatible with a given social situation" (van Compernolle, 2018)[31]. Appropriateness entails the sociocultural and pragmatic effectiveness of a given utterance that is formally possible and feasible "in relation to a context in which it is used and evaluated" (Hymes, 1972b). The appropriateness of a given utterance depends on its relationship to specific sociocultural activities (van Compernolle, 2018)[35].

Scales of politeness and indicators of use such as "vulgar," "formal," or "rare" are all relative and can serve as only the most general guide to appropriateness. It would be of far greater benefit to the learner if teachers attempted to make explicit the types of choices which underlie pragmatic decision-making. It is at this point that we must turn for help to pragmatic theory.

Van Dijk (1977b)[199] sees the goal of pragmatic theory as being to: "...formulate the general and particular conditions determining the full Intention—successfulness of illocutionary acts."

For an illocutionary act to succeed, the speaker must judge his/her position relative to his/her interlocutor by assessing (van Dijk, 1977a)[221]:

a. positions (e. g. roles, status, etc.)

b. properties (e. g. sex, age, etc.)

c. relations (e. g. dominance, authority)

d. functions (e. g. father, waitress, judge, etc.)

Brown et al. (1978) suggest that in order to compute the weightiness of a face-threatening act one must assess the social distance between S and H, the relative power of H over S, and the degree to which X is rated an imposition in that culture. Leech (1977) proposes almost identical criteria for gauging the amount of tact required in a given situation:

a. the more power H holds over S,

b. the more socially distant H is from S,

c. the more costly X is to H,
the more tact is required by the situation.

Raising consciousness

Pragmatic failure is not immediately apparent in the surface structure of utterances and can be revealed only by discussing with students what force they intended to convey. But first they must be given the tools to make such discussions possible. Teachers should develop a student's metapragmatic ability—the ability to analyze language use in a conscious manner—a process which Sharwood-Smith (1981) terms "consciousness-raising." This might be achieved by discussing language use in the light of the pragmatic parameters outlined above, or by doing as Candlin (1976) has suggested and taking a leaf from the ethnomethodologists' book and using "glossing" as a teaching/learning procedure. Short (1981)[200] proposes the discussion of drama to make pragmatic analysis explicit:

> The discussion of what is meant, implied, etc. by characters in dramatic dialogues can also be used in class to make students explicitly aware of the communicative nature of discourse. Mastery of the Gricean maxims would seem to be essential if the foreign learner is going to be able to understand English well and fit in socially when using English himself. This factor is extremely important as without it the confidence so important for good linguistic performance is likely to be undermined.

For the language teacher, however, the descriptions offered by theoretical pragmaticists are inadequate. It is not enough simply to make explicit the parameters within which pragmatic choices are made. House and Kasper (1981)[184] have indicated the need for teachers to alert their students to possible cross-cultural pragmatic differences:

> It seems also to be advisable for the teacher to explicitly point out to the learner that politeness markers are an integral part of the foreign cultural system, and should neither be used nor interpreted by reference to the learner's native system. More effective teaching of the behavioral component may minimize native cultural interference and prevent impolite, ineffective, or otherwise inappropriate behavior on the part of the learner.

Distinguishing pragmalinguistic from sociopragmatic failure

For those engaged in the teaching of English to people from other cultures, pragmatic failure raises issues which make it essential to distinguish two types:

a. Pragmalinguistic failure, which occurs when the pragmaticforce mapped by S onto a given utterance is systematically different from the force most frequently assigned to it by native speakers of the target language, or when speech act strategies are inappropriately transferred from L1 to L2.
b. Sociopragmatic failure, the social conditions placed on language in use.

While pragmalinguistic failure is basically a linguistic problem, caused by differences in the linguistic encoding of pragmatic force, socio-pragmatic failure stems from cross-culturally different perceptions of what constitutes appropriate linguistic behavior.

The language teacher is in the less fortunate position of having to be prescriptive, at least to a degree, whether he/she likes it or not. Correcting errors of any sort—grammatical or pragmatic—demands care and tact on the part of the teacher, but some areas are particularly sensitive. Pragmatics, "language in use," is the place where a speaker's knowledge of grammar comes into contact with his/her knowledge of the world. But both systems of knowledge are filtered through systems of beliefs—beliefs about language and beliefs about the world.

In order to interpret the force of an utterance in the way in which the speaker intended, the hearer must take into account both contextual and linguistic cues. Often, context alone will determine what force is assigned to an utterance. That "*Good luck*!" is interpreted as "I wish you well," while "*Bad luck*!" is assigned the force of "commiseration" rather than "malediction," has nothing to do with the linguistic form, but with what force is conventionally assigned to it and with what is a plausible interpretation in context. We live in a world in which it is unusual to ill-wish someone, or, at least, to do so openly. Consequently, if we want to curse someone in English, we must make the illocutionary force more explicit: "*I hope you have bad luck*!" Though Thomas (1983) would not wish to make more than a weak claim for this, it seems to her that the ability to determine what is "likely" in context is to some degree "universal," just as the "politeness principle" (Leech, 1983) is universal. It does not, on the whole, require explicit formalization and need not concern the language teacher unduly.

The point at which the student does need help is in interpreting the *linguistic* pragmatics. The types of information conveyed by pragmatics include:

Level 1: the attitude of the speaker towards the information (relative newness of information, topicalization and focusing of information, connotation, and presupposition);

Level 2: (a) the speech act or communicative intent of the utterance; (b) the attitude of the speaker towards the hearer (the degree of deference intended, perceptions of relative power, rights and duties, social distance, etc., existing between speaker and hearer).

As one moves from 2(a) to 2(b), one is moving from the pragmalinguistic to the sociopragmatic end of the continuum and at the same time from what is *language*-specific to what is *culture*-specific.

There is certainly a grey area in the middle where it is not possible to separate the two with any degree of certainty. The language-specific should be possible for the teacher to correct it quite straightforwardly. The culture-specific, a reflection of the student's system of values and beliefs, should not be "corrected," but only pointed out and discussed. Only by discussing the matter with the student would it be possible to establish, for example, whether an English speaker's overuse of "*Спасибо*" (meaning thank you) in Russian stems from:

a. ingrained habit—part of a "highly automatized system" inappropriately transferred from L1 to L2, and perhaps an example of covert grammatical error;
b. S's not knowing the pragmatic force of "*Спасибо*" in Russian, which might be an example of pragmalinguistic failure;
c. cross-culturally different perceptions of when or for what goods or services it is appropriate to thank, which would be an example of sociopragmatic failure.

At the extremes of the pragmatic failure continuum there is a very clear difference between, for example, failing to understand that "*can you close the window?*" usually carries the pragmatic force of a request in English, and having a different opinion from most British people as to what questions it is proper to ask. The first stems from uncertainty as to the pragmatic force attached to a particular utterance (i. e. it is basically a linguistic problem), whilst the second stems more from uncertainty as to what is socially appropriate linguistic behaviour (i. e. it is as much a cultural as a linguistic problem).

Conclusion

Once a student is exposed to a target culture, he/she rapidly begins to acquire pragmatic competence. Yet pragmatic competence can never simply be "grafted" on to grammatical competence.

Much effort is expended in writing nugatory texts explaining low-level rules of grammar, such as third person singular "-s" (which, since it is readily observable in the surface structure, requires little explicit formalization). Pragmatic failure, meanwhile, like covert grammatical error, often passes unchecked by the teacher or, worse, it is attributed to some other cause, such as rudeness, and the student is criticized accordingly. This problem can be overcome only by giving the student the tools to make the processes of pragmatic decision-making explicit.

Sensitizing learners to expect cross-cultural differences in the linguistic realizations of politeness, truthfulness, etc., takes the teaching of language beyond the realms of mere training and makes it truly educational. Helping students to understand the way pragmatic principles operate in other cultures, encouraging them to look for the different pragmatic or discoursal norms which may underlie national and ethnic stereotyping, is to go some way towards eliminating simplistic and ungenerous interpretations of people whose linguistic behavior is superficially different from their own. Such techniques are desirable both pedagogically and politically. To give the learner the knowledge to make an informed choice and allowing him/her the freedom to flout pragmatic conventions, is to acknowledge his/her individuality and freedom of choice and to respect his/her system of values and beliefs. Students who feel that their view of the world is being dismissed out of hand or who feel unable to express themselves as they wish are scarcely likely to develop positive attitudes towards learning a foreign language.

Recognizing the pragmalinguistic/sociopragmatic distinction means allowing the foreign student the right to flout in exactly the same way as the native-speaker does, and acknowledging that "speaking good English" does not necessarily mean conforming to the norms of the culturally hegemonic strata. Our only concern as language teachers is to ensure that the learner knows what he/she is doing. Making the distinction between pragmalinguistic and sociopragmatic failure removes much that non-Western learners, in particular, find objectionable in contemporary "communicative" approaches to language teaching.

Exercises, Questions and Tasks

1. Multiple Choices.

(1) Which level of the following meaning can be speaker's intention?

A. abstract meaning B. contextual meaning

C. utterance meaning D. the force of the utterance

(2) Which of the following is NOT TRUE of abstract meaning?

A. It is the utterance meaning.

B. It applies to single words.

C. It applies to phrases or even to whole sentences.

D. It is concerned with what a word, phrase, sentence, etc. could mean.

(3) Which one is NOT TRUE of utterance meaning?

A. It is contextual meaning.

B. It is the second level of speaker meaning.

C. It is a process to assign sense to a word, phrase or sentence.

D. It is a sentence-context pairing.

(4) It is one's ________ knowledge which provides the range of possible meanings of multiply ambiguous sentences.

A. discourse B. strategic C. grammatical D. pragmatic

(5) Pragmatic failure has occurred on any occasion except where a hearer perceives ________.

A. the force of S's utterance as stronger than S intended he/she should perceive it

B. as an order an utterance which S intended he/she should perceive as a request

C. S's utterance as ambivalent where S intended no ambivalence

D. the force of the speaker's utterance, relying on a system of knowledge or beliefs which they share.

(6) Pragmalinguistic failure occurs when ________ mapped onto a linguistic token or structure is systematically different from that normally assigned to it by native speakers.

A. the abstract meaning B. the pragmatic force

C. the contextual meaning D. the utterance meaning

(7) Which of the following might NOT be a teaching-induced pragmalinguistic failure?

A. Complete sentence responses

B. lack of marking for modality

C. pragmatically inappropriate transfer of syntactically equivalent structure

D. inappropriate prepositional explicitness

(8) Which of the following act might NOT cause sociopragmatic failure?

A. assigning certain pragmatic force to certain utterances

B. making judgements according to the social scales of value

C. abandoning an attempt at a face-threatening act

D. evaluating relative power

(9) Which one of the following cannot dictate which principle prevails when two pragmatic principles conflict?

A. circumstances　　B. abstract meaning

C. the personality of the speaker　　D. the vulnerability of the hearer

(10) Which of the following is least likely to assess by a speaker judging his/her position relative to his/her interlocutor for an illocutionary act to succeed?

A. the degree to which X is rated an imposition in that culture

B. the social distance between S and H, the relative power of H over S

C. the amount of tact required in a given situation

D. the standard grammatical code

2. Fill in each blank with an appropriate word.

(1) Pragmatic failure refers to the ________ to understand "what is meant by what is said."

(2) Pragmatic principles are ________ rather than prescriptive.

(3) The inappropriate ________ of speech act strategies from L1 to L2 is a frequent cause of pragmalinguistic failure.

(4) Appropriateness refers to a social judgment of the ________ of some instance of language in context.

(5) Teachers should develop a student's metapragmatic ability—the ability to analyze language use in a conscious manner—a ________ process.

3. Mark "True" or "False" for the following statements and explain why.

(1) What the words actually meant on could only be determined in context.

(2) A speaker's utterance meaning and its force are inseparable.

(3) A far more important source of difficulty in communication is that we often fail to understand the ambiguities of sense, reference and structure.

(4) For the language teacher, pragmatic failure can be revealed only by discussing with students what force they intended to convey.

(5) In order to interpret the force of an utterance in the way in which the speaker intended, the hearer must take into account contextual cues, neglecting linguistic ones.

4. Discuss the following questions.

(1) What do you know about the seriousness of pragmatic failure compared with grammatical errors?

(2) How can you be considered pragmatically competent?

(3) What should teachers do to help students to be pragmatically competent?

(4) Why have teacher and textbook writers alike almost completely ignored prag matic failure?

(5) How can you interpret the educational dimension of language teaching?

Suggested Readings

BARDOVI-HARLIG K, 2017. Acquisition of L2 pragmatics [M]// LOEWEN S, SATO M. The Routledge handbook of instructed second language acquisition[M]. New York: Routledge, 224 - 245.

BARDOVI-HARLIG, K, 2020. Pedagogical linguistics: A view from L2 pragmatics[J]. Pedagogical Linguistics, 1(1): 44 - 65.

GÓNZALEZ-LLORET M, 2019. Technology and L2 pragmatics learning (Review) [J]. Annual Review of Applied Linguistics, 39: 113 - 127.

KASPER G, ROSE K R, 2006. Pragmatics in language teaching[M]// ROSE K R, KASPER G. Pragmatics in language teaching. Beijing: Beijing World Publishing Corporation, 1 - 10.

LEECH G, 2018. The Pragmatics of politeness[M]. Shanghai: Shanghai Foreign Language Education Press.

MCGEE P, 2019. Cross-cultural pragmatic failure[J]. Training, Language and Culture, 3(1): 73 - 84.

SÁNCHEZ-HERNÁNDEZ A, BARÓN J, 2021. Teaching second language pragmatics in the current era of globalization: An introduction[J]. Language Teaching Research, 26(2): 163 - 170.

TAGUCHI N, 2015. Instructed pragmatics at a glance: Where instructional studies were, are, and should be going (Review)[J]. Language Teaching, 48(1): 1 - 50.

THOMAS J, 1983. Cross-cultural pragmatic failure[J]. Applied Linguistics, 4(2): 91 - 112.

THOMAS J, 2010. Meaning in interaction: An introduction to pragmatics[M]. Beijing: Foreign Language Teaching and Research Press.

VAN COMPERNOLLE R A, 2018. Sociocultural theory and L2 instructional pragmatics[M]. Beijing: Foreign Language Teaching and Research Press.

WOLFSON N, 1989. Perspectives: Sociolinguistics and TESOL[M]. Rowley, MA: Newbury House.

CHAPTER 9

Reflective Teaching in ELT

Focusing Question

- Imagine you have reached the midpoint of a course in which you have been conscientious in trying to be an effective teacher. Nevertheless, you notice that many of the students seem disinterested in the course. How could you find out what some of the problems might be?
- You notice that a majority of the students seem very reluctant to participate in class. How could you get them to be more involved?
- Suppose you are very excited about a series of new teaching procedures you are testing out in a secondary school classroom. How can you document that constructive changes are taking place in the course as you are offering it?

Introduction

Gaining teaching experience, participating in teacher-development courses, thinking about and discussing published scholarship, attending conferences, consulting colleagues, and getting to know students better are but some of the many ways that English language teachers can grow as professionals. Yet, teachers need to look inward, both within themselves and within the courses they offer, to access information and inspiration about their efforts in language classrooms (Murphy, 2006)[499].

Definition of Terms

Reflective Teaching

Richards and Lockhart (1994) define reflective teaching as an approach to second language classroom instruction in which current and prospective teachers "collect data about teaching, examine their attitudes, beliefs, assumptions, and teaching practices, and use the information obtained as a basis for critical reflection" about their efforts in language courses. They posit five basic assumptions:

1. An informed teacher has an extensive knowledge base about teaching.
2. Much can be learned about teaching through self-inquiry.
3. Much of what happens in teaching is unknown to the teacher.
4. Teaching experience alone is insufficient as a basis for continuing development.
5. Critical reflection can trigger a deeper understanding of teaching.

Why would we spend the time and energy it takes to develop understandings through reflective teaching?

We may find the answer by considering both our continuing needs as teachers and, even more importantly, the needs of the language learners we serve. Reflective teachers are capable of learning from, and further developing, their personal understandings and explanations of life within language classrooms. A central reason to be interested in reflective teaching "is to gain ***awareness*** of our teaching beliefs and practices" and to learn "to see teaching differently" (Gebhard et al., 1999)[4].

A rationale to support reflective teaching certainly includes such insights, but it also extends beyond them. Besides, an integral part of reflective teaching is to learn to take action, when possible, on whatever we might be learning about ourselves as teachers and about students' responses, for the purpose of enhancing the quality of learning opportunities we are able to provide in our classrooms. Taking action might involve exploring instructional innovations, trying out alternatives, and modifying—or even breaking—routines in teaching based upon what we learn (Murphy, 2006)[500].

Professional Development

Teacher development is a term used in the literature to describe a process of continual intellectual, experiential, and attitudinal growth of teachers (Lange, 1990). His use of the term allows for "continued growth both before and throughout a career." He adds that "the intent here is to suggest that teachers continue to evolve in the use, adaptation, and application of their art and craft" (Bailey et al., 2009)[4].

It is argued that the teacher's professional development should be addressed within the context of reflective action (Wallace, 1991; Zeichner et al., 1987), aiming to enable teachers to develop awareness of their own teaching. Reflective perspectives on professional development stress that an awareness raising component plays a significant role in the teacher learning process. According to Farrell (2004), if teachers can become more aware of what happens in their classroom and can monitor accurately both their own behaviour and that of their students, they can function more effectively, similarly to what is described by Jay et al. (2002) as an individual and collaborative process involving experience and uncertainty, which entails identifying questions and key elements of a matter that has emerged as significant, then taking one's thoughts into dialogue with oneself and with others (Wright et al., 2023)[229].

Self-awareness and self-observation are the cornerstones of all professional development. They are essential ingredients, even prerequisites, to practicing reflective teaching (Bailey et al., 2009)[22].

Descriptive Model of Teaching: The Constituents

Diane Larsen-Freeman (1983) has written that teachers need the following in order to "make informed choices" about their teaching:

1. heightened awareness;
2. a positive attitude that allows one to be open to change;
3. various types of knowledge needed to change;
4. the development of skills.

Awareness is a necessary (but not a sufficient) condition for professional development to occur. Donald Freeman (1989a) used these same concepts in developing a descriptive model of the constituents of teaching (Figure 9.1).

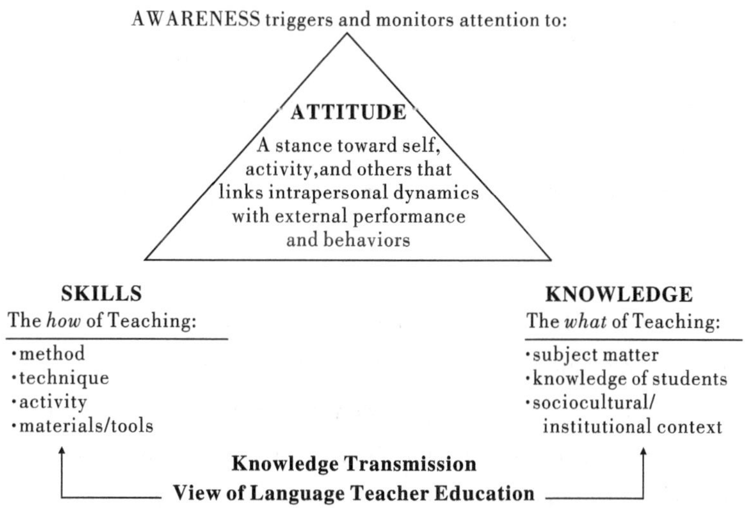

Figure 9.1 Descriptive model of teaching: The constituents

Freeman's model portrays the relationship among these four key constituents:

1. Awareness serves the function of triggering our attention to attitude, skills, and knowledge.
2. Attitude is described as "a stance toward self, activity, and others."
3. Skills, which constitute "the *how* of Teaching," include our methods, techniques, activities, materials, and other tools.
4. Knowledge embodies "the *what* of Teaching," which includes our subject matter and our knowledge of the students, as well as the sociocultural and institutional context.

According to Freeman, the traditional knowledge transmission model of teacher education only addresses the last two components-skills and knowledge. Yet long-lasting change and development must start with our awareness and our attitudes (Bailey et al., 2009)[23-24].

Evidence-Based Reflective Practice

How does the teacher know for sure if the class had in fact not worked out well for him or her?

Reflection occurs when a teacher consciously seeks answers to the following questions (Farrell, 2007):

- What do you do in the classroom and how do you do it?
- Why do you do this?
- What is the result?
- Will you change anything based on the information gathered from answering the previous questions?

Reflective teaching is evidence-based; teachers collect data or evidence about their work and then reflect on this evidence to make informed decisions about their practice.

Engaging in evidence-based reflective practice enables teachers to articulate to themselves (and others) what they do, how they do it, why they do it, and what the impact of one's teaching is on student learning. The results of engaging in such reflective practice may mean an affirmation of current practices or making changes, but these changes will not be based on impulse, tradition, or the like; they will emerge as a result of analysis of concrete evidence.

As such, reflective practice is based on the belief that both experienced and novice language teachers can improve their understanding of their own teaching by consciously and systematically reflecting on their teaching experiences. It starts with the internal rather than the external and the real center of the process is teaching itself, and it uses the teacher's actual teaching experiences as a basis for reflection. By making systematic reflections on teaching that produce concrete evidence of what teachers do, they can become free from making too many impulsive decisions about what to teach, when to teach and why to teach it. Teachers can thus move beyond designing routine activities for their students to complete just because they have always done these, as well as move on from making routine decisions in their classrooms. The reason is that reflective practice enables teachers to act in a more deliberate and intentional manner, because they will use the information/data gathered from their systematic reflections to make more informed decisions (rather than routine decisions) about what to do, thus creating better opportunities for their students to learn in their classes (Farrell, 2013)[7].

Experience as a teacher is not enough to being an effective teacher, for we do not learn much from experience as much as we learn from reflecting on that experience. As Dewey (1933) pointed out, experience combined with reflections leads to growth. Teachers who do not bother to reflect on their work are slaves to routine and are guided by impulse, tradition, and authority than by informed decision making (structured reflection). You can see these teachers huddled together in many staff rooms in many schools throughout the world complaining about how bad the system is, but are unwilling to reflect on it (both inside and outside the classroom). Unfortunately, these teachers tend to be the most vocal and also tend to burnout quickly. The more reflective teachers are busy trying to improve on their practice to become more effective teachers (Farrell, 2013)[14].

Purposes of Reflective Teaching

The purposes of reflective teaching are three-fold (Murphy, 2006)[499-500]:

1. to expand one's understanding of the teaching-learning process;
2. to expand one's repertoire of strategic options as a language teacher;
3. to enhance the quality of learning opportunities one is able to provide in language classrooms.

Those interested in reflective teaching take steps to deepen awareness of teaching and learning behaviors by working to improve their abilities to:

1. gather information on whatever is taking place within a language course;
2. examine such information closely in an effort to better understand what they collect;
3. identify anything puzzling about the teaching-learning process;
4. build awareness and deepen understanding of current teaching and learning behaviors;
5. locate and collaborate with others interested in processes of reflective teaching;
6. pose and refine questions tied to one's teaching that are worth further exploration;
7. locate resources that may help to clarify whatever questions are being posed;
8. make informed changes in teaching, even if only modest changes;
9. document changes in teaching-learning behaviors and responses;
10. continue such efforts over time and share emerging insights with others.

Why should we bother with reflective teaching? The best reason is stated in the introduction to Zeichner and Liston's (1996) book:

> Many educational issues engage and affect our heads and our hearts. Teaching is work that entails both thinking and feeling and those who can reflectively think and feel will find their work more rewarding and their efforts more successful.

In highlighting the value of working with colleagues, Gary Birch (1992)[290] draws a helpful analogy between practicing reflection and learning a new language:

> Reflection is potentially threatening. It involves the possible deconstruction of a belief system with which one has become familiar and its replacement with an alternative that may, in the initial stages, prove uncomfortable. In this it is analogous to the learning of another language, where a habitual system is discarded, to be replaced by an alien system of equal complexity, for which attempts at mastery may be traumatic.

Critical Reflection: Asking Questions about Teaching

A reflective approach to teaching is one in which teachers and student teachers collect data about teaching, examine their attitudes, beliefs, assumptions, and teaching practices, and use the information obtained as a basis for critical reflection about teaching. Critical reflection involves asking the following questions:

1. How can I collect information about my own teaching?
2. What are my beliefs about teaching and learning, and how do these beliefs influence my teaching?
3. Where do these beliefs come from?
4. What kind of teacher am I?
5. What beliefs do my learners hold about learning and teaching?
6. How do these beliefs influence their approach to learning?
7. What learning styles and strategies do my learners favor?
8. What kind of planning decisions do I make use of?
9. What kind of on-the-spot decisions do I make while I teach?
10. What criteria do I use to evaluate my teaching?
11. What is my role as a teacher?
12. How does this role contribute to my teaching style?
13. How do my learners perceive my role as a teacher?
14. What form or structure do my lessons have?
15. How do I communicate goals to my learners?
16. How effectively do I utilize learning opportunities within a lesson?
17. What kinds of interaction occur in my classroom?
18. What interactional styles do my learners favor?
19. What kind of grouping arrangements do I use and how effective are they?
20. What kind of learning activities do I employ?
21. What is the purpose of these activities?
22. What patterns of language use occur when I teach?
23. How do I modify my language to facilitate teaching and learning?
24. What opportunities do learners have for authentic language use in lessons?

It is necessary to reflect critically on what one discovers. The information obtained through the process of exploring teaching can (Richards et al., 2000)[1-2]:

1. help achieve a better understanding of one's own assumptions about teaching as well as one's own teaching practices;
2. lead to a richer conceptualization of teaching and a better understanding of teaching and learning processes;

3. serve as a basis for self-evaluation and is therefore an important component of professional development.

Key Attitudes for Teachers to be Reflective

Zeichner and Liston (1996)[1] point out: "If a teacher never questions the goals and the values that guide his or her work, the context in which he or she teaches, or never examines his or her assumptions, then it is our belief that this individual is not engaged in reflective teaching." By definition, this practice involves critical examination of our motivation, thinking, and practice.

According to Zeichner and Liston (1996)[11], a reflective teacher:

1. examines, frames, and attempts to solve the dilemmas of classroom practice;
2. is aware of and questions the assumptions and values he/she brings to teaching;
3. is attentive to the institutional and cultural contexts;
4. takes part in curriculum development and is involved in school change efforts;
5. takes responsibility for his or her own professional development.

This practice must include "reflection about the unexpected outcomes of teaching because teaching, even under the best conditions, always involves unintended as well as intended outcomes." This element of unpredictability can lead us into troublesome areas. Sometimes reflection leads us to uncomfortable awareness:

> Teachers need to be able to consider their practice in an informed and dispassionate way. This implies an extensive knowledge base and an attitude of mind that is sufficiently courageous to face the reality of one's own teaching, which may at times be unpalatable (Birch, 1992)[284].

In other words, a certain level of maturity and openness is needed to address aspects of our "blind selves" (Luft, 1969).

John Dewey (1933) felt that three key attitudes are necessary in order for teachers to be reflective: open-mindedness, responsibility, and wholeheartedness. Zeichner and Liston (1996)[11] state that "open-mindedness and responsibility must be central components in the professional life of the reflective teacher." Wholehearted teachers "regularly, examine their own assumptions and beliefs and the results of their actions and approach all situations with the attitude that they can learn something new." They further cite Dewey (1933)[17] as saying that reflection "emancipates us from merely impulsive and routine activity… [and] enables us to direct our actions with foresight and to plan according to ends in view of purposes of which we are aware" (Bailey et al., 2009)[39-40].

Five Dimensions of Reflection

Zeichner and Liston (1996) describe five dimensions of reflection (Figure 9.2). The behaviors that characterize dimensions of reflection range from split-second on-line decision-making to long-term reformulation of our practical theories.

Figure 9. 2 Dimensions of reflection

1. Rapid Reflection	Immediate and automatic Reflection-in-Action
2. Repair	Thoughtful Reflection-in-Action
3. Review	Less formal Reflection-on-Action at a particular point in time
4. Research	More systematic Reflection-on-Action over a period of time
5. Retheorizing and Reformulating	Long-term Reflection-on-Action informed by public academic theories

The first two dimensions occur during reflection-in-action, while the remaining three are part of reflection-on-action, to use Schön's term (1983).

The first level is part of our on-line decision making while we are teaching. Of necessity, such decision making happens very fast, almost constantly, and often privately. This kind of rapid reflection happens so quickly that such responses are thought of as "routine and automatic" (Zeichner et al., 1996)[45].

In the case of repair, a teacher makes a decision to alter his or her behavior in response to cues from students (e. g., novel ideas that they contribute, evidence that they didn't understand, and so on).

Review occurs before or after our teaching. In review, a teacher thinks about, discusses, or writes about some element of his or her teaching or the students' learning. As Zeichner and Liston note (1996)[46], review "is often interpersonal and collegial." It can be as simple as an after-class conversation with colleagues, or it can be more systematic, such as writing a report on a child's progress.

At the research level "teachers' thinking and observation become more systematic and sharply focused around particular issues". This is a long-term process that involves collecting data over time. Action research and teaching journals are two professional development procedures that entail this level of reflection.

The last dimension consists of retheorizing and reformulating. These processes are described as "more abstract and more rigorous than the other dimensions". In this dimension, "while teachers critically examine their practical theories, they also consider these theories in light of public academic theories". Retheorizing and reformulation are long term processes that can continue for years (Bailey et al., 2009)[40-42].

Topics Explored by Reflective Teachers

English language teaching (ELT) and language learning are processes embedded within complex arrays of dynamic and socially interactive events. Early stages of reflective teaching begin with a classroom teacher's desire to better understand the dynamics of a single language course as it is being experienced by a group of learners and their teacher. Most teachers find an individual course to be the most useful place to initiate what eventually becomes systematic efforts at reflective teaching. Some general topic areas reflective teachers often explore are (Murphy, 2006)[500]:

1. communication patterns in the classroom;
2. teacher decision making;
3. ways in which learners apply knowledge;
4. the affective climate of the classroom;
5. the instructional environment;
6. a teacher's self-assessment of growth and development as a professional.

Reflection Break #1

What are some other areas you think reflective teachers who work in ELT settings might profitably explore? Alternatively, what might be some specific examples of the six areas listed above?

Communication patterns in the classroom

Teachers who are interested in patterns of communication in language classrooms often explore classroom management issues, such as:

1. Who is doing what during lessons?
2. As the teacher, am I the sole source of power and control?
3. Do learners sometimes have an impact on what takes place?

Most of us are interested in better understanding how communications between everyone present in the classroom may influence teaching and learning processes. For example, a teacher might examine recurring features within the instructional routine to better understand students' learning preferences. A teacher interested in communication patterns might ask if lessons usually begin and end in the same way. With video support, it is possible to divide a language lesson into a series of manageable segments for analysis. Multiple viewing reveals how lessons begin (openings which tend to be broadly focused), introductions to specific activities (setting things up, giving directions, clarifying, providing support for what is to follow), core lesson segments (individual activities that tend to reflect preplanned teaching decisions), ways in which the teacher and the class move from one activity to another (transitions between lesson segments), how lesson segments are sequenced (pre-, core-, and post-activity phases), how students respond to teacher feedback, and the teacher's way of drawing a lesson to a close (calling for attention, assigning homework, previewing upcoming events).

An interesting way to increase understanding of current ways of teaching is to gather information on how you structure, pace, and sequence lesson segments. By generating an audio or video recording of their teaching, for example, and then moving between macro- and micro level examinations of whole lessons, reflective teachers can begin to better understand such features. Close review of their ways of teaching leads many teachers to then consider ways of manipulating lesson segments, and some of the features embedded with them, to increased effect.

Lesson Participant Interactions

Another helpful topic to explore is to examine more specific patterns of learner-to-learner and teacher-to-learner(s) interactions in the classroom. Who speaks to whom, how often, in what sequence, and for how long? How are speaking turns distributed? Is the teacher the only one who controls their distribution? How are topics and shifts in topic development introduced? What are some of the ways in which learners take the floor as speakers in the midst of classroom communications? Are there learners who are relatively more or less participatory during particular lesson phases? Do patterns of communication in the classroom provide opportunities for learners to take the initiative?

Teacher decision making

Acts of language teaching spring from sources within us that include our cognitive and emotional responses to external classroom events. Because all of us depend upon knowledge, values, and beliefs about teaching and learning in order to function as teachers in the classroom, our internal understandings and expectations contribute to our teaching decisions and behaviors.

Specialists sketch an intriguing territory of teacher decision making which Richards and Lockhart (1994) divide into pre-, during-, and post-lesson decisions.

Before a lesson can be taught it must be planned. Decisions at this stage are called *planning decisions*. During the lesson itself, another level of decision making is involved. The teacher has to make on-the-spot decisions concerning different aspects of the lesson, many of which may not have been planned. These are known as *interactive decisions*. After the lesson, the teacher must make decisions about its effectiveness and what the follow-up to the lesson will be. These are known as *evaluative decisions*.

Planning decisions

Planning decisions are made after a process of reflection (Neely, 1986), during which the teacher has to consider questions such as the following:

1. What do I want my students to learn from this lesson?
2. Why should I teach this lesson?
3. How well do I understand the content of the lesson?
4. What activities will be included in the lesson?
5. How will the lesson connect to what students already know?
6. How much time will I need for each activity?
7. How will I organize the lesson into stages or sections?
8. How will I begin and conclude the lesson?
9. Is the lesson going to be too easy/difficult for this class?
10. How will I deal with different student ability levels in the class?
11. What attention do I need to give the other students while I'm working with this small group?
12. What students have special needs that should be attended to during the lesson?
13. How will I check on student understanding?

14. What role will I take on during this lesson?
15. What discipline and management techniques will I incorporate?
16. What grouping arrangements will I use?
17. How will I handle interruptions to limit interference in this lesson?
18. What are my alternative plans if problems arise with some aspect of the lesson?
19. What will I do if I have too little or too much time?

Interactive decisions

Although planning decisions may form the starting point of a lesson, they are not the sole determinant of what happens during a lesson. Lessons are dynamic in nature, to some extent unpredictable, and characterized by constant change. Teachers therefore have to continuously make decisions that are appropriate to the specific dynamics of the lesson they are teaching. These kinds of decisions are called interactive decisions.

The ability to make appropriate interactive decisions is clearly an essential teaching skill, since interactive decisions enable teachers to assess students' response to teaching and to modify their instruction in order to provide optimal support for learning. A teacher whose teaching is guided solely by a lesson plan and who ignores the interactional dynamics of the teaching-learning process is hence less likely to be able to respond to students' needs.

There are a number of components to an interactive decision:

1. monitoring one's teaching and evaluating what is happening at a particular point in the lesson;
2. recognizing that a number of different courses of action are possible;
3. selecting a particular course of action;
4. evaluating the consequences of the choice.

The ability to monitor one's own instruction and evaluate it in terms of its appropriateness within a specific and immediate context is central to interactive decision making. It involves observing a lesson as it proceeds and asking questions of the following kind:

1. Do the students understand this? Are my instructions clear and understood?
2. Do I need to increase student involvement in this activity?
3. Is this too difficult for the students?
4. Should I try teaching this a different way?
5. Is this taking too much time?
6. Is this activity going as planned?
7. How can I get the students' attention?
8. Do students need more information?
9. Do I need to improve accuracy on this task?
10. Is this relevant to the aims of the lesson?
11. Do students have the vocabulary they need in order to do this task?
12. Is this teaching students something that they really need to know?

13. Am I teaching too much rather than letting the learners work it out for themselves?

In monitoring and evaluating his or her own teaching, the teacher may decide:

1. that the lesson is proceeding satisfactorily and let the lesson continue, or
2. that some sort of intervention is necessary in order to respond to a problem that has been identified.

In the case of during lesson decisions, teachers have very little time to follow through on what they decide to do since the process unfolds in collaboration with—and in front of—a group of learners. At such moments, a teacher's decisions may seem nearly instantaneous although they are informed by the teacher's background and previous experiences.

Evaluative decisions

Evaluative decisions are those which a teacher makes after a lesson has been taught. They arise from asking the following kinds of questions about a lesson:

1. Was this lesson successful? Why or why not?
2. What were the main strengths and weaknesses of the lesson?
3. Did the students learn what they were intended to learn?
4. What did the students get out of the lesson?
5. Did the lesson address the students' needs?
6. Was the lesson at an appropriate level of difficulty?
7. Were all students involved in the lesson?
8. Did the lesson arouse students' interest in the subject matter?
9. Did I do sufficient preparation for the lesson?
10. Do I need to re-teach any aspect of the lesson?
11. What would be a suitable follow-up to the lesson?
12. Should I have employed alternative teaching strategies?
13. Will I teach the material in the same way next time?

The study illustrates that as teachers gain experience in teaching and develop a deeper conceptualization of teaching, the criteria they use for evaluating teaching change to reflect their new assumptions, beliefs, and levels of awareness. Richards et al. (1992) also found that the evaluative decisions the teachers made provided input to planning decisions that they make on subsequent occasions. Hence, planning, interactive, and evaluative decisions are interconnected.

Reflection Break #2

Generate a list of topics related to your own teaching that you think would be worth learning more about See if you can come up with at least four examples not mentioned in the preceding section. Once your list is complete, compare it to that of one or more other language teacher (s). How might you set about increasing your understanding of at least some of the topics of interest to you!

Communication patterns in classrooms, lesson participant interactions, and teacher decisions making are just a few of the topics often explored by reflective teachers. A more complete listing would include learning to identify and explore:

1. the teacher's ways of giving instructions, responding to students' errors, providing feedback, using language, introducing new teaching strategies, encouraging language use beyond the classroom, identifying and attending to learners' needs, working with reluctant learners, responding to their errors;
2. learners' ways of requesting clarifications, responding to feedback, applying knowledge, using language, interacting with their peers, responding to changes in teaching, using learning strategies;
3. more general topics such as the affective climate of the classroom, debilitative and facilitative anxiety, cultural considerations, the instructional environment, the physical setup of the classroom, textbooks and other resources, student-generated materials, resources beyond the classroom.

The above list illustrates the kinds of topics that all language teachers are interested in learning more about but that reflective teachers take deliberate action to explore.

Tools for Reflective Teaching/Gathering Information

Just as there are many topics to be explored by reflective teachers, there are also many different ways to gather information. Figure 9. 3 depicts a more comprehensive listing of some of the major tools reflective teachers use.

Figure 9. 3 Some tools of reflective teaching: Ways of gathering information

- Formative feedback from learners
  - Five-minute papers
  - Teacher assessment surveys
  - Questionnaires
  - Dialogue journals
  - Written assessments
  - Student focus groups
- Formative feedback from other teachers
  - Peer collaborations (Murphy, 1992)
  - "Case" interviews
  - Field notes and classroom ethnographies
  - Dialogue with a supervisor (Master, 1983)
  - Observation schedules
  - Score charts
  - Classroom observation (Wajnryb, 1992)

Continued

■ Self-generated sources of information
Retrospective field notes
Teaching journals and teaching logs
Classroom diagrams and maps
Lesson plans and lesson reporting
Audio recordings
Video recordings
Transcript analysis
Protocol analysis
Stimulus recall
■ Course descriptions
■ Summative feedback from learners at the end of the course
■ Action research

Teachers use different tools to access different sorts of information. By combining two or more tools over the span of an entire course, a teacher gains access to alternative vantage points.

Expanding on Figure 9.3, Murphey (2006) discusses five tools that should be especially useful to teachers interested in becoming more involved in processes and procedures of reflective teaching. These tools are: five-minute papers, formative teacher assessment surveys, student focus groups, retrospective field notes, and formative feedback from peers.

Five-Minute Papers

Regular use of five-minute papers is a direct way of finding out how learners are perceiving and responding to our efforts as teachers. A few minutes before the end of the lesson, the teacher asks everyone to take out a sheet of paper and to write responses to one or two open-ended prompts such as:

1. What is the one thing you are likely to remember from today's class?
2. What was the most confusing concept we covered?
3. Is there anything you would like to know more about?
4. Is there anything you think I should be doing differently?

Learner responses to such questions are especially useful if the teacher emphasizes that their purpose is to provide formative feedback on how the course is going. In many ELT courses teachers are able to ask students to compose five-minute papers in English. In settings where it is possible, students might be given the option of writing five-minute papers in their first language(s). Though five-minute papers take time away from the regular part of a lesson, using them at the end of class can better inform a teacher's post-lesson decisions. When introducing them for the first time, Murphey explains to students that:

1. Their names should not appear on their papers (their writings will be kept in confidence).

2. When reading the papers I will *not* be looking at things like grammar, spelling, or vocabulary choice but only for the ideas they convey.
3. As their teacher I will be reading for the purpose of improving my teaching in the course and not to evaluate their progress.

Invariably, Murphey finds something of value in what students have to say. He occasionally asks a colleague to read the papers first, and then discuss with him the "gist of students" comments. Involving someone else is a small step toward gaining access to an outside perspective on his work. As well as providing an opportunity to talk about his teaching with another teacher, it helps to ensure he will be responsive to what students have to say.

In courses that meet two or three times a week, once every two or three weeks is often enough. Using them wisely can serve as vivid reminders to students that their responses to the course are valued and given serious attention.

Formative Teacher Assessment Surveys

A complement to five-minute papers is to schedule several surveys of students' perceptions of how well the course is going. These might be included in the course syllabus on the first day of class so students will know from the start that their impressions will be valued, when their impressions will be solicited, and what the survey will include. Some advantages of formative assessment surveys are that they can be clearly structured in advance, it is easy to keep students' comments anonymous, a lot of information can be gathered at one time, and the procedure may be carried out at regular intervals. One option is to implement such surveys three times during the span of an entire course.

The following is an illustration of a formative teacher assessment survey Murphey (2006) included in the syllabus for a high-intermediate level ESL Oral Communication course he offers.

Formative Feedback (1st of 3) to the Instructor

Please complete and place in a stack on the front desk at the end of our 8th day of class, Wednesday, September ×× (Alternatively you are welcome to place it in my mailbox in the main office).

Directions: Please do not sign your name. We are three weeks into the course. This is a time for some formative feedback from you as a course participant. You are welcome to use both sides of this page.

Thanks.

1. What are some features of the course that you think are working out pretty well (features you would like to see continued for the remainder of the course)?
2. What are some possible changes you would like to see incorporated into the course from this point forward?

Another option is to follow similar procedures but to use a format that involves less writing by providing a list of items to which students can respond on an easily accessible scale, such as:

□Yes, I agree. □I agree somewhat. □No, I do not agree.

Illustrations of sample items to include are:

In general, the textbooks, materials, and assignments in this course:

1. are interesting and useful;
2. are at the right level;
3. help me to practice and improve my language skills;
4. require the right amount of homework;

In general, the teacher of this course:

1. presents well-organized lessons;
2. speaks in a way that is clear and easy to understand;
3. is knowledgeable about the subjects we cover;
4. answers my questions well;
5. grades assignments and tests fairly;
6. makes good use of class time;
7. returns work (that I hand in) on time;
8. gives me individual help when I need it (or when I ask for it);
9. encourages me to do my best relates well to students;
10. provides appropriate opportunities for me to participate in class;

Reflection Break #3

Have you ever had an opportunity to receive learner feedback on your teaching! If so, what did you learn from the experience? If not, do you think such sources of information might be useful? Would you expect the quality of learner feedback to vary depending upon learners' cultural backgrounds! If so, what could you do to compensate for cultural differences?

A final survey item might ask: *If you were in a conversation with a friend, would you recommend taking a course from this teacher? Why or why not?*

Student Focus Groups

The use of student focus groups is a simple idea, yet one underutilized in our field. It is more involved than five-minute papers or student surveys and takes careful planning. In language teaching, student focus groups engage either all members of a class or a subset of learners in a discussion of how a course is going. Either the classroom teacher or a colleague consultant may serve as focus group discussion leader. Some options are as follows.

Make arrangements for a colleague you trust, and with whom you have a constructive working relationship, to serve as the focus group facilitator. Students focus groups work best when they are not being used for formal evaluative purposes.

Invite your colleague to visit the class for a lesson during which you will not be present but for which students have been prepared in advance. As agreed upon with the class, your colleague's role is to lead the whole class in a discussion of broad topics such as:

1. How is the course going?
2. What do you like about the course (or the teacher)?

3. What are your least favorite things?
4. Does the course textbook—or other instructional material—seem helpful?
5. What are some characteristics of the teacher's instructional style that work well?
6. What are some characteristics you find to be less helpful?
7. Do assessment procedures seem fair?
8. What are some of the ways in which the course might be improved?

The facilitator could distribute a handout listing the above questions or he or she might use a copy of the teacher assessment survey from the preceding section. Students can then pick and choose their preferred topics for discussion. Prior to the day of the focus group and at the start of the actual discussion, students need to be assured that their comments will be kept in confidence. The facilitator's role is to listen carefully and empathetically, keep the discussion on track, and take notes (when possible) on what students have to say.

When the class is finished, the facilitator composes a written report (not to be used for formal evaluation purposes) that provides a synopsis for the teacher of the students' suggestions for the course. No names should appear in the report; it needs to be phrased to protect students' identities. Once it is completed, the visiting colleague gives the classroom teacher a copy and makes arrangements to discuss what took place.

A very effective situation for those interested in student focus groups is to build toward a reciprocal peer arrangement in which two teachers may serve as the discussion facilitator for each other's classes. Ideally, a mutually supportive collaboration evolves between teachers that could develop over time. One modification to the focus groups is to avoid involving the whole class, but to discuss the focus group process with them and ask for only a few members of the class (e. g., 20-25 percent) to volunteer to participate. In this option, students choose whether to participate. Many language teachers find the kind of information revealed as a result of student focus groups to be tremendously helpful for fine-tuning their planning decisions and increasing awareness of their strengths as well as areas they could improve.

Retrospective Field Notes

The word *retrospective* signals that such field notes are not generated during lessons but only after a lesson has finished. Since acts of teaching are complex and keep teachers incredibly busy, a teacher's field notes ideally should be generated immediately following the lesson. It takes discipline to compose retrospective field notes on a regular basis and it is important to start writing soon after the end of a class (for example, within 30-60 minutes). The activity is

> **Reflection Break #4**
>
> Collaborate with someone else (a pre- or in-service teacher) to produce a list of five to eight questions you could use as prompts for composing retrospective field notes. Plan them so each writing prompt targets different dimensions of classroom teaching and learning.

similar to keeping a personal journal or diary, with the difference that retrospective field notes focus on course-related events.

General guidelines are to try to keep track of classroom issues that seem relevant to the lesson recently completed and to treat field notes as an ethnographer treats raw data. Reflective teachers using this procedure save their notes over time, review them on a regular basis, and look for what their notes may reveal about recurring patterns. After you have reworked your notes by deleting or modifying anything that might be personally uncomfortable, a colleague might be invited to read them and discuss whatever concerns you about a course.

Retrospective field notes can become a valuable source of information about one's understandings and a richly textured record of one's explanations of teaching over time. Some general ways to frame field notes are to respond to questions about yourself as a teacher, the teaching process, students in the class, the learning process, or anything tied to the dynamics of the lesson itself.

Formative Feedback from Peers

A classic way of gaining access to formative feedback is to invite a peer that is, another language teacher whose opinion you respect—to visit one or more of your classes. For purposes of reflective teaching, such visits should be planned to be different from the kinds of observations carried out by supervisors (Murphy, 1992).

In setting up a peer's non-supervisory visit to the classroom, it is important to discuss and clarify the visitor's purpose in advance. Fanselow (1988) points out that the primary purpose for observing another person teach is to gather descriptive information on what takes place during the lesson. A staring point to prepare for a classroom visit from a peer is for both parties to be aware of the importance of staying attentive, interested in the lesson, and open-minded. Though some visitors may be able to gather useful information by merely observing what takes place, visitor's recollections are more reliable and tend to be more helpful as starting points for discussion once the lesson is over if the visitor has written things down.

Two Underlying Concerns

It is important to acknowledge two fundamental challenges facing those interested in processes of reflective teaching: the search for multiple perspectives, and the question of learner involvement.

The Search for Multiple Perspectives

The search for multiple perspectives relates to two essential stages of reflective teaching: gathering information (the data collection stage) and making sense of what we find (the interpretation stage).

In the first stage, reflective teachers find ways of gathering information on teaching and learning that include outsider perspectives. As a result of our immersion within the process of language teaching, we are often too close to recognize our strengths and weaknesses. By way of illustration, most of us are somewhat surprised the first time we view a video recording of our teaching. In response to a video recording, we might notice ourselves thinking such things as:

"Oh, my voice sounds terrible! That's not what I sound like."

"Is that what I really look like?"

"Why am I walking around so much (or so little)?"

"No wonder students are having trouble following my directions; I really wasn't very clear."

A video recording of teaching-in-action brings to the fore evidence of how others may view us. Recordings sometimes surprise us because they are serving as an *estrangement* device. An estrangement device is any tool we might use to gain an outsider's perspective on what we may be doing in the classroom. Anthropologists refer to such a vantage point as an *etic* perspective (an outsider's view).

To complement the inclusion of etic perspectives within the reflective teaching process, it is useful to gather information from course participants as well. As participants in the process, learners' vantage points represent *emic* perspectives. Just as an anthropologist might search for ways to learn about the perceptions and understandings of the members of another culture, reflective teachers depend upon learners' perceptions and understandings. Freeman (1998) explains the importance of the search for multiple perspectives succinctly: etic perspectives provide us with information on "what outsiders see" while emic perspectives provide information on "what insiders know." Figure 9.4 summarizes etic versus emic distinctions that we can apply to either the collection or examination of classroom information.

Figure 9.4 Continuum of vantage points for either the collection or interpretation of information on teaching-learning processes

etic	**etic**
outsider's view	insider's view
participant understandings	consultant understandings
what outsiders see	what insiders know
teacher-peers' and colleagues' perceptions	classroom teacher' and learners' perceptions

The need for multiple perspectives challenges reflective teachers to find ways of gathering information on teaching-learning processes not only through their own perceptions and understandings, but also through those of learners who are participating in the course, and through colleagues' perceptions.

The Question of Learner Involvement

In connection with emic perspectives, a second set of questions for reflective teachers to ask is, "Do I want to involve learners in my efforts as a reflective teacher, and if so, to what degree?" There are many ways to collect information about what goes on within courses we teach. A distinction we can make is between ways that are "less intrusive" as opposed to those that are relatively "more intrusive" with respect to their potential impacts on learners' classroom experiences. Less intrusive means of gathering information depend upon little or no involvement from learners. Teachers interested in less intrusive means do their best to avoid direct impact on inside-the-classroom events. For instance, a teacher might gather information about teaching on a daily basis but only after the completion of individual lessons. To do so, some teachers keep private teaching journals of which learners remain unaware. Other non-intrusive options are, after a lesson has ended, to compose field notes of what happened inside the classroom only, or to look back on completed lessons through other retrospective procedures such as "lesson reporting." (A lesson report is similar to a lesson plan but with the following twist: lesson reports are generated following, not preceding, a lesson. By composing, saving, and reviewing them over time, a teacher is able to produce a substantive record of teaching that can be shared and discussed with others).

An alternative approach to lesson reporting is simply for the teacher to spend a few minutes after a lesson writing answers to questions such as the following:

1. What were the main goals of the lesson?
2. What did the learners actually learn in the lesson?
3. What teaching procedures did I use?
4. What problems did I encounter and how did I deal with them?
5. What were the most effective parts of the lesson?
6. What were the least effective parts?
7. Would I do anything differently if I taught the lesson again?

Through adoption of such nonintrusive procedures, it is possible for teachers to gain considerable information about the teaching process without involving learners.

Even with less intrusive procedures, reflective teachers are able to incorporate multiple perspectives into their efforts by inviting colleagues whose opinions they respect to review and discuss whatever information the teacher is able to gather from the classroom. Two or more teachers might collaborate to review a video or audio recording of teaching, transcripts of lesson segments, journal entries, samples of student work, or students' responses to a survey questionnaire on how the course is going. Some of these options feature learner participation to some degree. A teacher might, for example, arrange for a lesson to be videotaped for later review. If a video camera is in the room, the teacher has already taken a step in the direction of involving learners. The presence of any recording device in a classroom inevitably has some impact on lesson events. Of course, as a classroom teacher, you can lessen such impacts by taking steps ahead of time to familiarize students with whatever might be the procedure you would like to follow. You can: (1) discuss what you are planning to do, (2) ask for learners' permissions, (3) take time at an earlier point in the course to introduce whatever the procedure or recording device might be, and/or (4) include it as a part of normal classroom routine.

In the example of video cameras, some suggestions are to work with as small a camera as possible, position it in the back of the room—or at least out of students' direct lines of vision—

and involve one or more members of the class in its operation. Learners may perceive a teacher's use of recording equipment as perfectly normal and part of what they have already come to anticipate from the course. The point is to be aware of the potential impacts of such procedures and to make informed decisions on what you, your colleagues, and your students might consider to be (un)acceptable levels of learner involvement in reflective teaching procedures.

Figure 9. 5 provides a synopsis of several issues by featuring a matrix of two intersecting continua for gathering information on teaching.

Figure 9. 5　Two-way matrix for gathering information

Perspective	Degree of Intrusive	
	More Intrusive	Less Intrusive
ETIC	(A) * videotaping (video + audio) * video- (or audio-) taping for the first time * large, bulky video camera at the front of the room * learners participate in analyzing video recordings of lessons during class time * trained observer inside the classroom * in-class observer is someone unknown to learners * in-class observer takes notes or completes an observation schedule live in the classroom * a supervisor gathers information on teaching for formal assessment-of-teaching purposes	(B) * audiotaping (only) * video- (or audio-) taping for the fifth time * camera is small or out of sight * learners participate in analyzing video recordings of lessons only after a course has ended * trained observer watches video recording of lesson * in-class observer is someone learners know and are comfortable with * in-class observer watches and listens, tries to blend into the background, composes field notes only after the lesson has ended * teacher gathers information on teaching through self-initiated collaborations with peers/colleagues
EMIC	(C) * students compose journals in which they discuss their experiences as learners in the course and how they perceive the course * teacher conducts student focus groups * frequent student interviews * whole class, inside the classroom discussions of learners' perceptions and preferences while the course is in process * student focus group with whole class participating * teacher serves as focus group facilitator * students complete several instructor assessment forms at different points in the course (formative) * five-minute papers, frequent and on a regular basis * stimulated recall while the course is in process * teacher and learners collaborate to gather information on the teaching-learning process together	(D) * teacher keeps a diary or personal journal * teacher engages in lesson reporting * a third party conducts student focus groups in which learners' comments are kept anonymous * infrequent student interviews * outside-of-class discussions with individual learners of their perceptions and preferences while the course is in process * student focus group with only some class members participating * teacher-colleague serves as focus group facilitator * students complete a single end-of-term instructor assessment form (summative) * transcripts generated for discourse analysis of lesson events * stimulated recall only after the course is over * teacher gathers information on teaching while working alone [may collaborate with colleague(s)]

Procedures in quadrant A combine outsiders' perspectives with relatively more intrusive means of gathering information on teaching. Quadrant D is just the opposite, since these procedures tap into insiders' perspectives through somewhat less intrusive means. Quadrant B is weighted toward outsider perspectives through less intrusive means. With the procedures in quadrant C, the teacher involves course participants in sharing what they think about the course in ways that may impact students' learning experiences to varying degrees.

Teachers might set as a professional development goal exploring one or more of the options listed in each of its four quadrants.

As we continue to learn more about these and other pathways to reflective teaching, as well as the particular topics, we would like to explore within the language courses we teach, this chapter can remind us of the rewards of self-discovery, the importance of multiple perspectives, and the potentially facilitating impacts of learners' and colleagues' contributions to our efforts.

Suggested Activities

Make arrangements to consult two or more practicing language teachers. Ask if they have ever heard of traditions such as reflective or exploratory teaching. (Be aware that some teachers use different terms and phrases for similar concepts). Try to discover if they have ever been involved in such efforts. If they have, gather as much information as you can on how their efforts have made a difference in their teaching. If they have not, try to find out what might be some of the other things they do to grow and develop as language teachers.

For this activity you need to place yourself in the position of a language learner. If you had a language teacher who was interested in reflective teaching, how would you want the teacher to involve you in such efforts? Make a list of the kinds of things you would be willing to do. Also, think of a specific language class you either are teaching now or some other course in which you were once a language learner. From the perspective of a learner in that course, what would be some of the topics you think would be worthy ones for the teacher to explore? As a learner in the class, what contributions would you be willing to make?

Exercises, Questions and Tasks

1. Multiple Choices.

(1) Which of the following is more likely to promote reflective teaching?

A. Attending conferences.

B. Gaining teaching experience.

C. Thinking about and discussing published scholarship.

D. Accessing information and inspiration about efforts in language classrooms.

(2) Which one is not a purpose of reflective teaching?

A. Enhance the quality of learning opportunities for students.

B. Enhance the quantity of learning opportunities for students.

C. Expand one's repertoire of strategic options as a language teacher.

D. Expand one's understanding of the teaching-learning process.

(3) Those interested in reflective teaching take steps working to improve their abilities to ________.

A. make informal changes in teaching

B. answer some questions tied to one's teaching

C. identify anything puzzling about the teaching-learning process

D. keep changing in teaching-learning behaviors and responses

(4) Reflective teaching is an approach to second language classroom instruction in which teachers will not ________.

A. collect data for their teaching

B. examine their attitudes, beliefs, assumptions

C. design a lot of accuracy practices

D. use the information obtained as a basis for critical reflection

(5) Which of the following is not likely to be a basic assumption posited by reflective teachers?

A. The teacher knows much of what happens in teaching.

B. Critical reflection can trigger a deeper understanding of teaching.

C. An informed teacher has an extensive knowledge base about teaching.

D. Much can be learned about teaching through self-inquiry.

(6) The information obtained through the process of exploring teaching cannot ________.

A. serve as a basis for self-evaluation

B. lead to a richer conceptualization of teaching

C. help achieve a better understanding of one's own assumptions about teaching

D. guarantee professional development

(7) Which of the following might not be beneficial for reflective teachers gathering information with video support?

A. better control the class

B. examine recurring features within the instructional routine

C. consider ways of manipulating lesson segments

D. closely review their ways of teaching

(8) Which of the following questions might not be good to examine more specific patterns of interactions in the classroom?

A. How are speaking turns distributed?

B. How are topics and shifts in topic development introduced?

C. Do patterns of communication in the classroom provide opportunities for learners to take the initiative?

D. What are some of the ways in which teachers take the floor as speakers in the midst of classroom communications?

(9) During lessons, a teacher's decisions may seem nearly ________.

A. spontaneous B. instantaneous
C. impulsive D. sensible

(10) Which one of the following might not be true of regular use of five-minute papers?

A. A teacher can ask students to compose them after each class.
B. Students can provide formative feedback on how the course is going.
C. It can better inform a teacher's post-lesson decisions.
D. It is a direct way of finding out how learners are perceiving and responding to our efforts as teachers.

2. Fill in each blank with an appropriate word.

(1) A central reason to be interested in reflective teaching "is to gain ________ of our teaching beliefs and practices" and to learn "to see teaching differently."

(2) Three key attitudes are necessary in order for teachers to be reflective: open-mindedness, responsibility, and ________.

(3) Early stages of reflective teaching begin with a classroom teacher's desire to better understand the ________ of a single language course.

(4) Acts of language teaching spring from sources within us that include our ________ and emotional responses to external classroom events.

(5) A survey early in the course serves as a window into students' ________ responses to the course.

3. Mark "True" or "False" for the following statements and explain why.

(1) Communications between everyone present in the classroom may influence teaching and learning processes.

(2) Using Five-Minute Papers wisely can serve as vivid reminders to students that their responses to the course are valued and given serious attention.

(3) As participants in the process, learners' vantage points represent etic perspec-tives.

(4) Through adoption of intrusive procedures, it is possible for teachers to gain considerable information about the teaching process without involving learn ers.

(5) The primary purpose for observing another person teach is to gather descriptive information on what takes place during the lesson.

(6) The presence of any recording device in a classroom has no impact on lesson events.

(7) Teachers interested in intrusive means do their best to avoid direct impact on inside-the-classroom events.

(8) With less intrusive procedures, reflective teachers are able to incorporate multiple perspectives into their efforts to gather from the classroom.

(9) Awareness is a necessary condition for professional development to occur.

(10) According to Freeman, what the traditional knowledge transmission model of teacher education addresses is about skills and knowledge, but not about awareness and our attitudes.

4. Discuss the following questions.

(1) What would you do if you have finished a lesson only to find your mind racing with thoughts about it?

(2) How does a reflective teacher better understand how communication patterns in their language classrooms influence teaching and learning processes?

(3) How important are the three attitudes identified by Dewey (1933) for reflective teaching? Circle the number that best represents your view of each construct:

	Not Important			Very Important	
Open-mindedness	1	2	3	4	5
Responsibility	1	2	3	4	5
Wholeheartedness	1	2	3	4	5

Now assess the extent to which you think you possess these attitudes:

	Not All			To a Great Extent	
Open-mindedness	1	2	3	4	5
Responsibility	1	2	3	4	5
Wholeheartedness	1	2	3	4	5

If you compare the same attribute on the two scales above (e. g. , responsibility as rated on the two scales), how do your judgments of the importance of these traits match up with your assessment of these traits as part of your own attitudes?

(4) If you feel you would like to utilize some of the dimensions more fully in Table 9. 2, which one(s) would you like to address? How would you begin to do so?

(5) Should classroom tasks in fact relate to the world outside the classroom?

Suggested Readings

MURPHY J M, 2006. Reflective teaching in ELT[M]// CELCE-MURCIA M. Teaching English as a second or foreign language[M]. Beijing: Foreign Language Teaching and Research Press, 499-514.

BAILEY K M, CURTIS A, NUNAN D. 2009. Pursuing professional development: The self as source[M]. Beijing: Foreign Language Teaching and Research Press.

RICHARDS J C, LOCKHART C, 2000. Reflective teaching in second language classrooms[M]. Beijing: People's Education Press.

FARRELL T S C, 2013. Reflective practice: reawakening your passion for teaching[M]. Beijing: Foreign Language Teaching and Research Press.

WRIGHT T, BEAUMONT M, 2023. Experiences of second language teacher education[M]. Beijing: Foreign Language Teaching and Research Press.

APPENDIX 1

Reflection Questions

Questions about your teaching

1. What did you set out to teach?
2. Were you able to accomplish your goals?
3. What teaching materials did you use? How effective were they?
4. What techniques did you use?
5. What grouping arrangements did you use?
6. Was your lesson teacher dominated?
7. What kind of teacher-student interaction occurred?
8. Did anything amusing or unusual occur?
9. Did you have any problems with the lesson?
10. Did you do anything differently than usual?
11. What kinds of decision making did you employ?
12. Did you depart from your lesson plan? If so, why? Did the change make things better or worse?
13. What was the main accomplishment of the lesson?
14. Which parts of the lesson were most successful?
15. Which parts of the lesson were least successful?
16. Would you teach the lesson differently if you taught it again?
17. Was your philosophy of teaching reflected in the lesson?
18. Did you discover anything new about your teaching?
19. What changes do you think you should make in your teaching?

Questions about the students

1. Did you teach all your students today?
2. Did students contribute actively to the lesson?
3. How did you respond to different students' needs?

4. Were students challenged by the lesson?
5. What do you think students really learned from the lesson?
6. What did they like most about the lesson?
7. What didn't they respond well to?

Questions to ask yourself as a language teacher

1. What is the source of my ideas about language teaching?
2. Where am I in my professional development?
3. How am I developing as a language teacher?
4. What are my strengths as a language teacher?
5. What are my limitations at present?
6. Are there any contradictions in my teaching?
7. How can I improve my language teaching?
8. How am I helping my students?
9. What satisfaction does language teaching give me?

REFERENCES

ALLWRIGHT R L, 1977. Language learning through communication practice[J]. ELT Documents, 76(3): 2 - 14.

ABRAHAM R, VANN R, 1987. Strategies of two language learners: a case study[M]// WENDEN A, RUBIN J. Learner strategies in language learning. Englewood Cliffs, N. J.: Prentice Hall.

ALLWRIGHT D, 1990. Autonomy in language pedagogy. (CRILE Working Paper No. 6.) [M]. Lancaster, UK: Centre for Research in Education, University of Lancaster.

ALPTEKIN C, ATAKAN S, 1990. Field dependence-independence and hemisphericity as variables in L2 achievements[J]. Second Language Research, 6(2): 139 - 149.

ANDERSON R C, PICHERT J W, GOETZ E T, et al., 1976. Instantiation of general terms [J]. Journal of Verbal Learning and Verbal Behavior, 15(6): 667 - 679.

ANDERSON R C, SHIFFRIN Z, 1980. The meaning of words in context[M]// SPIRO R J, BRUCE B C, BREWER W F. In Theoretical issues in reading comprehension. Hillsdale, N. J.: Erlbaum.

ASHER J, 1977. Learning another language through actions: The complete teacher's guide book [M]. Los Gatos, Calif: Sky Oaks Productions.

ASHER J, KUSUDO J A, DE LA TORRE R, 1974. Learning a second language through commands: The second field test[J]. The Modern Language Journal, 58(1): 24 - 32.

ASHER J J, GARCIA R, 1969. The optimal age to learn a foreign language[J]. Modem Language Journal, 53(5): 33 - 41.

AUSTIN J L, 1962. How to do things with words[M]. Oxford: Oxford University Press.

AUSTIN J L, 1970. Philosophical papers[M]. Oxford: Oxford Paperbacks.

AUSUBEL D, 1968. Educational psychology: A cognitive view[M]. New York: Holt, Rinehart, and Winston.

AUSUBEL D, NOVAK J D, HANESIAN H, 1978. Educational psychology: A cognitive view [M]. 2nd ed. New York: Holt, Rinehart, and Winston. (Reprinted by Werbel and Peck, 1986)

BACON S, 1987. Differentiated cognitive style and oral performance[M]// VANPATTEN B,

DVORAK T R, LEE J F. Foreign language learning: A research perspective. Rowley, MA: Newbury House.

BANCROFT W J, 1972. The psychology of suggestopedia or learning without stress[J]. The Educational Courier (February): 16 - 19.

BARCELOS A, 2003. Researching beliefs about SLA: a critical review[M]// KALAJA P, BARCELOS A. Beliefs about SLA: New Research Approaches. Dordrecht: Kluwer.

BARDOVI-HARLIG, K, 2013. Developing L2 pragmatics[J]. Language Learning, 63 suppl. 1, 68 - 86.

BARTLETT F C, 1932. Remembering: A Study in Experimental and Social Psychology[M]. Cambridge: Cambridge University Press. (Reprinted, 1950)

BECKER A L, 1984. Toward a post-structuralist view of language learning[M]// GUIORA A Z. An epistemology for the language sciences. Michigan: Wayne State University Press.

BECKNER C, BLYTHE R, BYBEE J, et al., 2009. Language is a complex adaptive system: Position paper[J]. Language Learning, 59 (Suppl. 1): 1 - 26.

BEEBE L, 1980. Measuring the use of communication strategies[M]// SCARCELLA R, KRASHEN, S. Research in second language acquisition. Rowley, Mass.: Newbury House, 173 - 181.

BELL J, BURNABY B, 1984. A handbook for ESL literacy[M]. Toronto: Ontario Institute for Studies in Education.

BELZ J A, THORNE S L, 2005. Internet-mediated intercultural foreign language education [M]. Cengage Learning.

BENSON P, REINDERS H, 2011. Beyond the language classroom[M]. New York: Palgrave Macmillan.

BERNS M, 1990. Contexts of Competence[M]. London: Pergamon.

BIGGS J, TELFER R, 1987. The process of learning[M]. 2nd ed. Sydney: Prentice-Hall.

BIRCH G J, 1992. Language learning case study approach to second language teacher education [M]// Flowerdew J, Brock M N, Hsia S. Perspectives on second language teacher education. Hong Kong: City Polytechnic of Hong Kong, 283 - 294.

BLOCK D, 2014. Social class in applied linguistics[M]. New York: Routledge.

BLOOMFIELD L, 1933. Language[M]. New York: Holt.

BREEN M, CANDLIN C N, 1980. The essentials of a communicative curriculum in language teaching[J]. Applied Linguistics, 1(2): 89 - 112.

BREEN M, 1984. Process syllabuses for the language classroom[M]// BRUMFIT C. General English syllabus design. Oxford: Pergamon.

BRONFENBRENNER, U. 1979. The ecology of human development: Experiments by nature and design[M]. Cambridge, MA: Harvard University Press.

BROOKS, N. 1964. Language and language learning: Theory and practice[M]. 2nd ed. New York: Harcourt Brace.

BROWN H, 1980. Principles of language learning and teaching[M]. Englewood Cliffs: Prentice

Hall.

BROWN P, LEVINSON S, 1978. Universals in language usage[M]// Goody E N. Questions and Politeness. Cambridge: Cambridge University Press.

BURSTALL C, JAMIESON M, COHEN S, et al., 1974. Primary French in the Balance[R]. Slough: NFER.

BYRNE D, 1976. Teaching Oral English[M]. London: Longman.

BYRNE D, 1978. Materials for language teaching: Interaction packages[M]. London: Modern English Publications.

CANALE M, SWAIN M, 1980. Theoretical bases of communicative approaches to second language teaching and testing[J]. Applied Linguistics, 1(1): 1-47.

CANDLIN C N, 1976. Communicative language teaching and the debt to pragmatics[M]// RAMEH C. 27th Round Table Meeting. Washington, D. C.: Georgetown University Press, 237-256.

CANDLIN C N, 1979. The status of pedagogical grammars[M]// BRUMFIT C, JOHNSON K. The communicative approach to language teaching. Oxford: Oxford University Press.

CARRELL P L, 1981. Culture-specific schemata in second-language comprehension[C]// OREM R, HASKELL J. Selected Papers from the Ninth Illinois TESOL/BE Annual Convention, the First Midwest TESOL Conference. Chicago, 123-132.

CARRELL P L, 1988. Some Causes of Text-Boundedness and Schema Interference in ESL Reading[M]// CARRELL P L, DEVINE J E, ESKEY D, 2006. Interactive approaches to second language reading Cambridge: Cambridge University Press, 101-113.

CARRELL P L, EISTERHOLD J, 1983. Schema theory and ESL reading pedagogy[J]. TESOL Quarterly, 17 (4): 553-573.

CARRELL P L, 1979. Indirect speech acts in ESL: Indirect answers[J]. On TESOL, 79: 297-307.

CARROLL J B, 1965. The contributions of psychological theory and educational research to the teaching of foreign languages[J]. The Modern Language Journal, 49(5): 273-281.

CARROLL J B, 1966a. The contributions of psychological theory and educational research to the teaching of foreign languages[M]// Valdman A. Trends in language teaching. New York: McGraw-Hill, 93-106.

CARROLL J B, 1966b. Research in foreign language teaching: The last five years[M]// Mead Jr. R G. Language teaching: Broader contexts. Northeast Conference Reports on the Teaching of Foreign Languages: Reports of the Working Committees. New York: MLA Materials Center, 12-42.

CARROLL J B, 1981. Twenty-five years of research on foreign language aptitude[M]// DILLER K C. Individual differences and universals in language learning. Rowley, MA: Newbury House, 83-118.

CARROLL S, 2001. Input and evidence: The raw material of second language acquisition[M]. Amsterdam: John Benjamins.

CHAN L, DÖRNYEI Z, HENRY A, 2015. Learner archetypes and signature dynamics in the language classroom: A retrodictive qualitative modelling approach to studying L2 motivation [M]// DÖRNYEI Z, MACINTYRE P, HENRY A. Motivational dynamics in language learning. Bristol: Multilingual Matters, 238 - 259.

CHAPELLE C, ROBERTS C, 1986. Ambiguity tolerance and field independence as predictors of proficiency in English as a second language[J]. Langrage Learning 36(1): 27 - 45.

CHOMSKY N, 1957. Syntactic structures[M]. The Hague: Mouton.

CHOMSKY N, 1959. A review of B. F. Skinner's verbal behavior[J]. Language, 35(1): 26 - 58.

CHOMSKY N, 1965. Aspects of the theory of syntax[M]. Cambridge, MA. : MIT Press.

CHOMSKY N, 1966. Linguistic theory. [M]// Allen P B, Van Buren P. Chomsky: Selected Readings. London: Oxford University Press. 152 - 159.

CHRISTISON M, 1997. An introduction to multiple intelligences theory and second language learning[M]// REID J. Understanding learning styles in the second language classroom. Englewood Cliffs, N. J. : Prentice Hall/Regents, 1 - 14.

CHRISTISON M, 1999. Multiple Intelligences: Teaching the whole student[J]. ESL Magazine 2(5): 10 - 13.

CLAXTON C, RALSON Y, 1978. Learning styles: Their impact on teaching and administration (AAHE-ERIC Higher Education Report No. 10) [R]. Washington, DC: American Association for Higher Education.

CLYNE D, 1991. The Bulletin Magazine[Z]. December.

CLYNE M, 1981. Culture and discourse structure[J]. Journal of Pragmatics, 5: 61 - 66.

COHEN A D, 1998. Strategies in learning and using a second language[M]. Essex, UK: Longman.

COHEN A D, WEAVER S J, 2006. Styles and strategies-based instruction: A teachers' guide [M]. Minneapolis, MN: Center for Advanced Research on Language Acquisition, University of Minnesota.

COLEMAN A, 1929. The teaching of modern foreign languages in the United States[M]. New York: Macmillan.

COOK V, 1986. Experimental approaches to second language acquisition[M]. Oxford: Oxford University Press.

CRONBACH L, 2002. Remaking the concept of aptitude: Extending the legacy of Richard E. Snow. Mahwah, NJ: Lawrence Erlbaum Associates.

CROOKES G, 1986. Task Classification: A cross-disciplinary review[R]. Technical Report No. 4. Honolulu: Center for Second Language Classroom Research.

CRYSTAL D, 1997. The Cambridge encyclopedia of language[M]. 2nd ed. Cambridge: Cambridge University Press.

CURRAN C A, 1972. Counseling-learning: A whole-person model for education[M]. New York: Grune and Stratton.

CURRAN C A, 1976. Counselinglearning in second languages[M]. Apple River, IL: Apple River Press.

DE BOT K, LOWIE W, VERSPOOR M, 2007. A dynamic systems theory approach to second language acquisition[J]. Bilingualism: Language and Cognition, 10(1): 7-21.

DE SWAAN A, 2001. Words of the world: The global language system[M]. Cambridge: Polity.

DECKER B C, 1983. Cultural diversity: Another element to recognize in learning styles[J]. National Association of Secondary School Principals Bulletin, 67(464): 43-48.

DEKEYSER R, 2015. Skill acquisition theory[M]// VANPATTEN B, WILLIAMS J. Theories in second language acquisition: An introduction. New York: Routledge, 94-112.

DEWEY J, 1933. How we think[M]. Madison, WI: University of Wisconsin Press.

DILLER K C, 1978. The language teaching controversy[M]. Rowley, MA.: Newbury House.

DIXON N M, 1985. The implementation of learning style information[J]. Lifelong Learning, 9(3): 16-18, 26-27.

DONALDSON M, 1978. Children's minds[M]. London: Fontana.

DÖRNYEI Z, 1998. Demotivation in foreign language learning[C]. Paper presented at the TESOL'98 Congress, Seattle, WA.

DÖRNYEI Z, 2001. Teaching and researching motivation[M]. Harlow, UK: Longman.

DÖRNYEI Z, 2005. The psychology of the language learner: Individual differences in second language acquisition[M]. Mahwah, NJ: Lawrence Erlbaum.

DÖRNYEI Z, KUBANYIOVA M, 2014. Motivating learners, motivating teachers: Building vision in the language classroom[M]. Cambridge: Cambridge University Press.

DÖRNYEI Z, 2009a. Individualdifferences: Interplay of learner characteristics and learning environment[J]. Language Learning, 59(1): 230-248.

DÖRNYEI Z, 2009b. The psychology of second language acquisition[M]. Oxford: Oxford University Press.

DULAY H, BURT M, KRASHEN S, 1982. Language two[M]. New York: Oxford University Press.

DURANTI A, GOODWIN C, 1992. Rethinking context: An introduction[M]// DURANTI A, GOODWIN C. Rethinking context: Language as an interactive phenomenon. Cambridge: Cambridge University Press, 1-42.

EDMONDSON W, 1983. Kann der Lehrer Fehler erzeugen? Uberlegungen zum Korrekturverhalten im Fremdsprachenunterricht[M]// HEID M. Kommunikation im Klassenzimmer und Fremdsprachenlernen. New Yorker Werkstattgespräch 1982. München: Goethe Institut.

ELLIS N C, WULFF S, 2015. Usage-based approaches to SLA[M]// VANPATTEN B, WILLIAMS J. Theories in second language acquisition: An introduction. New York: Routledge, 75-93.

ELLIS N C, LARSEN-FREEMAN D, 2009. Language as a complex adaptive system[M]. Oxford: Wiley-Blackwell.

ELLIS R, 1997. SLA research and language teaching [M]. Oxford: Oxford University Press.

ELLIS R, 2005. Instructed second language acquisition: A literature review[M]. Wellington: Ministry of Education, New Zealand.

ELLIS R, 2015. Understanding second language acquisition[M]. 2nd ed. Oxford: Oxford University Press.

ELLIS R, SHINTANI N, 2014. Exploring language pedagogy through second language acquisition research[M]. New York: Routledge.

ELLIS R, 2001. The metaphorical construction of second language learners[M]// BREEN M. Learner contributions to language learning: New directions in research. Harlow: Longman.

ELLIS R, ROBERTS C, 1987. Two approaches for investigating second language acquisition in context[M]// Ellis R. Second Language Acquisition in context. Englewood Cliffs, N. J.: Prentice-Hall International.

ELY C, 1986. An analysis of discomfort, risktaking, sociability, and motivation in the L2 classroom[J]. Language Learning, 36(1): 1 - 25.

ERVIN-TRIPP S, 1976. Is Sybil there? The structure of American English directives[J]. Language in Society, 5(1): 25 - 66.

EYSENCK S, CHAN J, 1982. A comparative study of personality in adults and children: Hong Kong vs England[J]. Personality and Individual Differences, 3(2): 153-160.

FANSELOW J, 1988. "Let's see": Contrasting conversations about teaching[J]. TESOL Quarterly 22(1): 113 - 130.

FARELL T S C, 2004. Reflective practice in action[M]. Thousand Oaks, CA: Corwin Press.

FARELL T S C, 2007. Reflective language teaching: From research to practice[M]. London: Continuum Press.

FEEZ S, 1998. Text-Based Syllabus Design[M]. Sydney: National Centre for English Teaching and Research.

FERGUSON C, 1971. Absence of copula and the notion of simplicity: a study of normal speech, baby talk, foreigner talk and pidgins[M]//HYMES D. Pidginization and creolization of languages. Cambridge: Cambridge University Press, 141 - 150.

FINOCCHIARO M, BRUMFIT C, 1983. The functional-notional approach: From theory to practice[M]. New York: Oxford University Press.

FLEXNERS B, HAUCK L C, 1988, Random House dictionary of the English language[M]. 2nd ed. New York: Random House.

FOWLER R, 1986. Linguistic criticism[M]. Oxford: Oxford University Press.

FRANKE E, 1884. Die praktische spracherlernung auf grund der psychologie und der physiologic der sprache dargestellt[M]. Leipzig: O. R. Reisland.

FREEMAN D, 1989a. Teacher training, development and decision making: A model of teaching and related strategies for language teacher education[J]. TESOL Quarterly, 23 (1): 27 - 45.

FREEMAN D, 1989b. Learning to teach: Four instructional patterns in language teacher education[J]. Prospect, A Journal of Australian TESOL, 4 (2): 31 - 47.

FREEMAN D, 1998. Doing teacher research: From inquiry to understanding[M]. New York: Heinle & Heinle.

FUJII A, ZIEGLER N, MACKEY A, 2016. Peer interaction and metacognitive instruction in the EFL classroom[M]// SATO M, BALLINGER S. Peer interaction and second language learning: Pedagogical potential and research agenda. Amsterdam: John Benjamins, 63 – 89.

GASS S, 1988. Integrating research areas: A framework for second language studies[J]. Applied Linguistics, 9(2): 198 – 217.

GASS S, MACKEY A, 2007. Data elicitation for second and foreign language research[M]. Mahwah, NJ: Lawrence Erlbaum Associates.

GATTEGNO C, 1972. Teaching foreign languages in schools: The silent way [M]. 2nd ed. New York: Educational Solutions.

GATTEGNO C, 1976. The common sense of teaching foreign languages[M]. New York: Educational Solutions.

GAZDAR G, 1979. Pragmatics: implicature, presupposition and logical form[M]. New York: Academic.

GEBHARD Y, OPRANDY R, 1999. Langrage teaching awareness: A guide to exploring beliefs and practices[M]. New York: Cambridge University Press.

GEDDES M, STURTRIDGE G, 1979. Listening links[M]. London: Heinemann.

GIBSON J J, 1979. The Ecological Approach to Visual Perception[M]. Hillsdale, NJ: Erlbaum.

GOFFMAN E, 1981. Forms of talk[M]. Philadelphia: University of Pennsylvania Press.

GOFFMAN E, 1967. Interaction ritual: Essays on face-to-face behavior[M]. New York: Garden City.

GOH C, 1998. Strategic processing and metacognition in second language listening[D]. Lancaster, UK: Lancaster University.

GONZALES A, 2013. Development of politeness strategies in participatory online environments: A case study[M]// TAGUCHI N, SYKES J M. Technology in interlanguage pragmatics research and teaching. John Benjamins, 101 – 120.

GONZÁLEZ-LLORET M, 2018. Pragmatics in technology-mediated contexts[M]// SÁNCHEZ-HERNÁNDEZ A, HERRAIZ-MARTÍNEZ A. Learning second language pragmatics beyond traditional contexts. Peter Lang, 17 – 48.

GOO J, 2012. Corrective feedback and working memory capacity in interaction-driven L2 learning[J]. Studies in Second Language Acquisition, 34 (3): 445 – 474.

GOODWIN C, 1981. Conversational organization. Interaction between speakers and hearers [M]. New York: Academic Press.

GRASHA A, 1984. Learning styles: The journey from Greenwich Observatory (1796) to the college classroom (1984) [J]. Improving College and University Teaching, 32(1): 46 – 53.

GREENO J G, 1994. Gibson's Affordances[J]. Psychological Review, 101(2): 336 – 342.

GREGG K, 1984. Krashen's Monitor and Occam's razor[J]. Applied Linguistics, 5 (2): 79 – 100.

GRIFFITHS R, SHEEN R, 1992. Disembedded figures in the landscape: a reappraisal of L2 research on field dependence/independence[J]. Applied Linguistics, 13(2): 133 - 147.

GUIORA A, 1972b. Construct validity and transpositional research: toward an empirical study of psychoanalytic concepts[J]. Comprehensive Psychiatry, 13(2): 139 - 150.

GUIORA A, ACTON W, ERARD R AND STRICKLAND, et al. , 1980. The effects of benzodiazepine (valium) on permeability of language ego boundaries[J]. Language Learning, 30 (2): 351 - 361.

GUIORA A, BRANNON R, DULL C, 1972a. Empathy and second language learning[J]. Language Learning, 22(1): 111 - 130.

HALL E T, 1977. Beyond culture[M]. Garden City, NY: Anchor.

HALLIDAY M A K, 1978. Language as social semiotic. The social interpretation of language and meaning[M]. London: Arnold.

HALLIDAY M A K, 1989. Context of situation[M]// HALLIDAY M A K, HASAN R. Language, context, and text: Aspects of language in a social-semiotic perspective. Oxford: Oxford University Press.

HALLIDAY M A K, 1990. New ways of meaning: A challenge for applied linguistics[C]. Plenary address at the tenth AILA Congress, Thessaloniki, Greece.

HANLEY J, HERRON C, COLE S, 1995. Using video as an advance organizer to a written passage in the FLES classroom[J]. The Modern Language Journal, 79(1): 57 - 66.

HANSEN J, STANSFIELD C, 1981. The relationship of field dependent-independent cognitive styles to foreign language achievement[J]. Language Learning, 31(2): 349 - 367.

HANSEN L, 1984. Field dependence-independence and language testing: evidence from six Pacific Island cultures[J]. TESOL Quarterly 18(2): 311 - 24.

HATCH E, 1978. Acquisition of syntax in a second language[M]// RICHARDS J. Understanding second and foreign language learning: Issues and approaches. Rowley, MA: Newbury House, 34 - 70.

HERBERT P A, 1988. Comparing teaching and learning English in the Republic of China and in Japan[J]. Chinese Culture: A Quarterly Review, 29: 85 - 92.

HEYDE A, 1979. The relationship between self-esteem and the oral production of a second language[D]. Ann Arbor: University of Michigan.

HOGAN R, 1969. Development of an empathy scale[J]. Journal of Consulting and Clinical Psychology, 33: 307 - 316.

HOLDEN C, SYKES J M, 2013. Complex L2 pragmatic feedback via place-based mobile games [M]// TAGUCHI N, SYKES J M. Technology in interlanguage pragmatics research and teaching. John Benjamins, 155 - 184.

HOLDEN C, SYKES J, 2011. Leveraging mobile games for place-based language learning[J]. International Journal of Game-Based Learning, 1(2): 1 - 18.

HONEYFIELD J, 1993. Responding to task difficulty[M]// TICKOO M. Simplification: theory and practice. Singapore: Regional Language Center, 127 - 138.

HORWITZ E, I987a. Surveying student beliefs about language learning[M]// WENDEN A, RUBIN J. Learner strategies in language learning. New York: Prentice Hall.

HORWITZ E, 1999. Cultural and situational influences on foreign language learners' beliefs about language learning: a review of BALLI studies[J]. System, 27 (4): 557 - 576.

HOSENFELD C, 1978. Students' mini-theories of second language learning[J]. Association Bulletin, 29: 2.

HOUSEN A, PIERRARD M, 2005. Investigations in instructed second language acquisition [M]. Berlin: Mouton de Gruyter.

HOWATT A P R, 1984. A history of English language teaching[M]. Oxford: Oxford University Press.

HSU F L K, 1981. Americans and Chinese: Passage to different worlds[M]. 3rd ed. Honolulu: The University of Hawaii Press.

HUDSON T, 1982. The effects of induced schemata on the "Short Circuit" in L2 reading: Non-decoding factors in L2 Reading Performance[J]. Language Learning, 32 (1): 1 - 31.

HUDSON-ROSS S, DONG Y R, 1990. Literacy learning as a reflection of language and culture: Chinese elementary school education[J]. Reading Teacher, 44 (2): 110 - 123.

HYMES D, 1972a. On communicative competence[M]// PRIDE J B, HOLMES J. Sociolinguistics. Harmondsworth: Penguin, 269 - 293.

HYMES D, 1972b. Models of the interaction of language and social life[M]// GUMPERZ J J, HYMES D. Directions in Sociolinguistics: The Ethnography of Communication. New York: Holt, Rinehart, & Winston, 35 - 71.

HYMES D, 1974. Foundations in sociolinguistics: An ethnographic approach[M]. Philadelphia: University of Pennsylvania Press.

JAEMYUNG GOO, 2012. Corrective feedback and working memory capacity in interaction-driven L2 learning[J]. Studies in Second Language Acquisition, 34(3): 445 - 474.

JAMES C D R, 1973. A cognitive style approach to teacher-pupil interaction and the academic performance of black children[D]. New Brunswick, NJ: Rutgers University.

JAY J, JOHNSON K L, 2002. Capturing complexity: A typology of reflective practice for teacher education[J]. Teaching and Teacher Education, 18(1): 73 - 85.

JOHNSON K, 1982. Communicative syllabus design and methodology[M]. Oxford: Pergamon.

JOHNSON K, 1984. Skill psychology and communicative methodology[C]. Paper presented at the RELC seminar, Singapore.

JOHNSON K, JOHNSON H, 1998. Communicative methodology[M]// JOHNSON K, JOHNSON H. Encyclopedic dictionary of applied linguistics, Oxford: Blackwell, 68 - 73.

JOHNSON P, 1982. Effects on reading comprehension of building background knowledge[J]. TESOL Quarterly, 16(4): 503 - 516.

JORDEN E, 1992. Culture in the Japanese language classroom: A pedagogical paradox// KRAMSCH C, MCCONNELL-GINET. Text and context: Cross-disciplinary perspectives on language study. Lexington, MA: D. C. Heath.

KASPER G, 1982. Teaching-induced aspects of interlanguage discourse[J]. Studies in Second Language Acquisition, 4(2): 99 - 113.

KEEFE J W, 1979. Student learning styles: Diagnosing and prescribing programs [M]. Reston, VA: National Association of Secondary School Principals.

KELLY, L G, 1976. Twenty-five centuries of language teaching: 500 BC-1969[M]. Rowley, MA. : Newbury House.

KERN R, I995. Students' and teachers' beliefs about language learning[J]. Foreign Language Annals, 28 (1): 71 - 91.

KIM Y, 2012. Task complexity, learning opportunities and Korean EFL learners' question development[J]. Studies in Second Language Acquisition, 34(4): 627 - 658.

KIM Y, 2013. Effects of pretask modelling on attention to form and question development[J]. TESOL Quarterly, 47(1): 8 - 35.

KIM Y, TAGUCHI N, 2015. Promoting task-based pragmatics instruction in EFL classroom context: The role of task complexity[J]. Modern Language Journal, 99 (4): 656 - 677.

KIM Y, TAGUCHI N, 2016. Learner-learner interaction during collaborative pragmatic tasks: The role of cognitive and pragmatic task demands[J]. Foreign Language Annals, 49(1): 42-57.

KOGAN N, WALLACH M, 1967. Risk taking as a function of the situation, the person and the group. New Directions in Psychology III[M]. New York: Holt, Rinehart and Winston.

KORMOS J, CSIZÉR K, 2008. Age-related differences in the motivation of learning English as a foreign language: Attitudes, selves and motivated learning behavior[J]. Language Learning, 58(2): 327 - 355.

KRAMSCH C, MCCONNELL-GINET S, 1992b. Conversational epilogue[M]// KRAMSCH C, MCCONNELL-GINET. Text and context: Cross-disciplinary perspectives on language study. Lexington, MA: D. C. Heath.

KRASHEN S, 1981. Second language acquisition and second language learning[M]. Oxford: Pergamon.

KRASHEN S, 1976. Formal and informal linguistic environments in language acquisition and language learning[J]. TESOL Quarterly, 10(2): 157 - 168.

KRASHEN S, 1978. Individual variation in the use of the monitor[M]// RITCHIE, W. Second language acquisition research. New York: Academic Press, 175 - 183.

KRASHEN S, 1980. The input hypothesis[M]// ALATIS J. Current issues in bilingual education. Washington D. C. : Georgetown University Press, 168 - 180.

KRASHEN S, 1982. Principles and Practice in Second Language Acquisition [M]. Oxford: Pergamon Press.

KRASHEN S, 1985. The input hypothesis: Issues and implications[M]. New York: Longman.

KRASHEN S, Terrell T D, 1983. The natural approach: language acquisition in the classroom [M]. Oxford: Pergamon Press.

LA FORGE P G, 1983. Counseling and culture in second language acquisition[M]. Oxford: Pergamon.

LAKOFF R, 1974. What you can do with words: politeness, pragmatics, and performatives[J]. Berkeley Studies in Syntax and Semantics I, XVI－1－XVI－55.

LAMBERT W E, 1981 Lambert, W. E. (1981) Bilingualism and language acquisition[M]// WINITZ H. Native Language and Foreign Language Acquisition, Annals of the New York Academy of Sciences: 379. New York: New York Academy of Sciences: 9－22.

LAMBERT W E, 1990. Persistent issues in bilingualism[M]// HARLEY B, ALLEN P, CUMMINS J, et al. The Development of Second Language Proficiency. Cambridge: Cambridge University Press.

LANGE D L, 1990. A blueprint for a teacher development program[M]// Richards J C, Nunan D. Second language teacher education. Cambridge: Cambridge University Press.

LARSEN-FREEMAN D, 1995. Grammar dimensions[M]. Boston: Heinle & Heinle.

LARSEN-FREEMAN D, 2015. Ten "lessons" from Complex Dynamic Systems Theory: What is on offer[M]// DÖRNYEI Z, MACLNTYRE P D, HENRY A. Motivational dynamics in language learning. Bristol: Multilingual Matters, 11－19.

LARSEN-FREEMAN D, CAMERRON L, 2008. Complex systems and applied linguistics[M]. Oxford: Oxford University Press.

LARSON-HALL J, 2010. A guide to doing statistics in second language research using SPSS [M]. New York: Routledge.

LEECH G N, 1977. Language and tact[Z]. LAUT Series A, Paper 46. University of Trier.

LEECH G N, 1980. Explorations in Semantics and Pragmatics[M]. Amsterdam: John Benjamins.

LEECH G N, 1983. Principles of pragmatics[M]. London: Longman.

LENNEBERG E, 1967. Biological foundations of language[M]. New York: Wiley and Son.

LEOW R P, 2015. Explicit learning in the L2 classroom: A student-centered approach[M]. New York: Routledge.

LI S, 2013. The interactions between the effects of implicit and explicit feedback and individual differences in language analytic ability and working memory. Modern Language Journal, 97 (3): 634－654.

LICHTMAN K, VanPatten B, 2021. Krashen forty years later: Final comments[J]. Foreign Language Annals, 54(2): 336－340.

LITTLE D, SINGLETON D, SILVIUS W, 1984. Learning second languages in Ireland: Experience, attitudes and needs[M]. Dublin: Trinity College, Centre for Language and Communication Studies.

LITTLE D, 1991. Learner autonomy 1: Definitions, issues, and problems[M]. Dublin: Authentik.

LITTLEWOOD W, 1981. Communicative language teaching[M]. Cambridge: Cambridge University Press.

LITTLEWOOD W, 1984. Foreign and second language learning: Language acquisition research and its implications for the classroom[M]. Cambridge: Cambridge University Press.

LITTLEWOOD W, 2014. Communication-oriented language teaching: Where are we now? Where do we go from here? [J]. Language Teaching, 47(3): 349 - 362.

LOCASTRO V, 2003. An introduction to pragmatics: Social action for language teachers. Ann Arbor, MI: The University of Michigan Press.

LOEWEN S, 2015. Introduction to instructed second language acquisition[M]. New York: Routledge.

LOEWEN S, SATO M, 2017. The Routledge handbook of instructed second language acquisition[M]. New York: Routledge.

LONG M, CROOKES G, 1992. Three approaches to task-based syllabus design[J]. TESOL Quarterly 26(1): 27 - 56.

LONG M, CROOKES G, 1993. Units of analysis in course design - the case for task[M]// CROOKES G, GASS S. Tasks in a pedagogical context: Integrating theory and practice. Clevedon: Multilingual Matters.

LONG M H, 1981. Input, interaction and second language acquisition[M]// WINITZ H. Annals of the New York Academy of Sciences, 379. New York: Academy of Sciences, 259 - 278.

LONG M H, 1983. Native speaker/non-native speaker conversation in the second language classroom[M]//CLARKE M A, HANDSCOMB J. On TESOL'82: Pacific perspectives on language learning and teaching. Washington, D. C. : TESOL, 207 - 225.

LONG M H, 1991. Focus on form: a design feature in language teaching methodology[M]// DE BOT K, GINSBERG R, KRAMSCH C. Foreign language research in cross-cultural perspective. Amsterdam: John Benjamins, 39 - 52.

LONG M H, 1996. The role of the linguistic environment in second language acquisition[M]// RITCHIE W, BHATIA T. Handbook of second language acquisition. San Diego: Academic Press, 413 - 468.

LONG M H, 2017. Instructed second language acquisition (ISLA): Geopolitics, methodological issues, and some major research questions[J]. Instructed Second Language Acquisition, 1(1): 7 - 44.

LOEWEN S, SATO M, 2017. The Routledge handbook of instructed second language acquisition[M]. New York: Routledge.

LOZANOV G, 1978. Suggestology and outlines of suggestopedy[M]. New York: Gordon and Breach.

LUFT J, INGRAM H, 1969. Of human interaction[M]. New York: National Press Books.

LYONS J, 1977. Semantics, Vols. 1 and 2[M]. Cambridge: Cambridge University Press.

MACINTYRE P, SERROUL A, 2015. Motivation on a per-second timescale: Examining approach-avoidance motivation during L2 task performance[M]// DÖRNYEI Z, MACINTYRE P, HENRY A. Motivational dynamics in language learning. Bristol: Multilingual Matters, 109 - 138.

MACINTYRE P, NOELS K A, 1996. Using social-psychological variables to predict the use of language learning strategies[J]. Foreign Language Annals, 29(3): 373 - 386.

MACINTYRE P D, LEGATTO J J, 2011. A dynamic system approach to willingness to communicate: Developing an idiodynamic method to capture rapidly changing affect[J]. Applied Linguistics, 32 (2): 149 - 171.

MACKEY A, 2006. Feedback, noticing and instructed second language learning[J]. Applied Linguistics, 27(3): 405 - 430.

MACKEY A, ABBUHL R, GASS S, 2013. Interactionist approach[M]// GASS S, MACKEY A. The Routledge handbook of second language acquisition. New York: Routledge, 7 - 24.

MACKEY A, GASS S M, 2015. Second language research: Methodology and design[M]. 2nd ed. New York: Routledge.

MACKEY A, PHILP J, FUJII, A, et al., 2002. Individual differences in working memory, noticing of interactional feedback and L2 development[M]// Robinson P. Individual differences and instructed language learning. Philadelphia, PA.: John Benjamins, 181 - 208.

MACKEY A, SACHS R, 2012. Older learners in SLA research: A first look at working memory, feedback, and L2 development[J]. Language Learning, 62(3): 704 - 740.

MARCKWARDT A D, 1972. Changing winds and shifting sands[J]. MST English Quarterly, 21, 3 - 11.

MASTER P, 1983. The etiquette of observing[J]. TESOL Quarterly, 17(3): 497 - 501.

MCCARTHY M, 2001. Issues in applied linguistics[M]. Cambridge: Cambridge University Press.

MCDONOUGH K, MACKEY A, 2013. Second language interaction in diverse educational contexts[M]. Amsterdam: John Benjamins.

MCLAUGHLIN B, ROSSMAN T, MCLEOD B, 1983. Second language learning: An information-processing perspective[J]. Language Learning, 33(2): 135 - 158.

MILLER G A, 1974. Psychology, language and levels of communication[M]// SILVERSTEIN A. Human communication: theoretical explorations. Hillsdale, New Jersey: Lawrence Erlbaum Associates, 1 - 17.

MOLINSKY S J, BLISS B, 1989. Side by Side[M]. 2nd ed. Book 1. Englewood Cliffs, NJ.: Prentice-Hall.

MOSKOWITZ G, 1978. Caring and sharing in the foreign language class[M]. Rowley, Mass.: Newbury House.

MOULTON W, 1963. Linguistics and language teaching in the United States 1940 - 1960[J]. International Review of Applied Linguistics, 1 (1): 21 - 41.

MOWRER D, 1950. Learning theory and personality dynamics[M]. New York: Ronald Press.

MURPHY J, 1992. An etiquette for the nonsupervisory observation of L2 classrooms[J]. Foreign Language Annals, 25(3): 215 - 225.

NAIMAN N, FROHLICH M, STERN H H, et al., 1978. The good language learner[M]. Toronto: Ontario Institute for Studies in Education.

NASSAJI H, 2009. Effects of recasts and elicitations in dyadic interaction and the role of feedback explicitness[J]. Language Learning, 59(2): 411 - 452.

NEISSER U, 1987. From direct perception to conceptual structure[M]// Neisser U. Concepts and conceptual development: Ecological and intellectual factors in categorization. Cambridge: Cambridge University Press.

NORTON B, TOOHEY K, 2011. Identity, language learning and social change[J]. Language Teaching, 44(4): 412 - 446.

NUNAN D, 1989. Designing tasks for the communicative classroom[M]. New York: Cambridge University Press.

NYIKOS M, OXFORD R L, 1993. A factor-analytic study of language learning strategy use: Interpretations from information processing theory and social psychology[J]. Modern Language Journal, 77(1): 11 - 23.

O'MALLEY J M, CHAMOT A U, 1990. Learning strategies in second language acquisition [M]. Cambridge: Cambridge University Press.

OMAGGIO A C, 1977. The effects of selected pictorial contexts on measures of reading comprehension in beginning college French[D]. Columbus: The Ohio State University.

OMAGGIO A C, 1979. Pictures and second language comprehension: Do they help? [J]. Foreign Language Annals, 12(2): 107 - 116.

ORTEGA L, 2015. Second language learning explained? SLA across 10 contemporary theories [M]// VanPatten B, Williams J. Theories in second language acquisition: an introduction. New York: Routledge, 245 - 272.

OXFORD R, 1990. Language learning strategies: What every teacher should know[M]. New York: Newbury House.

OXFORD R L, 1996. Language learning strategies around the World: Cross-cultural perspectives[M]. Manoa: University of Hawaii Press.

OXFORD R L, 2011. Teaching and researching language learning strategies[M]. Harlow, UK: Longman/Pearson Education.

PALMER H E, 1921. Principles of Language Study[M]. New York: World Book Co.

PALMER H E, 1923. The Oral Method of Teaching Languages[M]. Cambridge: Heffer.

PALTRIDGE B, PHAKITI A, 2015. Research methods in applied linguistics: A practical resource[M]. London: Bloomsbury.

PEREZ-VIDAL C, 2014. Language acquisition in study abroad and formal instruction contexts [M]. Amsterdam: John Benjamins.

PERVIN L A, CERVONE D, 2010. Personality: Theory and research[M]. 11th ed. Hoboken, NJ: John Wiley and Sons.

PHILIPS S, 1972. Participant structures and communicative competence: Warm spring children in community and classroom[M]// CAZDEN C, JOHN V P, HYMES D, 1972. Functions of language in the classroom. New York: Teachers College Press.

PICA T, KANAGY R, FALODUN J, 1993. Choosing and using communicative tasks for second language instruction[M]// CROOKES G, GASS S. Tasks and language learning: Integrating theory and practice. Clevedon: Multilingual Matters, 9 - 34.

PICA T, KANAGY R, FALODUN J, 1994. Choosing and using communication tasks for second language research and instruction[M]// CROOKES G, GASS S. Tasks in pedagogical context: Integrating theory and practice. Clevedon: Multilingual Matters.

PIENEMANN M, 1998. Language processing and second language development: processibility theory[M]. Amsterdam: John Benjamins.

PIENEMANN M, LENZING A, 2015. Processability theory[M]// VANPATTEN B, WILLIAMS J. Theories in second language acquisition: an introduction. New York: Routledge, 159 - 179.

PIEPHO H E, 1981. Establishing objectives in the teaching of English[M]//CANDLIN C. The communicative teaching of English: Principles and an exercise typology. London: Longman.

PINIEL K, CSIZÉR K, 2015. Changes in motivation, anxiety, and self-efficacy during the course of an academic writing seminar[M]// DÖRNYEI Z, MACINTYRE P, HENRY A. Motivational dynamics in language learning. Bristol: Multilingual Matters, 164 - 194.

PITTMAN G, 1963. Teaching structural English[M]. Brisbane: Jacaranda.

RAINIE L, WELLMAN B, 2012. Networked: The new social operating system[M]. Cambridge: MIT Press.

REBUSCHAT P, 2013. Measuring implicit and explicit knowledge in second language research [J]. Language Learning, 63 (3): 595 - 626.

REID J, 1987. The learning style preferences of ESL students[J]. TESOL Quarterly, 21 (1): 87 - 111.

RICHARDS J C, 1985. Conversational competence through role-play activities[J]. RELC Journal, 16(1): 82 - 100.

RICHARDS J C, RODGERS T, 1986. Approaches and methods in language teaching[M]. Cambridge: Cambridge University Press.

RICHARDS J C, HO B, GIBLIN K, 1992. Learning how to teach: a study of EFL teachers in pre-service training[R]. Department of English Research Report No. 19, City Polytechnic of Hong Kong.

RICHARDS J C, LOCKHART C, 1994. Reflective teaching in second language classrooms[M]. New York: Cambridge University Press.

RUBIN J, 1975. What the "good language learner" can teach us[J]. TESOL Quarterly, 9(1): 41 - 51.

RUBIN J, THOMPSON I, 1982. How to be a more successful language learner[M]. Boston: Heinle and Heinle Publishers.

RUMELHART D, 1977. Understanding and summarizing brief stories[M]// LABERGE D, SAMUELS S. Basic processes in reading: Perception and comprehension. Hillsdale, NJ: Lawrence Erlbaum Associates.

RUMELHART D, 1980. Schemata: The building blocks of cognition[M]// SPIRO R, BRUCE B, BREWER W. Theoretical issues in reading comprehension. Hillsdale, NJ: Lawrence Erlbaum Associates.

RUTHERFORD W, 1980. Aspects of pedagogical grammar[J]. Applied Linguistics, I(1): 60-73.

SATO C. 1988. Origins of complex syntax in interlanguage development[J]. Studies in Second Language Acquisition, 10(3): 371 - 395.

SATO M, LYSTER R, 2012. Peer interaction and corrective feedback for accuracy and fluency development: Monitoring, practice, and proceduralization[J]. Studies in Second Language Acquisition, 34(4): 591 - 626.

SAVIGNON S, 1983. Communicative competence: theory and classroom practice[M]. Reading, Mass. : Addison-Wesley.

SAVILLE-TROIKE, M. 1992. Cultural maintenance and "vanishing" Englishes[M]// KRAMSCH C, MCCONNELL-GINET. Text and context: Cross-disciplinary perspectives on language study. Lexington, MA: D. C. Heath.

SCARCELLA R C, OXFORD R L, 1992. The tapestry of language learning[M]. Boston, MA: Heinle & Heinle.

SCHANK R, ABELSON R, 1977. Scripts, plans, goals, and understanding: An inquiry into human knowledge structures[M]. Hillsdale, NJ: Lawrence Erlbaum Associates.

SCHMIDT R, MCCREARY C, 1977. Standard and superstandard English: Recognition and use of prescriptive rules by native and non-native speakers[J]. TESOL Quarterly, 11(4): 415-429.

SCHMIDT R W, RICHARDS J C, 1980. Speech acts and second language learning[J]. Applied Linguistics, I(2): 129 - 157.

SCHÖN D A, 1983. The reflective practitioner: How professionals think in action[M]. New York: Basic Books.

SCHUMANN J, HOLROYD J, CAMPBELL R, et al. , 1978. Improvement of foreign language pronunciation under hypnosis: a preliminary study[J]. Language Learning 28(1): 143 - 148.

SCOTT R, PAGE M, 1982. The subordination of teaching to learning: A seminar conducted by Dr. Caleb Gattegno[J]. ELT Journal, 36(4): 273 - 274.

SCOVEL T, 1978. The effect of affect on foreign language learning: A review of the anxiety research[J]. Language Learning 28(1): 129 - 142.

SCOVEL T, 1979. Review of suggestology and outlines of suggestopedy[J]. TESOL Quarterly, 13(2): 255 - 266.

SELINKER L, 1974. Interlanguage[M]// SCHUMANN J H, STENSON N. New frontiers in second-language learning. Rowley, MA. : Newbury House, 114 - 136.

SHAOFENG LI, 2010. The effectiveness of corrective feedback in SLA: A meta-analysis[J]. Language Learning, 60(2): 309 - 365.

SHARWOOD-SMITH M, 1981. Consciousness-raising and the second language learner[J]. Applied Linguistics, II(2): 159 - 168.

SHAVELSON R, HUBNERJ, STANTON G, 1976. Self-concept: validation of construct interpretations[J]. Review of Educational Research 46(3): 407 – 441.

SHEHADEH A, COOMBE C, 2012. Task-based language teaching in foreign language contexts: Research and implementation[M]. Amsterdam: John Benjamins.

SHORT M H, 1981. Discourse analysis and the analysis of drama[J]. Applied Linguistics, II (2): 180 – 202.

SKEHAN P, 1996. Second language acquisition research and task-based instruction[M]// WILLIS J, WILLIS D. Challenge and change in language teaching. Oxford: Heinemann, 17 – 30.

SKEHAN P, 1998. A cognitive approach to language learning[M]. Oxford: Oxford University Press.

SKEHAN P, 1991. Individual differences in second language learning[J]. Studies in Second Language Acquisition, 13(2): 275 – 298.

SKINNER B, 1957. Verbal behavior[M]. New York: Appleton-Century-Crofts.

SMITH B, 2005. The relationship between negotiated interaction, learner uptake, and lexical acquisition in task-based computer-mediated communication[J]. TESOL Quarterly, 39(1): 33 – 58.

SPADA N, 1997. Form-focused instruction and second language acquisition: a review of classroom and laboratory research[J]. Lang Teach, 30(2): 73 – 87.

SPIELBERGER C, I983. Manual for thestate-trait anxiety inventory (form Y) [M]. Palo Alto, Calif: Consulting Psychologists Press.

SPOLSKY B, 1989. Conditions for second language learning[M]. Oxford: Oxford University Press.

STENHOUSE L, 1975. An introduction to curriculum research and development[M]. London: Heinemann.

STERN H H, 1983. Fundamental concepts of language teaching [M]. Reprinted London: Oxford University Press.

STERN H H, 1975. What can we learn from the good language learner? [J]. The Canadian Modern Language Review, 31(4): 304 – 318. Reprinted in Croft 1980.

STERN H H, 1983. Fundamental concepts of language teaching[M]. Oxford: Oxford University Press.

STEVICK E W, 1980. Teaching languages: A way and ways[M]. Rowley, Mass. : Newbury House.

STOCKWELL G, 2010. Effects of multimodality in computer-mediated communication in tasks. [M]// THOMAS M, REINDERS H. Task-based language learning and teaching with technology. London: Continuum International, pp. 83 – 104.

STORTI C, 1999. Figuring foreigners out: A practical guide[M]. Yarmouth, ME: Intercultural Press.

SWAFFAR J K, ARENS K, MORGAN M, 1982. Teacher classroom practices: Redefining method as task hierarchy[J]. The Modern Language Journal, 66(1): 24 – 33.

SWAIN M, 1985. Communicative competence: Some roles of comprehensible input and comprehensible output in its development[M]// GASS S, MADDEN C. Input in second language acquisition. Rowley, MA: Newbury House: 235 - 253.

SWAIN M, 1995. Three functions of output in second language learning[M]// Cook G, SEIDLHOFER B. Principle and practice in applied linguistics: Studies in honour of H. G. Widdowson. Oxford: Oxford University Press, 125 - 144.

SWAIN M, LAPKIN S, 1998. Interaction and second language learning: Two adolescent French immersion students working together[J]. The Modern Language Journal, 82(3): 320 - 337.

SWEET H, 1899. The practical study of languages[M]. Reprinted London: Oxford University Press.

SYKES J, 2012. Synthetic immersive environments and second language pragmatic development [M]// CHAPELLE C, SAURO S. The encyclopedia of applied linguistics. Blackwell.

SYKES J, 2014. TBLT and synthetic immersive environments: What can in-game task restarts tell us about design and implementation? [M]// GONZÁLEZ-LLORET M, ORTEGA L. Technology mediated TBLT: Researching technology and tasks. John Benjamins, 149 - 182.

SYKES J M, 2021. Researching digital discourse in second language pragmatics [M]// FÉLIXBRASDÉFER C, SHIVELY R. New directions in second language pragmatics. De Gruyter Mouton, 197 - 207.

TAGUCHI N, KIM Y, 2018. Task-based approaches to teaching and assessing pragmatics[M]. John Benjamins.

TAGUCHI N, ROEVER C, 2017. Second language pragmatics[M]. Oxford University Press.

TAGUCHI N, SYKES J M, 2013. Technology in interlanguage pragmatics research and teaching [M]. John Benjamins.

THE DOUGLAS FIR GROUP, 2016. A transdisciplinary framework for SLA in a multilingual world[J]. The Modern Language Journal, 100-S1: 19 - 47.

TREICHLER P A, KRAMARAE C, 1983. Women's talk in the ivory tower[J]. Communication Quarterly, 31(2): 118 - 132.

TRUSCOTT J, SHARWOOD S M, 2004. Acquisition by processing: A modular perspective on language development. Bilingualism: Language and Cognition, 7(1): 1 - 20.

TYLER R, 1949. Basic principles of curriculum and instruction[M]. New York: Harcourt Brace.

USHIODA E, 2003. Engaging with the curriculum through the European language portfolio[J]. Neusprachliche Mitteilungen, 56(3): 147 - 153.

USHIODA E, 2015. Context and complex dynamic systems theory[M]// DÖRNYEI Z, MACLNTYRE P D, HENRY A. Motivational dynamics in language learning. Shanghai: Shanghai Foreign Language Education Press, 47 - 54.

VAN DIJK T A, 1977a. Context and cognition: knowledge frames and speech act comprehension [J]. Journal of Pragmatics, 1(3): 211 - 232.

VAN DIJK T A, 1977b. Text and context: Explorations in the semantics and pragmatics of discourse[M]. London: Longman.

VAN LIER L, 1988. The classroom and the language learner[M]. London: Longman.

VAN LIER L, 2004. The ecology and semiotics of language learning: A sociocultural perspective [M]. Boston: Kluwer Academic.

VANPATTEN B, 1993. Grammar teaching for the acquisition-rich classroom[J]. Foreign Language Annals, 26(4): 435-450.

VANPATTEN B, CADIERNO T, 1993. Explicit instruction and input processing[J]. Studies in Second Language Acquisition, 15(2): 225-243.

VANPATTEN B, ROTHMAN J, 2014. Against "rules" [M]// BENATI A, LAVAL C, ARCHE M J. The grammar dimension in instructed second language acquisition: Theory, research, and practice. London: Bloomsbury, 15-35.

WAJNRYB R, 1992. Classroom observation tasks [M]. New York: Cambridge University Press.

WALLACE M J, 1991. Training foreign language teachers: A reflective approach[M]. Cambridge: Cambridge University Press.

WENDEN A, 1986. What do second language learners know about their language learning? A second look at retrospective accounts[J]. Applied Linguistics, 7(2): 186-205.

WENDEN A, 1987. How to be a successful learner: insights and prescriptions from L2 learners [M]// WENDEN A, RUBIN J. Learner strategies in language learning. Englewood Cliffs, N. J.: Prentice Hall.

WHITE L, 1985. The"pro-drop" parameter in adult second language acquisition[J]. Language Learning, 35(1): 47-62.

WHITE L, 1987. Against comprehensible input: The input hypothesis and the development of L2 competence[J]. Applied Linguistics, 8(2): 95-110.

WHITE L, 2015. Linguistic theory, universal grammar, and second language acquisition[M]// VANPATTEN B, WILLIAMS J. Theories in second language acquisition: An introduction. 2nd ed. New York: Routledge, 34-53.

WIDDOWSON H G, 1978. Teaching language as communication[M]. Oxford: Oxford University Press.

WIDDOWSON H G, 1979. The communicative approach and its applications[M]// WIDDOWSON H G. Explorations in applied linguistics. Oxford: Oxford University Press, 251-264.

WIDDOWSON H G, 1984. Learning purpose and language use[M]. Oxford: Oxford University Press.

WILKINS D A, 1976. Notional syllabuses[M]. Oxford: Oxford University Press.

WILLIS J, 1996. A framework for task-based learning[M]. Harlow: Longman.

WRIGHT A, 1976. Visual material for the language teacher[M]. London: Longman.

WRIGHT T, 1987. Roles of teachers and learners[M]. Oxford: Oxford University Press.

YOU, C J, DÖRNYEI Z, CSIZÉR K, 2016. Motivation, vision, and gender: A survey of learners of English in China[J]. Language Learning, 66 (1): 94-123.

YULE G, MACDONALD D, 1991. Resolving referential conflicts in L2 interaction: The effect of proficiency and interactive role[J]. Language Learning, 40(4): 539 - 556.

YUM J O, 1988. The impact of Confucianism on interpersonal relationships and communication patterns in east Asia[J]. Communication Monographs, 55 (4): 374 - 358.

ZEICHNER K, LISTON O, 1987. Teaching student teachers to reflect[J]. Harvard Educational Review, 57(1): 23 - 48.

ZEICHNER K, LISTON O, 1996. Reflective teaching: An introduction[M]. Mahwah, NJ: Lawrence Erlbaum.

ZIEGLER N, 2016. Synchronous computer-mediated communication and interaction: A meta-analysis[J]. Studies in Second Language Acquisition, 38 (3): 553 - 586.

束定芳，庄智象，2008. 现代外语教学理论、实践与方法[M]. 上海：上海外语教育出版社.

